ACHIEVING INCLUSIVE GROWTH
IN THE ASIA PACIFIC

ACHIEVING INCLUSIVE GROWTH IN THE ASIA PACIFIC

EDITED BY ADAM TRIGGS
AND SHUJIRO URATA

Australian
National
University

PRESS

Pacific Trade and Development Conference Series
(PAFTAD)

ANU PRESS

Published by ANU Press
The Australian National University
Acton ACT 2601, Australia
Email: anupress@anu.edu.au

Available to download for free at press.anu.edu.au

ISBN (print): 9781760463816
ISBN (online): 9781760463823

WorldCat (print): 1159740071
WorldCat (online): 1159739893

DOI: 10.22459/AIGAP.2020

Cover design and layout by ANU Press

CONTENTS

FIGURES

TABLES

CONTRIBUTORS

Lisa Cameron is Professorial Research Fellow at the Melbourne Institute of Applied Economic and Social Research at the University of Melbourne.

Aekapol Chongvilaivan is an Economist (Public Finance) at the Asian Development Bank (ADB).

Miles Corak is Professor of Economics at The Graduate Center and Senior Scholar with the Stone Center on Socio-Economic Inequality, City University of New York.

Ryo Hasumi is Associate Professor at Musashi University and Specially Appointed Fellow at the Japan Center for Economic Research.

Himanshu is Associate Professor in the Centre for Economic Studies and Planning, at Jawaharlal Nehru University.

Zhi-An Hu is a PhD student at the National School of Development & China Center for Economic Research, Peking University.

Kazuki Kuroiwa is Supervisor at Aflac Life Insurance Japan Ltd, and formerly Trainee Economist at the Japan Center for Economic Research.

Saeko Maeda is Counsellor, Personnel Division, Cabinet Office, Government of Japan, and formerly principal economist at the Japan Center for Economic Research.

Kevin J Mumford is Associate Professor of Economics and Director of the Purdue University Research Center in Economics (PURCE), Department of Economics, Purdue University.

William Rowell is based in the Economic Development Division at the Australian Department of Foreign Affairs and Trade.

Sumio Saruyama is Lead Economist at the Japan Center for Economic Research.

Diana Contreras Suarez is Research Fellow at the Melbourne Institute of Applied Economic and Social Research at the University of Melbourne.

Adam Triggs is the Director of Research at the Asian Bureau of Economic Research at the Crawford School of Public Policy, The Australian National University, and a non-resident fellow at the Brookings Institution in the Global Economy and Development program.

Shujiro Urata is Professor at the Graduate School of Asia Pacific Studies, Waseda University, and Senior Research Adviser to the President, Economic Research Institute for ASEAN and East Asia (ERIA).

Yang Yao is a Cheung-Kong Scholar Chair Professor at the National School of Development (NSD), Peking University, Beijing, China.

Yixiao Zhou is Senior Lecturer in the School of Economics and Finance, Curtin Business School, Faculty of Business and Law, Curtin University.

Juzhong Zhuang is Senior Economic Advisor, Economic Research and Regional Cooperation Department, Asian Development Bank.

ABBREVIATIONS

ADB	Asian Development Bank
ADBI	Asian Development Bank Institute
AEC	ASEAN Economic Community
AI	artificial intelligence
AIDIS	All-India Debt and Investment Survey
APO	Asian Productivity Organization
ASEAN	Association of Southeast Asian Nations
ASI	Annual Survey of Industries
BEA	Bureau of Economic Analysis
BLS	Bureau of Labour Statistics
CCP	Chinese Communist Party
CFPS	China Family Panel Studies
CHIP	Chinese Household Income Project
CMIE	Centre for Monitoring Indian Economy
CPI AL	Consumer Price Index for Agricultural Labourers
CPI IW	Consumer Price Index for Industrial Workers
ELMO	Elbers, Lanjouw, Mistiaen, Özler
EUS	Employment-Unemployment Surveys
FAS	Foundation for Agrarian Studies
FDI	foreign direct investment
FLFP	female labour force participation
GDIM	Global Database on Intergenerational Mobility
GDP	gross domestic product
GFC	global financial crisis

GWR	Global Wealth Report
ICT	information and communications technology
IDB	Islamic Development Bank
IFR	International Federation of Robotics
IHDS	Indian Human Development Survey
ILO	International Labour Organization
IMF	International Monetary Fund
IoT	Internet of Things
IT	information technology
JCER	Japan Center for Economic Research
JHPS	Japan Household Panel Survey
MGNREGS	Mahatma Gandhi National Rural Employment Guarantee Scheme
MHLW	Ministry of Health, Labour and Welfare
MLD	mean log deviation
MPCE	monthly per capita expenditure
MRP	mixed recall period
MSP	minimum support prices
NAFTA	North American Free Trade Agreement
NCAER	National Council of Applied Economic Research
NDA	National Democratic Alliance
NDP	net domestic product
NIPSSR	National Institute of Population and Social Security Research
NSFIE	National Survey of Family Income and Expenditure
NSSO	National Sample Survey Office
OBC	other backward class
OECD	Organisation for Economic Co-operation and Development
OLS	ordinary least squares
PARI	Project on Agrarian Relations in India
PDS	Public Distribution System

PISA	Programme for International Student Assessment
PODES	Village Potential Statistics
PPP	purchasing power parity
PRC	People's Republic of China
REDS	Rural Economic and Demographic Survey
SAKERNAS	Indonesian National Labour Force Survey
SAR	Special Administrative Region
SC	scheduled castes
SEEA	System of Integrated Environmental and Economic Accounting
SMEs	small and medium enterprises
SNA	System of National Accounts
ST	scheduled tribes
SUSENAS	National Socioeconomic Survey
TFP	total factor productivity
TPP	Trans-Pacific Partnership
ULC	unit labour costs
VAT	value-added tax
VHLSS	Vietnam Household Living Standard Surveys
WDI	World Development Indicators
WIL	World Inequality Lab
WTO	World Trade Organization

PREFACE

The Pacific Trade and Development (PAFTAD) celebrated its 50th anniversary in 2018. The conference series has been at the forefront of analysing challenges facing the economies of East Asia and the Pacific since its first meeting in Tokyo in January 1968. The 39th PAFTAD conference was again held in Tokyo between 31 January and 2 February 2018 with the theme 'Growth, globalisation and intergenerational issues in the Asia Pacific'. The conference was hosted by the Japan Center for Economic Research (JCER) with financial support from the Economic Research Institute for ASEAN and East Asia (ERIA). The papers presented at the conference are collected in this volume.

The 39th PAFTAD conference met at a critical time to consider how Asian economies can drive inclusive economic growth against a backdrop of rising inequality, demographic change and the challenges from globalisation. Rapid demographic and technological change have characterised the region and it is increasingly important that new strategies for growth are pursued that have proper regard for sustainability and inclusiveness. Improving intergenerational welfare requires identifying barriers to labour and income mobility, investing effectively in human and social capital, and balancing shorter-term growth with the responsible use of resources. For many countries, it also means responding innovatively to the problems presented by an ageing population.

The chapters in the volume outline pathways to achieving more inclusive growth and greater social mobility. Close attention is paid to reviewing methods for measuring wealth and their implications for sustainable development. The impacts of automation on the future of work are examined alongside strategies to reduce income inequality and promote new employment opportunities. The role of female labour force participation in future growth and the impact of ageing populations are also examined. Investment in human and social capital, and commitment to trade-orientated growth and openness are further underscored as critical components to continued Asian economic development.

A distinguished group of economists from East Asia and the Pacific gathered in Tokyo to discuss Asia's strategies for achieving inclusive growth in this era of rapid economic change. PAFTAD is famous for extensive discussion and debate around each chapter at the conference, followed by extensive revision for publication.

The PAFTAD team is grateful to the contributors to the book who collaborated enthusiastically to bring this research to publication. Our debt to the authors in the volume is obvious. In addition, we are grateful for the invaluable and substantive contributions made by Peter Drysdale, Hugh Patrick, Mari Pangestu, Akira Kohsaka, Shiro Armstrong, Chul Chung, Chun Lee, David Dollar, Dhiraj Nayyar, Francis Hutchinson, Fukunari Kimura, Juan Palacios, Jung Taik Hyun, Jungsoo Park, Kazumasa Iwata, Lin Chen, Lin Chien-Fu, Muhamad Chatib Basri, Naohiro Yashiro, Narongchai Akrasanee, Nobuko Nagase, Ponciano S Intal Jr, Robert Scollay, Shankaran Nambiar, Shekhar Shah, Somkiat Tangkitvanich, Stephen Howes, Vivi Alatas, Vo Tri Thanh, Wendy Dobson, Yue-Chim Richard Wong, Zaw Oo and ZhongXiang Zhang. They helped to refine arguments and ideas at the conference and engage in thinking on the structural challenges facing Asian economies and the world.

We were honoured by the presence of Yasutoshi Nishimura, Member of Prime Minister Shinzo Abe's Cabinet and Deputy Chief Cabinet Secretary, who delivered the Keynote Speech at the public forum on 2 February at the Nikkei Building, Tokyo. Mari Pangestu, Muhamad Chatib Basri, Peter Drysdale, Zaw Oo and Yiping Huang participated in a stimulating and timely panel discussion at the forum, which focused on the principle challenges to maintaining high growth in Asia.

Former prime minister Yasuo Fukuda addressed the conference dinner, discussing the challenges for Japan and the region in an increasingly uncertain world. The dinner also celebrated Professor Peter Drysdale's contribution to PAFTAD over its 50 years.

We are indebted to Sam Hardwick of The Australian National University (ANU) and Koki Murai and the JCER team for all stages of the management of the PAFTAD conference that made it such a success.

This book would not exist if it were not for the hard work of Nishanth Pathy and later Dorothy Mason for managing PAFTAD, the publication process and the editors through to finalisation of the book in 2020.

The PAFTAD International Steering Committee and the PAFTAD International Secretariat are grateful for the generous support of the donors whose continuing support make this important work possible. They include the Ford Foundation, the Canadian International Development Research Center, the Korean Institute of International Economic Policy, the Asia Foundation of Toronto University, the National University of Singapore, the Taiwan Institute of International Economic Research, Colombia University, Sanaree Holdings and, last but not least, ANU.

May we extend our sincere thanks to Emily Tinker and ANU Press for working so patiently with us through the production process. We express our gratitude to Justine Molony for her excellent copyediting work.

This is an important collection of essays at a critical point in time for the global economy where Asia can lead a global effort to fostering more inclusive growth. Widening inequality and social discontent threaten economic success made possible by long-term commitment to open markets and economic integration. This volume helps to think of ways forward for Asia to extend the benefits of globalisation equitably across societies.

Adam Triggs and Shujiro Urata
Canberra, July 2020

1

INTRODUCTION

Adam Triggs and Shujiro Urata

The death of a former world leader is followed by much reflection. We reflect on their legacy, their policies and the decisions they made. The passing of former US president George HW Bush in 2018, however, was different. We reflected not only on the man and his legacy, but on how radically the United States, and its government, has changed since then.

In a 1989 debate, President Bush was asked about illegal immigration. In his answer, he referred to illegal immigrants in the United States as 'good people, strong people and part of my family'. He called them 'honourable, decent, family-loving people' and discussed practical options to balance their human rights with the need for an orderly immigration system.

On trade, President Bush strived for an open America. 'We don't want an America that is closed to the world,' he said in 1989 (Green 2018). President Bush signed the North American Free Trade Agreement (NAFTA) to 'build a common future built on shared values'. 'We recognise trade is an important part of our economic growth,' he said, 'Trade creates widespread prosperity and further enhances global stability' (Bush 1999).

How quickly times have changed.

The election of Donald Trump has seen a radical shift in US policies, and rhetoric, on openness and the role of the United States in the world. Illegal immigrants have been depicted as drug dealers, criminals, rapists and terrorists (BBC 2016). Trade deals have been scrapped. Trade wars have been started and characterised as being 'good' and 'easy to win'. He has declared himself 'a tariff man' as he deepens his trade war with

China (*Wall Street Journal* 2018). The President has refused to reappoint judges to the World Trade Organization (WTO) dispute settlement body, threatening to plunge the institution into crisis (Miles 2018). He has withdrawn from the Trans-Pacific Partnership (TPP) and the Paris Climate Accord, while other US lawmakers have considered abolishing institutions like the International Monetary Fund and the World Bank (Bergsten 2000).

Trump appears determined to undermine the rules-based global system that the United States spent 70 years creating, risking the very prosperity that this system has created. But Trump is a symptom rather than a cause. He represents a growing discontent with the direction in which the world is heading.

This discontent is by no means limited to the US rust belt. Advanced economies across the world are experiencing a sharp backlash against globalisation. It appears to be contagious. The critical question for this book is whether Asia, the most dynamic region in the world, will catch it next.

The citizens of many advanced economies now believe that globalisation is a bad thing. Less than half of those surveyed in France, the United States, Britain, Australia and Norway believe that globalisation is a force for good. Westerners believe the world is getting worse. Only 11 per cent of Americans believe that the world has improved in recent years (Smith 2016).

The numbers are worse in Europe, where 52 per cent of French citizens believe their country should not have to rely on imports. Only 13 per cent believe immigration is a good thing. Attitudes towards foreign investment are in sharp decline. The French, Australians, Norwegians and Americans oppose the idea of foreigners buying indigenous companies (Smith 2016).

The drivers of this backlash against globalisation are as numerous as the challenge is serious (Bergsten 2000). But most analyses suggest a common core: the rise in inequality, a lack of inclusive growth and the belief that openness has made it worse (Pastor & Veronesi 2018).

Inequality is high and rising in many advanced economies. Inequality can be measured in multiple ways, which are discussed in detail in this book. One way is to measure the percentage of national income that goes to the top 10 per cent of income earners. In Europe, the top 10 per cent of income earners receive about 37 per cent of national income. In the United States, Canada and Russia this figure is worse at around 47 per cent (World Inequality Lab (WIL) 2018).

This inequality has grown quickly. The share of national income going to the top 10 per cent has increased by a fifth in Europe since 1980. In the United States and Canada, it has increased by more than a third. In Russia it has doubled (WIL 2018).

The growth in inequality is even more pronounced when looking at the top 1 per cent of income earners. For this group of ultra-rich in the US, their share of national income has almost doubled from 11 per cent to 20 per cent since 1980. The share of the bottom 50 per cent has almost halved, from 21 per cent to 13 per cent (WIL 2018).

Many blame this rise in inequality on globalisation and the openness of economies. The most commonly cited evidence for this claim is the so-called 'Elephant chart' (Figure 1.1). Over the period of rapid globalisation from 1988 to 2008, the chart shows big income gains from globalisation at the very top (the trunk) and for those in the middle (the torso). But the cohort around the 75th and 85th percentile – sandwiched between their own country's ultra-rich and the booming middle classes in the emerging market economies – barely benefited at all. This cohort was pivotal in the election of Trump. It underpinned the Brexit vote and has fuelled the rise in European nationalism.

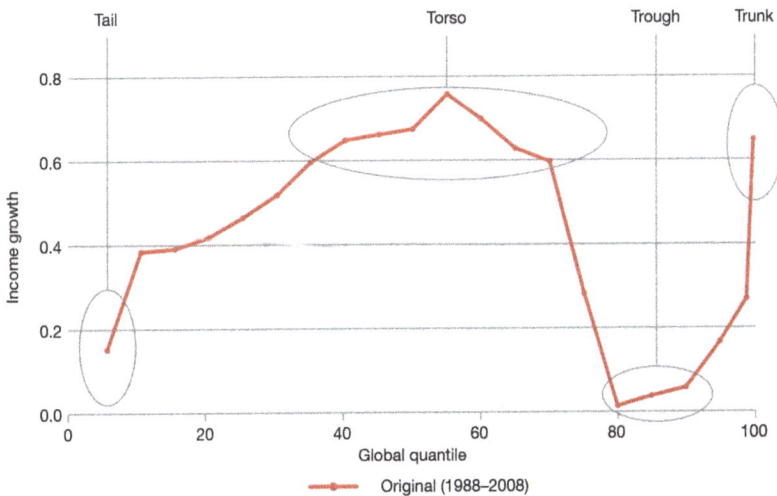

Figure 1.1. Christoph Lakner and Branko Milanovic's 'Elephant chart'
Source. Kharas & Siedel 2018

The research shows that much of this backlash against globalisation is misdirected. There is little evidence that immigration reduces native wages or hurts employment (Breunig et al. 2017). The size, scale and influence of foreign investment are often dramatically overstated and its benefits overlooked (RMIT 2013). The alleged negative effects of trade liberalisation on growth, employment and wages are often confused with the effects of technological automation, which replaces workers with machines (Cocco 2016). And many of the negative effects that flow from trade and investment liberalisation are due to poor domestic policies and weak social safety nets. Economies with strong social safety nets have weathered current transitions well. Those without them have not (Colford 2016).

But regardless of the causes of the current discontent, it is inescapably true that, in advanced economies, globalisation and openness are increasingly viewed with suspicion. This creates a predicament for Asia, which has seen spectacular growth in recent decades. It has benefited substantially from openness and the rules-based global order. Asia not only exports to the advanced economies, but it is also experiencing rising inequality. Much of Asia's growth has not been shared; it has not been 'inclusive growth'.

Inequality in Asia is increasing in wealth and incomes. It is also increasing between genders, races, ages and locations. Will Asia catch the anti-globalisation backlash? How can Asia reduce inequality? What are the forces that determine whether growth in the Asia–Pacific is inclusive or not? And what can be done to make Asia's growth more inclusive in the future? These are the questions explored in this book.

Economic theory and practical lessons for measuring equality of opportunity in the Asia–Pacific region, by Miles Corak

Ensuring that growth is inclusive in the Asia–Pacific means, among other things, ensuring there is more equality. But what exactly does 'equality' mean? And what does it mean to have more of it?

The push for equality has become a challenging political topic in many Asian countries. Much of this debate hinges on how we define equality and the policy solutions that flow from this definition. The area where there appears to be the most political agreement is that we should, at a minimum, strive for equality of opportunity. In Chapter 2, Miles Corak explores this difficult concept.

Theorists and philosophers continue to debate the definition of equality of opportunity, relying as it does on an inherent value judgement to distinguish between 'circumstance' and 'effort'. A young person may, for example, have access to good quality tertiary education through government-funded positions, scholarships or deferred-payment schemes. We may conclude, therefore, that this young person has equality of opportunity and any failure to take up these opportunities is the result of insufficient effort and bad decision-making on their part. But what if this individual has caring responsibilities in their family that are not accounted for? What if their school years failed to prepare them for tertiary education? What if they were raised by parents who did not value education and actively steered them away from it? Suddenly this notion of 'equality of opportunity' becomes much less clear.

The notion of equality of opportunity, however, rings true at some basic level for many citizens, regardless of their country and regardless of their political persuasion. It is one of the few areas of this debate that can be agreed upon by many across the political spectrum. For this reason alone, Corak argues, practitioners should grasp firmly onto whatever theoretical threads they can in order to offer practical indicators that are useful to identify problems and to guide policy solutions.

One commonly used indicator of equality of opportunity is intergenerational earnings elasticity. A high elasticity implies a significant fraction of income inequality will be passed on across generations. In this scenario, a child's adult income will continue to be correlated with their grandparents' income, putting aside any independent influence grandparent income may have on the transmission process.

Conversely, a low intergenerational elasticity suggests that any advantage that parents may have echoes only weakly among the next generation. With no tie at all between child and grandparent incomes, any income advantage or disadvantage is wiped out within two generations.

In the Asia–Pacific, India is estimated to stand at the upper end of this ranking with an intergenerational elasticity of 0.596. The elasticity in China is 0.399. This is somewhat lower than India and the United States, but is nonetheless a relatively high elasticity. Most of the higher income countries in the Asia–Pacific region have higher rates of mobility, whether compared to others in the region but also globally. Countries in South Asia tend to have lower mobility than those in East Asia and the Pacific.

Indicators like intergenerational elasticity are powerful tools. They help policymakers identify serious challenges and tailor policy solutions. But are they reliable?

Intergenerational elasticity, for example, assumes linearity in the mobility process. It assumes that mobility for the very rich is the same for the very poor. As such, it offers no specific sense of directional movement, which may vary across the parental income distribution. The upward movement from rags to riches may not be the same as the downward movement from riches to rags. Further, the elasticity cannot be given a causal interpretation and, though it informs discussions of 'equality of opportunity', it is not, on its own, a measure of this concept.

Corak explores the reliability and usefulness of this and other measures of equality of opportunity. He draws three lessons for the development of useful indicators.

First, existing data should be investigated to calculate standard summary measures of intergenerational mobility. New data should be developed for this purpose from administrative sources. Existing surveys should be enhanced with retrospective information.

Second, common descriptive statistics of mobility across generations should be complemented with other measures that speak more directly to policy concerns. These include measures of absolute mobility and an associated poverty rate based on the minimum level of resources needed to reasonably lower the risk of the intergenerational transmission of low status.

Finally, a dashboard of statistics should be developed to gauge equality of opportunity across different indicators. This involves organising existing information and developing new instruments to chart the relationship between family background and child development through the whole series of transitions that children make on their way to becoming successful and self-sufficient adults.

As many of the chapters in this book show, promoting inclusive growth in the Asia–Pacific requires politically difficult reforms. History shows that the political will to implement reforms can quickly evaporate when there is dispute over the nature of problem to be addressed. Ensuring we can properly measure, identify and understand the challenge of promoting inclusive growth is therefore critical.

Measuring wealth: Implications for sustainable development, by Kevin J Mumford

One of the World Bank's most influential reports is its annual publication of the Doing Business rankings. The rankings compare the business environments across countries, measuring how long it takes a firm to be registered, obtain electricity, secure a building permit, pay taxes and complete many of the other tasks necessary to start and run a business.

The Doing Business rankings have brought out the competitive spirit between countries. Many governments, like those in India and China, have sought to implement reforms to improve their ranking against other countries. But there is a downside. Many of these reforms, it seems, have been unusually specific. Rather than seeking to improve the business environment more generally, many reforms have targeted the specific areas that are measured by the World Bank. By gaming the World Bank's methodology, governments have been able to maximise their country's ranking while minimising their reform effort (*The Economist* 2018).

The impact of the Doing Business rankings is an important lesson: what we choose to measure strongly influences the focus of policy. This is the warning from Kevin Mumford in exploring how we think about, and measure, current and intergenerational wellbeing and wealth in Asia. In Chapter 3, he explores how to present income and wealth data from several Asia–Pacific countries. While he does not evaluate policies, he shows that what we measure determines our focus when choosing policies and strongly influences how we view our political leaders and how we vote.

Mumford uses the term 'current wellbeing' to describe the standard of living enjoyed in a country and the term 'intergenerational wellbeing' to describe the long-run standard of living that will be enjoyed by a country's future generations. Mumford argues that wealth accounting allows us to measure the productive base that provides for the wellbeing of future generations. As a theoretically based measure of intergenerational wellbeing, inclusive wealth, he argues, is the appropriate way to evaluate if economic development is sustainable.

The methods for calculating inclusive growth do not require assumptions about optimality, nor do they require forecasts of future quantities. They do, however, require high-quality price and quantity data for a variety of capital assets. Mumford presents inclusive wealth measures for several Asia–Pacific countries and the computed results make it clear that gross domestic product (GDP) growth does not necessarily indicate growth in inclusive wealth. Indonesia and Malaysia both have periods of GDP growth that occur simultaneously with decreases in inclusive wealth. In fact, he finds that GDP growth rates tend to be larger than inclusive wealth growth for most countries with the exception of Japan. Across most Asian countries, natural capital has experienced large decreases while produced and human capital has experienced large increases. An exception is the Republic of Korea (South Korea hereafter) where natural capital is increasing, driven by renewable natural resources including forests.

Wealth accounting, Mumford argues, will not replace GDP. Flow variables, like GDP, are directly related to current wellbeing. Stock variables, like inclusive wealth, are instead related to potential intergenerational wellbeing. An increase in inclusive wealth implies that future citizens will inherit a larger productive base and will therefore be able to enjoy higher levels of wellbeing. He adds, however, that this is only a statement about potential intergenerational wellbeing, not a claim that wellbeing will necessarily be higher.

Mumford encourages government statistical offices to augment their wealth accounts by measuring the value of human and natural capital. Just as firms create annual balance sheets, governments should prepare annual wealth accounts. Citizens need wealth measures to be able to hold their government accountable for the policies it enacts. Without wealth accounting, all citizens can do is look at the usually strong GDP per capita growth rate and hope that it will continue indefinitely.

Rising inequality amid rapid growth in Asia and implications for policy, by Juzhong Zhuang

Over the past three decades, developing Asia achieved economic growth and reduced poverty faster than any other region of the world at any time in history. There are some recent trends, however, that threaten to overshadow this phenomenal achievement.

Juzhong Zhuang analyses the recent trend of rising income inequality in developing Asia. While growth has increased substantially, the bulk of the region's population lives in countries with rising income inequality. This is in contrast both to the 'growth with equity' story that marked the transformation of the newly industrialised economies in the 1960s and 1970s, and to recent trends in some other parts of the developing world, particularly Latin America, where income inequality has been narrowing since the 1990s.

Zhuang identifies the factors driving this trend and, more importantly, what policies are required to reverse it and reduce income inequality. Zhuang observes that inequality of opportunity is prevalent in developing Asia and is a crucial factor in widening income inequality. Inequality of opportunity and of income can lead to a vicious circle, as unequal opportunities create income disparities, which in turn lead to differences in future opportunities for individuals and households. Zhuang argues that increasing inequality weakens the basis of economic growth.

Technological change, globalisation, and market-oriented deregulation have played a critical role in driving Asia's rapid growth. But they have also had significant implications for the distribution of wealth. These forces tend to favour owners of capital over labour, skilled over unskilled workers, and urban and coastal areas over rural and inland regions. The impacts of these forces have been compounded by various forms of unequal access to opportunity caused by institutional weaknesses and social exclusion. Zhuang shows that these forces have worked together to lead to a falling share of labour income in total national income, increasing premiums on human capital, growing spatial disparity, and widening wealth inequality – all of which contribute to rising income inequality. But how should Asian governments respond to rising inequality?

Zhuang argues that the three driving forces of economic growth – technological change, globalisation, and market-oriented deregulation – should not be obstructed, even if they cause rising inequality. Doing so would cause more harm than good. What is required, Zhuang argues, is to have policy measures deployed that confront rising inequality and focus on equalising opportunity. These policies include measures toward creating more high-quality jobs for the broader population; interventions that narrow spatial disparity; fiscal policies that reduce inequality in human capital and make the tax system more effective and fairer; and reforms that strengthen governance and institutions, level the playing field, bolster the social safety net and eliminate social exclusion.

Openness and inclusive growth in South-East Asia, by Aekapol Chongvilaivan

A lack of inclusive growth has contributed to a backlash against globalisation in both advanced and emerging economies alike. The Asian region has invested heavily in openness, however, as Zhuang shows, it has also experienced rising inequality in recent years. Are these two phenomena related? Is Asia's pursuit of openness helping or hindering inclusive growth?

Aekapol Chongvilaivan explores this question. Given the complex interplay between openness and inclusive growth, he empirically investigates the redistributive effects of trade and financial openness in the context of South-East Asian economies. The relationship between openness and inequality, it seems, is not as clear as anti-globalists suggest.

First, contrary to the opinion of the anti-globalists, trade openness has no significant impact on inequality. This is consistent with the literature. Studies that have looked at the relationship between openness and inequality, in South-East Asia and elsewhere, typically struggle to find any robust relationship.

Chongvilaivan, however, finds a different story when trade is broken down into its respective export and import components. He finds that the export and import components of trade openness have opposing effects on inequality. While export openness tends to mitigate inequality, more exposure to imports results in higher inequality. Although further research is required, the impact on wages is posited as a potential reason for this.

Importantly, Chongvilaivan finds that financial liberalisation, measured by the ratio of foreign assets to GDP, helps to reduce inequality. He argues that greater financial liberalisation provides greater access to financial resources and opportunities for the poor. There is a robust literature in support of this argument. Chongvilaivan argues that freer flows of cross-border capital may provide greater access to financial resources and economic opportunity to the poor.

Several policy insights flow from these findings. The interplay of exports and imports through the development of cross-border supply-chains across South-East Asian countries makes the distinction between exports and imports less clear. But the findings show that openness is by no means to blame for the observed increase in inequality. This is particularly the case for financial openness. Financial openness provides greater access to financial resources and opportunities for the poor and has played a critical role in reducing inequality.

Chongvilaivan's results are an important contribution. Combatting the rise in anti-globalisation sentiment will require many different solutions. Protectionism, Chongvilaivan shows, is not one of them.

Automation, the future of work and income inequality in the Asia–Pacific region, by Yixiao Zhou

Research shows that, when it comes to manufacturing-job losses in the advanced economies, trade is often unfairly blamed. A study found that 85 per cent of US manufacturing-job losses from 2000 to 2010 were caused by technological change – largely automation – rather than trade (Hicks & Deveraj 2015). For a region heavily invested in the global trading system, such analysis may be welcome news in Asia. But it raises critical questions about what automation and increased technological change might mean for the Asian region into the future.

Yixiao Zhou examines the impact of recent developments in technologies on employment and income distribution and identifies some important trends for the future. Based on his analysis, Zhou discusses development strategies and policies to nurture employment and growth while harnessing technological advances in the Asia–Pacific region.

Zhou observes that, despite sluggishness in the growth of total factor productivity in major economies since the global financial crisis (GFC), a new round of technological revolution characterised by automation, robotics, artificial intelligence, big data analytics and Industry 4.0 is rapidly approaching. The full impact of these new technologies, he argues, yet to be realised. Use of industrial robots has been growing quickly in Asia, surpassing their rate of adoption in Europe and the Americas. This growth in robotics is driven by firms' need to maintain competitiveness in international markets due to ageing populations and increases in labour costs in the Asia–Pacific region.

Zhou is not alone in his prediction. William Nordhaus, winner of the 2018 Nobel Prize in Economics, has made similar predictions (Nordhaus 2015). Analysis from Iraj Saniee and his co-authors at Bell Labs have predicted a productivity surge in the United States between 2028 and 2033, based on the historical time lags between technological advances and productivity booms (Saniee et al. 2017).

Zhou argues that technological progress will have positive impacts on firms' competitiveness and economic growth. But there may also be a downside. The rise of robotics will potentially cause unemployment and aggravate income inequality given that future technological progress may favour those with skills and be labour-saving for those with fewer skills. Two mechanisms with opposite effects on employment are identified: the labour-replacing effect and the productivity-enhancing effect, with the former reducing employment and the latter creating new jobs and tasks.

Income inequality is likely to rise in the short run if the labour-replacing effect dominates before new industries, tasks and jobs are generated. To deal with unemployment resulting from increased use of robots, it is important to improve the quality of workers through retraining. Zhou foresees that the rise of automation in major economies including China, South Korea, Japan, Germany and the United States will have significant impacts on the growth trajectory of emerging economies in Asia. If large-scale capital deepening continues in China, there is less hope that emerging economies can continue to follow the East–Asian growth model to prosperity, resulting in greater development gaps. Instead, firms in these countries could develop technological capability to integrate into the Industry 4.0 platforms of major economies and leverage these new technologies to leapfrog and ace in niche markets.

Zhou concludes that staying open and connected, investing in human capital, improving business environments, promoting flexible economies and stimulating entrepreneurship are strategies that will help firms in the Asia–Pacific region prosper in the new wave of technological progress.

History returns: Intergenerational mobility of education in China in 1930–2010, by Yang Yao and Zhi-An Hu

Education is referred to as the silver bullet in a world where there are no silver bullets. And the sheer scale of China means that policy outcomes there will reverberate throughout the region. When it comes to reducing inequality in Asia, education in China must therefore receive special attention.

Yao and Hu analyse intergenerational mobility in education in China by using the results of a widespread survey (China Family Panel Studies) conducted in 2010. The survey covered the intergenerational education of 62,219 people born between 1930 and 1985.

Intergenerational mobility in education is an important indicator for measuring educational equality. The survey results on educational attainment by different birth cohorts showed a continuous improvement in education in terms of school enrolment. Intergenerational mobility, however, changed dramatically during the period studied, with key implications for policy in the region.

The authors measured intergenerational mobility by computing the coefficient of correlation (transmission coefficient) between the educational achievements of two consecutive generations. A higher coefficient implies stagnant intergenerational mobility and thus slower improvement of educational equality.

According to the estimation, the coefficient formed a U–shaped curve with the lowest points situated at the birth cohorts of the mid-1950s. Intergenerational mobility was limited for people born in the early 1930s.

The coefficient dropped rapidly until the cohorts born around 1940. This shows that social mobility accelerated even before the communist revolution. After a short period of setback, the decline continued until the birth cohorts of the mid-1950s. Most of these people got their middle school and high school education during the Cultural Revolution. The political and social mobilisation during this period decisively accelerated social mobility within the Chinese population.

This process has reversed since 1978, however, when the Chinese Communist Party turned its focus to economic growth and spent less effort on social transformation. The transmission coefficient increased steadily across birth cohorts and, by the cohorts of the mid-1970s (who would finish their education by the end of the 1990s), it went back to the levels of the cohorts of the mid-1930s. In other words, educational inequality has been widening in China.

Yao and Hu point out several reasons for the decline in intergenerational mobility. One crucial reason is the disadvantageous educational environment in rural areas compared to urban areas; good high schools are concentrated in the city. Farm households' incentive to invest in their children's education has declined because of increased employment opportunity. As for university education, rural youths face the two disadvantages of poor-quality university education and high tuition fees.

Yao and Hu argue that, during 40 years of relentless economic growth, the Chinese Government and Chinese society have been firmly occupied by a single-minded belief in economic efficiency. Now that China is establishing a well-off society, it is time for the government to reintroduce social progress into its programs.

Inequality and intergenerational mobility in India, by Himanshu

Few countries embody the challenge of inclusive growth more than India. Analysis across income, consumption and wealth shows that inequality is much higher in India compared to other countries with similar levels of economic development. This has been confirmed on several dimensions, including aspects of human development such as education, health and nutrition.

Over the next five years, India is forecast to grow faster than China and the ASEAN+6 average. Even if growth moderates to 6 per cent, the economy will still double in size within two decades. A fifth of the world's workers will be Indian by 2025. The Indian economy is attracting significant global attention.

On human development indicators, India suffers from the twin problem of a high level of deprivation and low achievement on most indicators, but also from large inequalities in access and outcomes. More worrying are the trends over time that suggest a secular rise in inequality in almost all dimensions, albeit with some moderation in the most recent period.

India's rising inequality has followed significant economic growth in recent decades. The pattern of growth has increased incomes and reduced poverty but also led to a growing gap between those in the formal, service-based economy and a majority who are stuck in farming and in the informal sector with poor working conditions. The livelihood and wellbeing of these people are affected by the persistence of inequalities of caste, religion, geography and gender, all of which contribute to exclude and marginalise a large segment of the population.

Himanshu documents and analyses the trends in inequality in India, particularly in the last three decades, exploring the role of inequality in relation to mobility of households and individuals.

Himanshu finds that inequality in India has largely been driven by changes in the labour market. The rise in profit share of national income has accompanied the decline in wage share. Inequality in access to public services, such as health and education, has also risen in recent years. There are growing concerns of 'crony capitalism' in parts of India's economy.

Whether the process of growth will be sustained or not depends not just on economic policies but also policies on human development and inclusion. The evidence from intergenerational mobility provides a mixed picture. There is an overall increase in access to non-farm jobs by the poor and the disadvantaged but also a persistence of caste-based rigidities.

In the long run, inequality is not just a matter of moral and philosophical concern. Reducing it is also instrumental in sustaining economic growth by allowing a larger majority of disadvantaged to participate in and benefit from the growth process. India's success in reducing inequality will have critical economic and political implications throughout the region.

Intergenerational equity under increasing longevity, by Sumio Saruyama, Saeko Maeda, Ryo Hasumi and Kazuki Kuroiwa

People in Japan enjoy one of the highest life expectancies in the world. Lives are long in Japan, and they are forecast to get longer. This is undoubtedly a good thing. But it raises a range of challenges, including intergenerational equity.

Sumio Saruyama, Saeko Maeda, Ryo Hasumi and Kazuki Kuroiwa examine intergenerational equity by applying a simulation analysis to the case of Japan. They look at three representative generations: those born in 1950; the children of this generation, born in 1980; and the generation born 30 years later in 2010. These are referred to as generations 1, 2 and 3. If the current situation continues in the future, the younger the generation, the heavier will be the net burden and the greater the disadvantages from societal ageing.

In the simulation, life expectancies of these groups are assumed to be 85.8, 90, and 93.2, respectively. Along with longer life expectancy, working years are assumed to be extended by 10 years. The year in which people begin receiving their pension will be rolled back and they are assumed to continue paying pension-insurance premiums as they work.

Saruyama et al.'s main interests from the simulation are the impacts on consumption, generational accounting, government finance and GDP. According to the simulation results, thanks to increased longevity, Generation 3 will experience a 9–13 per cent increase in lifetime consumption. Generation 2 will see a 9–10 per cent increase. Another important finding is that the primary balance to GDP ratio would improve by 6–7 per cent over the baseline case because of the extension of working years and delay in pension payment. If the resulting fiscal surplus is then applied to reducing medical and nursing care premiums, it will be possible to lighten the burden on the younger generations.

Saruyama et al. argue that, in an age when people live to 100, exiting the workforce at the age of 65 – retirement age for many companies and institutions – is too early. Japan needs to build a system enabling people to work an additional 10 years. Extending people's healthy lifespan will also be important so that they can fully benefit from the additional consumption that longer lifespans make possible.

Having obtained the scenario, which is more favourable to business, the authors warn the need for Japan to enhance the sustainability of its social-insurance system and urgently institute reforms. These reforms must narrow the gaps between generations regarding burdens and benefits. If economic conditions deteriorate or a large-scale debt-reduction plan is required, there may not be a resolution for the young generation's disadvantage, even with the extension of the retirement age.

Female labour force participation in Indonesia: Why has it stalled? By Lisa Cameron, Diana Contreras Suarez and William Rowell

The policy objective that is integral to boosting inclusive economic growth – increasing female workforce participation – would advance human rights, grow the economy, raise household incomes, increase productivity and strengthen societies.

In 2014, the G20 committed to reduce the gap between male and female workforce participation in each of their economies by 25 per cent by the year 2025. If achieved, the Organisation for Economic Co-operation and Development (OECD) estimated that this would raise G20 GDP by more than 1 per cent, around US$1 trillion. This commitment was taken up by all G20 countries, including its six Asian members: Australia, China, India, Indonesia, Japan and Korea.

Achieving this commitment is a critical way to boost inclusive growth in Asia. But will Asia's G20 economies achieve this goal?

Lisa Cameron, Diana Contreras Suarez and William Rowell look at the interesting case of Indonesia. Despite dramatic economic advances having occurred since the late 1990s, female labour force participation in Indonesia has barely changed. Indonesia is below the average for ASEAN+3 economies. It is roughly on a par with Japan, Malaysia, Myanmar and the Philippines, but even these economies have seen female participation increase since 1995 (Japan being the other exception).

Not all news is bad. The modelling by Cameron et al. finds that, once you control for individual, household and village characteristics, there are signs that the underlying propensity for women to participate in the labour force has been increasing in Indonesia, particularly in urban areas. The problem, however, is that this increase is offset by forces reducing female participation. The most significant offsetting force is the continued decline in the relative importance of the agricultural sector to the Indonesian economy, given the importance of this sector to female employment.

If this underlying propensity for women to participate in the workforce continues to increase, the authors expect female labour force participation will similarly increase as older cohorts exit the labour market. But this will take time. It will likely be too late for the G20's 2025 commitment. In fact, under the authors' less-optimistic scenario (which the authors argue is more realistic), female workforce participation may even decrease by 2025 before it starts to rise.

There is another way. Using the results from their modelling on the drivers of female workforce participation in Indonesia, Cameron et al. identify a variety of policies that could be implemented to increase female workforce participation.

Their analysis finds that the main drivers of female workforce participation (cohort and age effects aside) are marital status, the number of children aged between 0 and 2 years of age in the household, educational attainment (particularly tertiary education) and the village industrial structure (with agriculture and manufacturing being female-friendly industries). These results suggest some practical ways in which the Indonesian Government could speed-up the progress in female workforce participation.

Policies that support women to return to work after childbirth are likely to have the most dramatic effects in increasing female labour force participation. These policies include the provision of some form of child care for women with young children and policies and laws that encourage employers to make part-time and family-friendly work available. Increasing the educational attainment of women, particularly in rural areas where educational attainment remains low, is also likely to assist.

No matter what new policies are put in place, the ongoing movement of the Indonesian economy away from the agricultural sector will continue to drag. Policies need to hit this head-on. Policies designed to provide women with access to employment in non-traditional industrial sectors, for example, through the provision of subsidised vocational education or campaigns that provide and promote opportunities for women in these sectors, are worthy of special attention.

Indonesia will be an important case study for the Asia–Pacific on female workforce participation. But will it be an example of what to do, or what not to do? As is often the case throughout this book, this will depend on the political will of the government.

References

BBC (2016). 'Drug dealers, criminals, rapists: What Trump thinks of Mexicans', *BBC News*, 31 August, www.bbc.com/news/av/world-us-canada-37230916/drug-dealers-criminals-rapists-what-trump-thinks-of-mexicans.

Bergsten, F (2000). 'The backlash against globalization', speech to the Trilateral Commission, Tokyo, Japan, 9 May. Petersen Institution for International Economics, piie.com/commentary/speeches-papers/backlash-against-globalization.

Breunig, B, Deutscher, N & Thi To, H (2017). 'The relationship between immigration to Australia and the labour market outcomes of Australian-born workers', *Economic Record*, 93(301), 255–76. doi.org/10.1111/1475-4932.12328.

Bush, GHW (1999). 'Free Trade @ 10', keynote address, 5 June. McGill University, Montreal, www.youtube.com/watch?v=zKeSAI8uS8g.

Cocco, F (2016). 'Most US manufacturing jobs lost to technology, not trade', *Financial Times*, 3 December.

Colford, C (2016). '"Making the case for trade": Winning voters' trust by strengthening social safety nets', *Private Sector Development Blog*, 15 May, World Bank Blogs, blogs.worldbank.org/psd/making-case-trade-winning-voters-trust-strengthening-social-safety-nets.

Green, L (2018). '"Conservative but not a nut": how Bush's party fell to Trump's troops', *The Guardian*, 3 December, www.theguardian.com/us-news/2018/dec/03/george-hw-bush-republicans-trump-1988-election-michael-dukakis.

Hicks, M & Deveraj, S (2015). 'The myth and the reality of manufacturing in America', Ball State University, June, projects.cberdata.org/reports/Mfg Reality.pdf.

Kharas, H & Siedel, B (2018). *What's happening to the world income distribution?*, April, Brookings Institution, Working Paper 114, www.brookings.edu/wp-content/uploads/2018/04/workingpaper114-elephantchartrevisited.pdf.

Miles, T (2018). 'US seen likely to win in effort to shut down WTO's appeals court', *Reuters*, 5 October, www.reuters.com/article/us-usa-trade-wto/u-s-seen-likely-to-win-in-effort-to-shut-down-wtos-appeals-court-idUSKCN1MF1NE.

Nordhaus, W (2015). *Are we approaching an economic singularity? Information technology and the future of economic growth*, September, Working Paper 21547. National Bureau of Economic Research, Cambridge, MA, www.nber.org/papers/w21547.pdf. doi.org/10.3386/w21547.

Pastor, L & Veronesi, P (2018). *Inequality aversion, populism, and the backlash against globalization*, Becker Friedman Institute, Working Paper 2018-53, bfi.uchicago.edu/sites/default/files/file_uploads/WP_2018-53.pdf. doi.org/10.3386/w24900.

RMIT (2013). 'Greens Senator Rachel Siewert's foreign ownership claim overstated', RMIT ABC FactCheck, 3 October.

Saniee, I, Kamat, S, Prakash, S & Weldon, M (2017). 'Will productivity growth return in the new digital era?' *Bell Labs Technical Journal*, 22, 1–18, ieeexplore. ieee.org/document/7951155. doi.org/10.15325/BLTJ.2017.2714819.

Smith, M (2016). 'International survey: globalisation is still seen as a force for good in the world', *YouGov*, 17 November, today.yougov.com/topics/politics/articles-reports/2016/11/17/international-survey.

The Economist (2018). 'Most criticisms of the Doing Business rankings miss the point', 1 November.

Wall Street Journal (2018). 'I am a tariff man', 4 December, www.wsj.com/articles/i-am-a-tariff-man-1543965558.

World Inequality Lab (2018). *World Inequality Report, 2018*, wir2018.wid.world/executive-summary.html.

2

ECONOMIC THEORY AND PRACTICAL LESSONS FOR MEASURING EQUALITY OF OPPORTUNITY IN THE ASIA–PACIFIC REGION[1]

Miles Corak

Introduction and major messages

My use of the word 'practical' in the title of this paper should not necessarily be interpreted as 'feasible'. Some of the suggestions I make for the development of a set of statistics appropriate for the measurement of equality of opportunity certainly are feasible, and while some can be introduced and used almost immediately, others can only be put into practice over a longer horizon and may well require a commitment of statistical resources. The point is to clarify the elements of a dashboard of equality-of-opportunity indicators that can be used to promote evidence-based policy by making comparisons, gauging progress, and possibly even setting targets. 'Practical' lessons are those that can in principle be put into practice, but also those that are grounded in our understanding of the theory of intergenerational mobility and equality of opportunity.

---

1   This paper is based upon and adapts my 2016 paper *Economic theory and practical lessons for measuring equality of opportunities* (No 2016/02, OECD Statistics Working Papers. Paris).

Theory, of course, rarely if ever gives direct guidance to empirical analysis and public policy. I draw two threads from economic theory, and pull them as long as I possibly can to inform specific recommendations for policymakers concerned with the measurement and monitoring of equality of opportunity in the Asia–Pacific countries. Economic theory first suggests that descriptive statistics associated with intergenerational mobility do not speak directly to equality of opportunity without accepting a value judgement that children should not be held responsible for circumstances beyond their control; and, second, the process of child development encourages a focus on different skills and competencies, as well as different stages in a child's life. These two threads of thought lead to three suggestions.

The first is to use data appropriate for the country at hand – and, indeed, where possible promote the development and use of new data, whether associated with the administration of government programs, survey data supplemented with retrospective questions, or linked survey and administrative data – to estimate summary measures of intergenerational mobility. These statistics include a measure of the average rate of income mobility, and a measure of directional rank mobility: (1) the intergenerational earnings elasticity, which can be thought of as a complement to cross-sectional indicators of inequality like the Gini coefficient; and (2) intergenerational income transition matrices, which depict the degree and direction of child mobility according to each parental rank.

The second suggestion is to develop measures of absolute mobility and, in particular, develop a poverty line based upon the monetary resources associated with possibly discrete changes in the lack of upward mobility for children whose parents are in the lower part of the income distribution. The headcount ratio of children living in families with less than this level of monetary resources is a more timely statistic than the intergenerational elasticity that can be regularly published, and offers an early warning sign of changes in intergenerational mobility.

The final suggestion is to describe socio-economic gradients in the health and wellbeing, numeracy, and literacy of young children and those in their early teens. This involves regularly publishing a host of appropriate statistics associated with important skills and competencies of children in a way that is framed by the theory of equality of opportunity. This should be based upon surveys of children in their early teen years, and children on the cusp of primary school. These age-appropriate statistics should be included – along with measures of family background – in repeatedly administered cross-sectional surveys.

What is intergenerational mobility?

There is no single answer to the question of what comprises intergenerational mobility, and certainly there is credibility in many of the different measures used across the various social sciences. Economic analysis is rooted in a perspective that stretches back to Francis Galton, whose work dates to the late 1800s, and continues to resonate today through a simple model of 'regression to the mean':

$$lnY_{i,t} = \alpha + \beta lnY_{i,t-1} + \epsilon_{i,t}$$

where Y is an outcome that we are interested in, usually taken to be permanent income by economists, i indexes families, and t generations. The best guess of a child's adult earnings (generally expressed in natural logarithms) is just the average income of his or her birth cohort – which can be thought as indicated by α – plus two deviations from the average, the first being some fraction of the earnings of his or her parent or parents, as represented by β – and the other representing residual influences not correlated with parental income. The value of β, the intergenerational income elasticity – usually estimated by least squares – is the parameter of interest, indicating to what degree the relative advantages or disadvantages of the parent are transmitted to the child. β expresses this in percentage terms, and is generally found to be positive but less than one: as it approaches zero, mobility is complete (with the best guess of a child's adult earnings being the cohort average); as it approaches one, mobility is limited and, in the extreme, children occupy the same position in the income distribution as their parents. Negative values indicate an intergenerational reversal in economic status, and values greater than one indicate divergence from, rather than regression to, the average.

As an exercise in description, this statistic is no more than what it is, though sometimes it is made out to be much more, possibly reflecting the fact that what is central to academic analysis may not align perfectly with what is of interest in public policy. It is the best overall measure of the average degree of intergenerational mobility. But, much in the same way that the Gini coefficient offers a broad indication of cross-sectional inequality, the intergenerational elasticity, like the Gini, misses important nuances. The elasticity assumes linearity in the mobility process, mobility for the very rich being the same for the very poor. As such, it offers no specific sense of directional movement should that vary across the parental income distribution; the upward movement from rags to riches may not be the same as the downward movement from riches to rags. Further, the elasticity cannot be given a causal interpretation and, though it informs discussions of 'equality of opportunity', it is not, on its own, a measure of this concept.

There is a long list of careful studies suggesting this statistic varies across the rich countries, lying somewhere between 0.4 and 0.6 for Italy, the United Kingdom and the United States; and as low as 0.2 or less in some Nordic countries. Björklund and Jäntti (2011), Black and Devereux (2011), Blanden (2013), Corak (2013; 2006), Mulligan (1997), and Solon (2002; 1999) review this literature. While this statistic has been estimated for men and women, for a host of different measures of income and earnings – both individual and family; for earnings; total market income; and for income after taxes and transfers – the largest number of estimates that permit cross-country comparisons refer to the market earnings of fathers and sons. This version of the statistic has been estimated for many more countries, with the World Bank offering the most recent and comprehensive list covering more than 70 countries (Narayan et al. 2018). Figure 2.1 uses this list, presenting the available intergenerational earnings elasticity for the Asia–Pacific countries. These statistics roughly refer to the adult outcomes of children born in the 1960s and 1970s.

There is a significant range, from as high as 0.702 to as low as 0.181. The World Bank report notes that mobility tends to be higher in high-income countries (Narayan et al. 2018, 139). The intergenerational elasticities among the 75 countries listed in the World Bank report range from 1.095 to 0.113, with a global unweighted average of 0.515. The range of estimates in Figure 2.1 comes close to spanning the global extremes. Most of the higher income countries in the region have higher rates of mobility, whether compared to others in the region but also globally. Countries in South Asia tend to have lower mobility than those in East Asia and the Pacific.

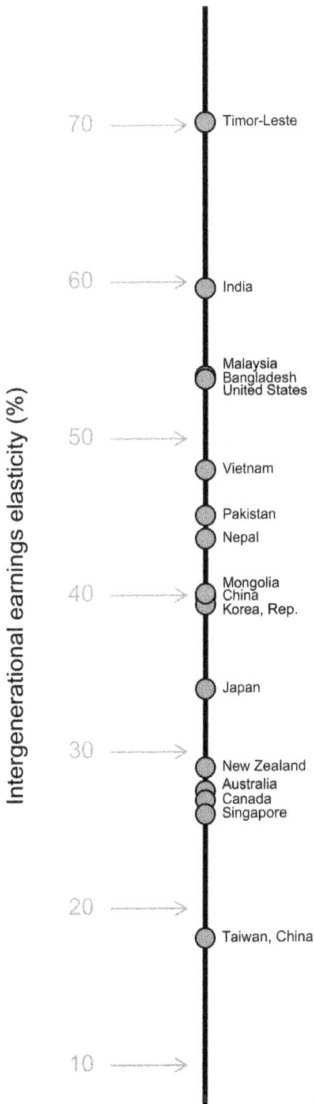

Figure 2.1. Seventeen Asia–Pacific countries ranked according to World Bank estimates of intergenerational earnings elasticity

Source. Derived by the author using the Global Database on Intergenerational Mobility (GDIM) (2018) (Development Research Group, World Bank. Washington DC)

An intergenerational earnings elasticity as high as 0.702 implies a significant fraction of income inequality will be passed on across generations and, on its own, suggests a sluggish rate of regression to the mean. In this scenario, a child's adult income will continue to be correlated with his or her grandparents' income, putting aside any independent influence grandparent income may have on the transmission process. An intergenerational elasticity as low as 0.181 suggests that any advantage that parents may have echoes only weakly among the next generation, with no tie at all between child and grandparent incomes and income advantage or disadvantage being wiped out in two generations. India is estimated to stand at the upper end of this ranking with an intergenerational elasticity of 0.596. The elasticity in China is 0.399, somewhat lower than India or, for that matter, the United States, but nonetheless a relatively high elasticity reflecting lower mobility than almost half of the countries in this list.

Finally, this statistic on its own makes no reference to absolute differences or directional changes: whether a generation is making more or less than the previous generation, whether particular children are making more or less than their parents, or whether mobility in one country is higher or lower than another because of more or less mobility in either an upward direction from the bottom, or a downward direction from the top.

Public policy is motivated not just by the overall average rate of mobility, but also by the direction of movement, particularly the chances of intergenerational cycles of low income, the chances of moving from the bottom to the middle or upper ranks, and even the chances of intergenerational cycles of privilege that may block children from lower or middle family backgrounds moving into the top ranks.

Even so, this is a valuable statistic as a backdrop to public policy discussion, and offers a complement to the Gini coefficient and other measures of cross-sectional inequality. It is a broad summary measure of mobility, indicating the degree to which relative income advantages are passed on between successive generations. But if there is confidence that a particular country has the statistical infrastructure in place to accurately produce this statistic, then it would do well to supplement it with a somewhat fuller descriptive account of mobility. As mentioned, the regression to the mean model assumes the mobility process is linear, and offers no sense of movement in specific directions. It is usefully complemented with the transition matrix between parent and child ranks in their respective income distributions. These transition matrices, an example of which is offered in Table 2.1, give a sense of both upward and downward mobility, and permit the public policy community to assess the degree of mobility from any set of parents with a common rank in the income distribution.

Table 2.1. Quintile transition matrix between parent and child incomes in the United States

Child quintile	Parent quintile				
	1	2	3	4	5
1	33.7%	24.2%	17.8%	13.4%	10.9%
2	28.0%	24.2%	19.8%	16.0%	11.9%
3	18.4%	21.7%	22.1%	20.9%	17.0%
4	12.3%	17.6%	22.0%	24.4%	23.6%
5	7.5%	12.3%	18.3%	25.4%	36.5%

Source. Chetty et al. (2014), Table II

This example is drawn from Chetty et al. (2014) using administrative data on the income taxation of the population of children born in the early 1980s, their filings at roughly the age of 30 and those of their parents decades earlier. The information in Table 2.1 shows that children raised by parents in the bottom 20 per cent of the income distribution have only a 7.5 per cent chance of moving to the top fifth, while those raised by parents in the top have an almost 37 per cent chance of being in the top fifth of their generation. It is in this sense that patterns of directional movement can be described.

But this example also makes clear that the data requirements may be particularly challenging, necessitating not just a direct intergenerational link between parent and child adult incomes – a longitudinal link of members of the same family that may have to span decades – but also relatively large sample sizes in order to derive transition probabilities between distinct parts of the income distribution. The use of high quality and comprehensive income tax data has allowed researchers in some of the rich countries to produce transition matrices as defined as finely as percentiles (Chetty et al. 2014; Corak 2018). This may not be possible, and poses a data challenge for other countries.

This said, promoting the upward mobility of children raised by bottom income parents is likely to be a relevant policy issue for all countries, and particularly those moving from low- and middle-income status to high-income status. The intergenerational earnings elasticity informs this discussion even under the assumption of linearity. A slow regression to the mean might raise the importance of not letting families fall too far below average income because mobility is so low. But a non-linear process heightens the matter even more, and may also give this public policy discussion particular salience in countries that have a high degree of regression to the mean.

What is left unanswered is just what income levels are critical to lowering the risk of an intergenerational stickiness of status at the bottom: where should we draw a poverty line if our concern is the risk associated with the loss of upward mobility? Further, should this be entirely income based, or should it include other crucial resources needed to promote upward mobility? Ranks don't answer these questions, and we can't fully answer them without an appreciation of the underlying causes. The development and regular publication of a poverty line of this sort – a measure of the minimal monetary and other resources below which the chances of the intergenerational transmission of poverty are distinctly higher – and its associated headcount ratio would be a valuable complement to existing poverty lines.

What is equality of opportunity?

The degree of regression to the mean in incomes, and associated transition matrices, are central descriptive statistics of intergenerational mobility. Without them we cannot begin a discussion about equality of opportunity. But they are not measures of equality of opportunity. John Roemer makes the case that a transition matrix in which all entries are the same – a completely level playing field with no differences in the association between child outcomes and family backgrounds – does not reflect a definition of equality of opportunity that most citizens would consider acceptable (Roemer 2004). It would involve public policy levelling all possible playing fields, compensating for all possible circumstances and, by implication, significantly curtailing the role of family autonomy in the raising of children.

For Roemer, equality of opportunity means that inequities of outcome are not defensible when they are the result of different 'circumstances' (Roemer 2000). To make this distinction, we need to know to what degree individuals are responsible for their outcomes in life: in other words, to what extent are these outcomes the result of circumstances beyond an individual's control (for which they should be compensated), and to what extent do they reflect an individual's effort (for which they should be responsible)?

His philosophical analysis of these issues asks us to accept that drawing a line between 'circumstance' and 'effort' requires a value judgement. Values are certainly a part of economic analysis, and it is fair to suggest that they mainly enter the analysis as a way of ranking the desirability of alternative outcomes. Philosophers, and a good deal of experimental evidence, however, tell us that most people also care about the ways in which outcomes are obtained: process matters. Equality of opportunity is about process, and value judgements are inherent to defining it.

As such, the development of statistics useful for public policy addressed to equality of opportunity cannot escape the need to make an explicit value judgement. Without doing so, theory will offer little guidance for the conduct of policy, and no practical suggestions for the development of appropriate statistical indicators beyond the purely descriptive. But this is nothing new. For example, while it is rare for the statistical agencies to adopt 'official' poverty lines, all these countries, or their supra-national representatives, draw these lines using some value judgement on the degree of absolute and relative deprivation that in some sense is not acceptable.

It is not self-evident what 'circumstances' policymakers should seek to level in order to promote equality of opportunity, but one way to advance the discussion is to focus measurement on children. Roemer and Trannoy suggest that 'all inequality regarding children should be counted as due to circumstances, and none to effort. More specifically, children should only become responsible for their actions after an "age of consent" is reached (which may vary across societies), so both nature and nurture fall within the ambit of circumstances for the child' (Roemer & Trannoy 2016, 1308). This may be a value judgement that most citizens are willing to accept, particularly when paired with a human rights perspective, informed by the UN Convention on the Rights of the Child, which almost all countries have ratified.

Economic theory makes clear that intergenerational mobility is determined by a host of factors, and that we can't parse these out by simply looking at the intergenerational income elasticity. Becker and Tomes (1986; 1979) offer a standard and widely used economic model underscoring this point. A simplified version would be based on the following three equations:

$$lnY_t = \phi lnY_{t-1} + \gamma H_t + \lambda E_t + v_t \tag{1}$$
$$H_t = \delta E_t + \theta lnY_{t-1} \tag{2}$$
$$E_t = \alpha + hE_{t-1} + V_t \tag{3}$$

The model is recursive, and this formalisation also links with increasingly accepted notions of child development. In my notation, t indexes generations, with t referring to children and t-1 to their parents. Children inherit from their parents an endowment associated with their underlying personality, competencies, or perhaps family culture (E), to the degree given by h. This endowment influences the development of their human capital (H), which may also be influenced by their parents' status, usually income status (but also possibly education status), to the degree given by θ, with $\theta \geq 0$. Human capital, in turn, is an important influence on adult outcomes, (Y), but endowments continue to play a direct role, as may also be the case for parental status, according to the values of λ and ϕ.

The important message, even at this level of abstraction, is that β, as Solon (2004) makes clear, will be a composite of:

- the degree of inheritability of innate endowments or family culture (h)
- the strength of the causal association between family circumstances and a child's human capital (θ)
- the returns to those components of human capital (γ), a clear marker for the degree of labour market inequality
- any direct influence parental status may have on earnings outcomes of children in adulthood (ϕ), through networks or nepotism, or through endowments (λ).

The observation that one country has a different β from another, or that there are upward or downward trends in β over time and cohorts within a country is not informative for public policy directed to equality of opportunity because this coefficient does not identify a particular causal force, and because we have not articulated as a public policy objective which – if any – of these factors cut against accepted notions of equality of opportunity.

If we focus on equation (1), most citizens might agree that differences in incomes associated with nepotism in the hiring process should be eliminated so that those with well-connected parents are not earning more than other children who are just as highly educated or have the same level of other characteristics that influence earnings. And most citizens might also agree on eliminating differences in outcomes associated with endowments that do not reflect differences in productivity – skin colour, height, beauty, and ethnicity. But we cannot know whether or not this is the case from observing β, which would also be influenced by the returns to characteristics, whether innate or through the efforts that went into getting more schooling and skills, that are associated with productivity differentials. A statistic derived from an equation like $lnY_{i,t} = \alpha + \beta lnY_{i,t-1} + \epsilon_{i,t}$ only starts this conversation, and a public policy conversation more closely tied to Roemer's notion of equality of opportunity first requires an understanding of how labour markets work and how access to jobs is determined, and then moves to placing emphasis on children, focusing on equation (2), the development of human capital, and its association with parental status.

This model may be too simplified to describe how human capital is developed. We need to appreciate the developments in the economics, psychology and child development literatures suggesting equation (2) might be more appropriately represented as a series of recursive equations, each representing a stage in which children develop specific competencies that then set a stage, and raise or dampen the risks of fully developing through the next stage. An important interaction in this process is that between the early years and subsequent development, as summarised by Jim Heckman's metaphor that 'skills beget skills' (Heckman & Mosso 2014). We need to also appreciate that the dimensions of human capital relevant for adult earnings may also be multidimensional and include not just cognitive skills but also aspects of health and wellbeing, as well as personality and other non-cognitive skills. Formal schooling and the associated credentials may only partially indicate or develop these skills.

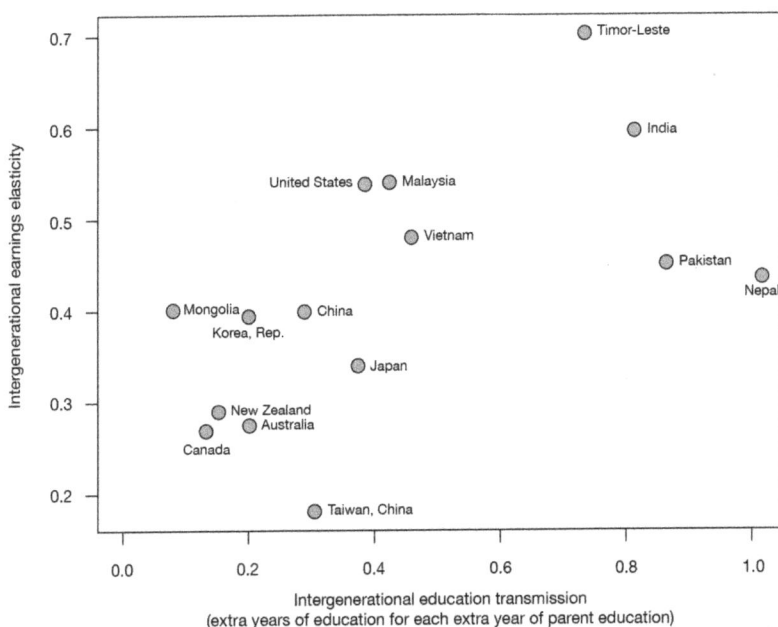

Figure 2.2. Intergenerational education transmission (extra years of education for each extra year of parent education). The intergenerational transmission of earnings is positively correlated with the intergenerational transmission of education among 15 Asia–Pacific countries

Source. Derived by the author using the Global Database on Intergenerational Mobility (GDIM) (2018) (Development Research Group, World Bank. Washington DC)

This said, statistical markers of equality of opportunity should be informed by the subsystem of recursive equations represented by equation (2). My view is that parental education is a preferred indicator of socio-economic status for these purposes, reflecting the capacity of parents to make both monetary and non-monetary investments in their children. We might profitably rewrite equation (2) to be $H_t = \delta E_t + \theta H_{t-1}$, letting H represent years of schooling, with lower values of θ representing a diminished role of circumstance in determining child outcomes.

This is the perspective taken in Figure 2.2, which ranks 15 Asia–Pacific countries along two dimensions. First, the horizontal direction offers an indicator of the degree to which education is transmitted between generations, a particular version of θ. Narayan et al. (2018) derive this statistic as the regression coefficient between child and parent years of schooling. Their derivation is based upon children old enough to have completed schooling, and whose parents have less than tertiary education. The latter restriction prevents a 'ceiling' bias from influencing the results since there is an upper limit to the amount of schooling that can be obtained. This intergenerational transmission statistic should be interpreted as the extra years of schooling a child is expected to obtain for each additional year of schooling among their parents. This is a summary measure of the relationship between the monetary and non-monetary resources to which parents may have access, including preferences and family culture, and the educational attainments of their children, a very broad representation of equation (2) and the subsystems it summarises. The intergenerational transmission of schooling varies significantly between the countries in the Asia–Pacific region for which this indicator is available. This gradient varies from as low as 0.08 to as high as 1.016: in some countries this playing field is relatively level, but in others extremely steep.

The figure also ranks the countries vertically by the intergenerational elasticity used in Figure 2.1 (Bangladesh and Singapore not appearing for lack of the intergenerational education data). There is a clear positive association between intergenerational mobility of incomes and education. The more strongly children's years of schooling are associated with their parents' years of schooling, the more tightly associated are child–parent incomes: a sharper socio-economic gradient in the development of human capital tends to suggest a sharper gradient in incomes. Broadly speaking, socio-economic differences in human capital development underpin, in some measure, socio-economic differences of incomes.

We can look to socio-economic inequalities in the human capital of children to refine a statistical dashboard depicting equality of opportunity. The intergenerational earnings elasticity and transition matrices are broad-picture statistics with long time lags, but the correlation in Figure 2.2 suggests that early warning signs of the direction in which they may move are offered by the socio-economic gradients in the development of human capital during important transitions in children's lives. These gradients are associated with a causal understanding of the process and can be produced more regularly, and in a more timely fashion, to directly inform public policy.

These statistics and even more finely defined statistics directly measuring skills, variations in children's literacy, numeracy, or social skills according to their parents' education, are abstractions neglecting variations in parental preferences. Nonetheless, we may imagine that regardless of parental preferences or capacities, all children should grow up in a way that develops their capacity to become all that they can be, and to function normally in our societies as they exist. So explicit measurement of these capacities at each important stage of child development is important for informing public policy, and measuring equality of opportunity in a way that is at least one level deeper than just description, even if in some degree it continues to formally remain that.

Figure 2.3, drawn from a four-country study by Bradbury et al. (2015), offers an example of competency in various dimensions of mathematics by 14-year-old children in the United States, according to whether the parent with the highest education held a college degree (labelled 'High education' in the figure) or, at the other extreme, had no more than a high school diploma (labelled 'Low education'). On average, less than four in 10 teens on the cusp of high school have mastered manipulating fractions. This average outcome is something public policymakers may wonder about, and they may even also wonder about the fact that just less than six in 10 children from the most advantaged backgrounds have mastered this skill. Overall averages – indicated by the horizontal lines in the figure – may continue to be a concern as policymakers are likely to have a clearer sense of what is socially acceptable in these sorts of domains, regardless of a child's family circumstances. If this is so, then they may also wonder about the falling away of competency among children with less-advantaged backgrounds. This dimension of the discussion opens a natural window onto equality of opportunity.

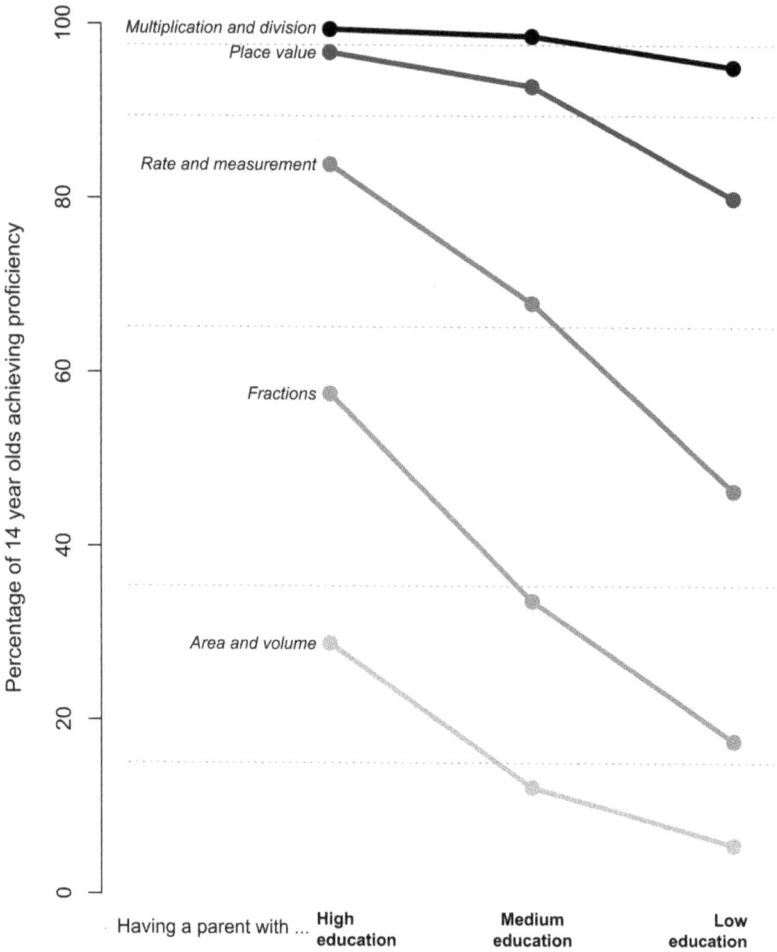

Figure 2.3. Proficiency in mathematics among 14-year-olds in the United States is much higher for children with better educated parents

Source. Adapted by the author from Bradbury et al. (2015)

Pictures of this sort have been, and can easily continue to be, provided by the Organisation for Economic Co-operation and Development (OECD) Programme for International Student Assessment (PISA) for similarly aged children in many rich countries. They should form a part of any dashboard of statistics associated with equality of opportunity among many more countries as they focus on indicators of skills and competencies, rather than education expenditures and inputs. The OECD tends to focus on a continuous index of competency that certainly has its merits, but loses something as a communication device. These indices can be directly associated with particular levels of competency that are more directly grasped in public policy, and they should be derived and communicated in this form.

But a continuous index reflecting a more finely nuanced notion of skills and competency also has a central place in Roemer's framework. He encourages use of the empirical cumulative distribution functions categorised by family circumstances, and proposes that equality of opportunity is reflected in the degree to which these functions are the same (Roemer & Trannoy 2016). If similarly ranked children across family-background types attain the same level of competency, then this indicates equality of opportunity. His view is that the rankings within socio-economic groups are a marker for 'effort'. The implication is that a top-ranked child among children of low-educated parents is similar in this sense to a top-ranked child among those with high-educated parents. If the former has less developed skills and competencies along some relevant domain for adult success, then this is the role of 'circumstance', indicating inequality of opportunity. The cumulative distribution functions across groups are comprehensive indicators of these populations, and the extent to which they differ, or even differ at particular points in the distribution, is a measure of inequality of opportunity.

Figure 2.4 offers an example. These are the same data used in Figure 2.3, but with a continuous indicator of mathematics skill, and displayed in the way Roemer suggests by offering on the vertical axis the cumulative percentage of children that have reached no more than a particular skill level indicated along the horizontal axis. The horizontal gaps between the curves indicate inequality of opportunity, if we accept that parental education is a circumstance in the sense used by Roemer. These gaps are widest in the broad middle of the distribution: the median ranked child of all children with parents having low education has a competency in mathematics much lower than the average test score, and notably lower than his or her counterpart with high educated parents, who scores well above the average. Equality of opportunity is evident where a child is extremely gifted: the achievement gaps of top percentile children being very small. But even among the top there is a significant gap in achievement. The children scoring in the top decile of the distribution of all children with low-education parents close somewhat the achievement gap relative to the top 10 per cent with medium-educated parents. But both groups – in spite of surely having nurtured talent, expending effort, or having innate ability – still score lower than the top decile from parents with college degrees. All of this leaves unquestioned the fact that, for the great bulk of the distribution, achievement is clearly distinguished by family background.

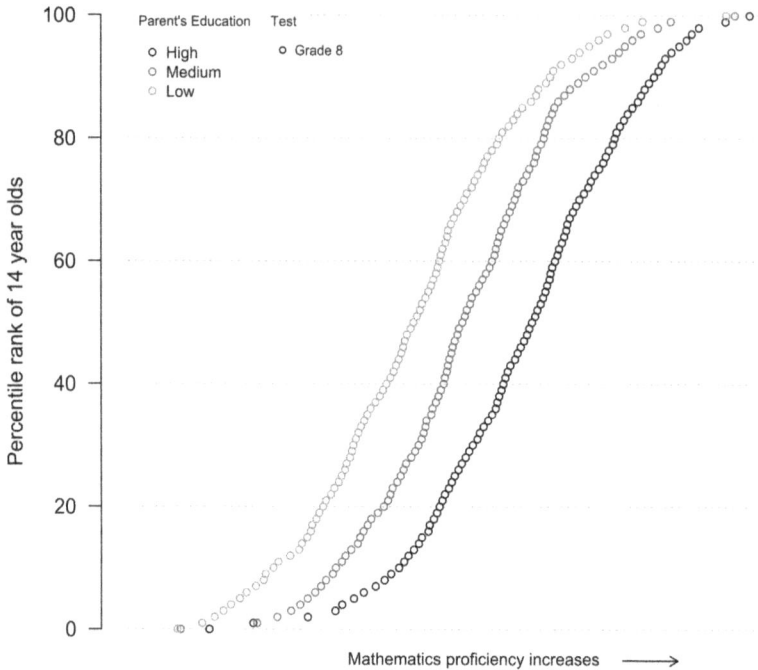

Figure 2.4. Roemer's equality-of-opportunity framework suggests organising test scores as cumulative distribution functions by family background, with achievement differences of similarly ranked students across groups indicating inequality of opportunity among Grade 8 students in the United States

Source. Adapted by the author from Bradbury et al. (2015)

These results are conditional on children being in their early to mid-teens. These results are powerful in better understanding how to design education policies for high school and adolescent years, but it may be misguided if the theory of child development wrapped up in our discussion of equation (2) is correct. If the early years also matter, then inequality of opportunity may be embedded in societal outcomes well before children reach the teen years. If we are to take the focus on children seriously, then indicators of equality of opportunity need to be provided at younger ages, particularly on the cusp of formal schooling so that family versus societal influences can have a hope of being distinguished.

Figure 2.5 adds the cumulative distribution function of standardised math scores collected at roughly age five, when these American children were starting kindergarten, to the information in Figure 2.4. The cumulative distribution functions are similar, whether measured at age five or 14. The differences in outcomes by parental education are evident when children first enter the schooling system, and do not change significantly during the years in primary education. This suggests both that the early years are very important in determining life chances, and also that the primary school system has accomplished little in offering disproportionate advantages to the relatively disadvantaged. I should emphasise that an analysis of this sort does not require a longitudinal survey of children, only a series of repeated cross-sections across countries, and at crucial ages in child development that have already been highlighted by the academic literature.

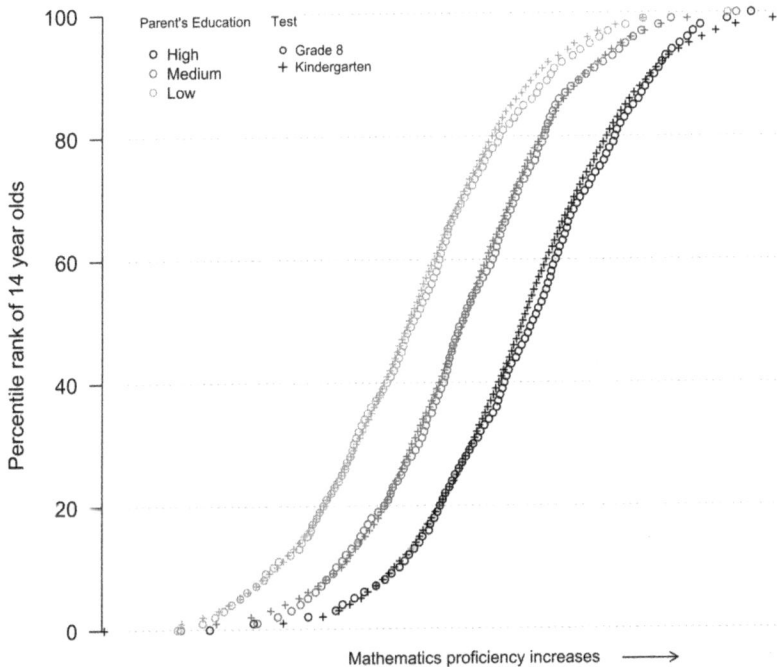

Figure 2.5. Roemer's equality-of-opportunity framework suggests organising test scores as cumulative distribution functions by family background, with achievement differences of similarly ranked students across groups indicating inequality of opportunity among Grade 8 and Kindergarten students in the United States

Source. Adapted by the author from Bradbury et al. (2015)

Conclusions

Equality of opportunity should be an aspect of how we understand economic performance and social progress. It puts a focus on process, not just on outcomes. It may be challenging to discern in a rigorous way, relying as it does on an inherent value judgement to distinguish between 'circumstance' and 'effort'. While theorists and philosophers will continue to debate its definition, the notion of equality of opportunity rings true at some basic level for many citizens of both rich and less rich countries. For this reason alone, practitioners should grasp firmly onto whatever theoretical threads they can in order to offer up practical indicators that are useful both to describe societies, and to guide policy interventions.

There is no measurement without theory, and I suggest three lessons for the development of useful indicators. These involve firstly uncovering existing data that is useful for the calculation of standard summary measures of intergenerational mobility, developing new data for this purpose from administrative sources, and enhancing existing surveys with retrospective information. Second, common descriptive statistics of mobility across generations should be complemented with other measures that speak more directly to policy concerns, including measures of absolute mobility and an associated poverty rate based on the minimal level of resources needed to reasonably lower the risk of the intergenerational transmission of low status. Finally, an ideal dashboard of statistics to gauge equality of opportunity would involve organising existing information and developing new instruments to chart the relationship between family background and child development through the whole series of transitions that children make on their way to becoming successful and self-sufficient adults.

References

Becker, GS & Tomes, N (1979). 'An equilibrium theory of the distribution of income and intergenerational mobility', *Journal of Political Economy*, 87(6), 1153–89. doi.org/10.1086/260831.

—— (1986). 'Human capital and the rise and fall of families', *Journal of Labor Economics*, 4(3), Part 2, S1–S39. doi.org/10.1086/298118.

Björklund, A & Jäntti, M (2011). 'Intergenerational income mobility and the role of family background'. In W Salverda, B Nolan & T Smeeding (eds), *The Oxford handbook of economic inequality* (pp 491–521). Oxford University Press. doi.org/10.1093/oxfordhb/9780199606061.013.0020.

Black, SE & Devereux, PJ (2011). 'Recent developments in intergenerational mobility'. In D Card & O Ashenfelter (eds), *Handbook of labor economics*, Vol. 4, Part B (pp 1487–541). Elsevier. doi.org/10.1016/S0169-7218(11) 02414-2.

Blanden, J (2013). 'Cross-country differences in intergenerational mobility: A comparison of approaches from economics and sociology', *Journal of Economic Surveys*, 27(1), 38–73. doi.org/10.1111/j.1467-6419.2011.00690.x.

Bradbury, B, Corak, M, Waldfogel, J & Washbrook, E (2015). *Too many children left behind: The US achievement gap in comparative perspective*. New York: Russell Sage Foundation.

Chetty, R, Hendren, N, Kline, P & Saez, E (2014). 'Where is the land of opportunity? The geography of intergenerational mobility in the United States', *Quarterly Journal of Economics*, 129(4), 1553–623. doi.org/10.1093/ qje/qju022.

Corak, M (2006). 'Do poor children become poor adults? Lessons from a cross-country comparison of generational earnings mobility'. In J Creedy & G Kalb (eds), *Research on economic inequality*, Vol. 13 (pp 143–88). Amsterdam: Elsevier. doi.org/10.1016/S1049-2585(06)13006-9.

—— (2013). 'Income inequality, equality of opportunity, and intergenerational mobility', *Journal of Economic Perspectives*, 27(3), 79–102. doi.org/10.1257/ jep.27.3.79.

—— (2016). *Economic theory and practical lessons for measuring equality of opportunities*, OECD Statistics Working Papers, No. 2016/02. Paris.

—— (2018). 'The Canadian geography of intergenerational income mobility', *The Economic Journal*, uez019. doi.org/10.1093/ej/uez019.

Heckman, JJ & Mosso, S (2014). *The economics of human development and social mobility*, No. 19925, NBER Working Paper. Cambridge, Mass.: National Bureau of Economic Research. doi.org/10.3386/w19925.

Mulligan, CB (1997). *Parental priorities and economic inequality*. University of Chicago Press.

Narayan, A, van der Weide, R, Cojocaru, A, Lakner, C, Redaelli, S, Gerszon Mahler, D, Ramasubbaiah, RGN & Thewissen, S (2018). *Fair progress? Economic mobility across generations around the world.* Washington DC: World Bank. doi.org/10.1596/978-1-4648-1210-1.

Roemer, J (2000). *Equality of opportunity.* Cambridge, Mass.: Harvard University Press.

—— (2004). 'Equal opportunity and intergenerational mobility: Going beyond intergenerational income transition matrices'. In M Corak (ed.), *Generational income mobility in North America and Europe* (pp 48–57). Cambridge University Press.

Roemer, J & Trannoy, A (2016). 'Equality of opportunity: Theory and measurement', *Journal of Economic Literature*, 54(4), 1288–332. doi.org/10.1257/jel.20151206.

Solon, G (1999). 'Intergenerational mobility in the labor market', In OC Ashenfelter & D Card (eds), *Handbook of labor economics*, Vol. 3A (pp 1761–800). Amsterdam: Elsevier Science. doi.org/10.1016/S1573-4463(99)03010-2.

—— (2002). 'Cross-country differences in intergenerational earnings mobility', *The Journal of Economic Perspectives*, 16(3), 59–66. doi.org/10.1257/089533002760278712.

—— (2004). 'A model of intergenerational mobility variation over time and place'. In M Corak (ed.), *Handbook of labor economics* (pp 38–47). Cambridge University Press.

3

MEASURING WEALTH: IMPLICATIONS FOR SUSTAINABLE DEVELOPMENT[1]

Kevin J Mumford

Introduction

This chapter is about measurement, not about evaluating specific policies. What we measure determines our focus when choosing policies and strongly influences how we view our political leaders and how we vote. As the costs of data collection and analysis have dropped, a host of new indices and dashboards of economic, demographic, social and environmental measures are posted for public consumption. One of the axioms of choice theory is that more of a good is preferred to less. The axiom can fail, however, when it comes to information. An overload of information can leave us worse off if the host of measures distracts us from what is relevant.

In this paper, I describe how we measure current wellbeing, what economic theory tells us about how to measure intergenerational wellbeing, and how to measure wealth. This paper provides a context in which to assess the economic and political value of wealth accounting. I present income and wealth data from several specific countries to illustrate the methods,

---

1   My thinking on this subject has benefited greatly from conversations and collaboration with Kenneth Arrow, Partha Dasgupta, Anantha Duraiappah, Larry Goulder, and Pablo Muñoz.

not to evaluate the political choices of those countries. Rather than trying to make a point about sub-optimal policies in the 1990s and 2000s in certain countries, this paper has the more far-reaching goal of influencing policy choices indirectly by changing what we measure.

Measuring current wellbeing

In this paper, I use the term 'current wellbeing' to describe the standard of living enjoyed in a country. I do not assume that people or governments have perfect foresight, nor do I assume that their policies and investment choices place the country on an optimal growth path. I use the term 'intergenerational wellbeing' to describe the long-run standard of living that will be enjoyed by a country's future generations.

The System of National Accounts (SNA) is the international standard for measuring consumption, investment, production and government expenditure flows. The SNA is designed to measure gross domestic product (GDP), which is the value of market production within a country and is the most widely used measure of economic activity. GDP is a flow variable, it measures current production of goods and services, not future production, and thus is commonly used as a proxy for the current wellbeing of a country.

The machines, computers and other capital assets used to produce goods and services wear out over time and become obsolete. Some fraction of total output has to be dedicated to maintaining the capital stock and replacing obsolete assets just to keep the stock of capital assets from declining. Net domestic product (NDP) is calculated by subtracting the depreciation of capital assets from GDP. As a measure of current wellbeing, NDP is generally better than GDP because goods and services dedicated to upkeep of capital assets are not available for consumption.[2] The reason GDP has been more widely used is that measuring depreciation of capital assets is difficult and, in practice, historical movements in NDP closely mirrored those in GDP, at least until the 1990s. Capital assets today have a shorter life expectancy than those of several decades ago, which means there is a higher rate of depreciation.

---

2   If investment is less than depreciation, the stock of capital assets will decline, which reduces the productive capacity of the county. This implies that wellbeing is higher in the current period than it will be in the future. In this scenario, GDP may be the better measure of current wellbeing.

Just like GDP, NDP is a flow variable, but Weitzman (1976) shows that NDP is the appropriate measure of intergenerational wellbeing in a world where (1) all goods and services are purchased in a competitive market and where (2) governments, firms and households optimally make savings and consumption decisions to maximise intergenerational wellbeing. Under these conditions, changes in NDP represent changes in both current wellbeing and intergenerational wellbeing. This is because the present discounted value of all future NDP is equivalent to the current wealth of the county.

My view is that neither of Weitzman's (1976) two assumptions holds. Many of the goods and services that we value are not purchased in a competitive market and are therefore not included in NDP. We value family, friendships, safety, meaningful work and recreation time. These are important sources of happiness and cannot generally be purchased directly. They all, however, depend on goods and services. For example, sporting goods and travel services are associated with recreation. Educational services help us to find meaningful work, develop friendships and become the kind of person we want to be. Therefore, NDP indirectly measures these important sources of happiness, at least to the extent that they are correlated with the consumption of market goods and services.

However, NDP does not take into account our current enjoyment of the natural environment. Polluted air and water have a large negative effect on current wellbeing, but they are not included in NDP because there is no competitive market for these environmental goods. In fact, NDP does not even account for changes in the stock of fossil fuels, minerals and forests that are bought and sold on markets. Hartwick (1990) points out that the depreciation of environmental capital assets that are employed in production should be subtracted from GDP when calculating NDP but, nearly 30 years later, this is still not the standard for the headline statistic. One must refer to the satellite accounts for environmental depreciation.

The System of Integrated Environmental and Economic Accounting (SEEA) has developed methods for estimating the social value of environmental services. Note that there is controversy about what methods to increase stocks of natural capital; that is, forest or fisheries growth. Should these natural increases be added to the measure of output? In principle, NDP accounting should be symmetric with the depreciation of all capital and environmental assets used in production subtracted from GDP and natural capital growth should be added. A related question is whether reductions of environmental services that have little direct impact on production be subtracted from GDP. In principle, the value of environmental services (for example, the direct benefit of clean air and water) as well as the value of leisure time and the value of unpaid work should all be treated identically to services produced by the market and added to GDP. Such a measure is generally called 'green GDP' and proponents argue that it is a better measure of current wellbeing.[3]

The World Bank's world development indicators measure the value of natural capital stock depletion for most countries from 1970 to 2015 (World Bank 2016). Barbier (2016) shows how to construct a natural capital depreciation rate that can be used to calculate green GDP or as a 'green' national income measure.

Why not dispense with these adjusted GDP measures and directly measure happiness instead? I believe that attempts to directly measure happiness are unlikely to be useful. Happiness surveys essentially ask people to report their happiness by selecting one of a few ordered categories such as 'very happy', 'somewhat happy', 'not very happy', etc. One can assign numerical values to these categories and then report how the average level of happiness in a country changes over time or in response to a certain policy. However, Bond and Lang (2014) show that it not possible to rank countries by happiness without imposing restrictive assumptions. They show that producing a cardinal measure of happiness from such surveys is not possible. Without some revolutionary advance in how we directly measure wellbeing, we are resigned to inferring wellbeing from GDP measures.

There is a fundamental problem with NDP, green GDP, and other adjusted GDP measures. They do not measure true economic growth, which is an expansion in the capacity to produce goods and services. They are only measures of the production or income itself. Mumford (2016) provides an analogy to attempting to evaluate firms by looking only at the income statement and ignoring the balance sheet, which reports the value of all assets and liabilities. If Weitzman's (1976) second assumption holds, that countries (or firms in the analogy) are on an optimal growth path, then we can safely ignore the balance sheet because the firm's current

---

3   See Harper et al. (2009) for a description of the US Bureau of Economic Analysis (BEA) and Bureau of Labour Statistics (BLS) efforts to value unpaid work by using productivity measures in the BEA satellite accounts.

profits characterise the firm's future profit potential. On the other hand, if some firms occasionally make short-sighted decisions to increase current profits at the expense of future profits, then ignoring the balance sheet is a mistake.

Arguments for the assumption that countries are on an optimal growth path are unconvincing. Examples of governments, firms and households making myopic decisions abound. No green GDP-like measure will be able to indicate if a country is over-consuming and underinvesting (Stiglitz et al. 2008).

Measuring intergenerational wellbeing

Here, I will review the methods used to measure intergenerational wellbeing and evaluate the sustainability of a country's consumption and investment policies. We begin by ignoring distributional considerations and population growth. Under these assumptions, the wellbeing of a country in period t is defined as $U(C_t)$. Current wellbeing is increasing in consumption per capita, or C_t. Consumption is an aggregation of the value of the goods and services consumed. There are trade-offs between the various goods and services and thus various ways of achieving any particular level of wellbeing $U(C_t)$. For example, consumption of a sufficient quantity of additional goods and services can compensate for an increase in air pollution. Similarly, people would be willing to give up some positive quantity of goods and services in exchange for less-polluted air. The amount of other goods and services that people are willing to give up for less-polluted air defines the social value of the flow of clean-air services.

Consumption growth, $C_{t+1} \geq C_t$ means that people are better off at the moment, but it does not guarantee that people will enjoy a higher standard of living in the future. Intergenerational wellbeing at period t is defined by Dasgupta and Mäler (2000) as the discounted sum of the flow of wellbeing into the infinite future

$$V_t = U(C_t) + (1-\delta)U(C_{t+1}) + (1-\delta)^2 U(C_{t+2}) + K = \sum_{s=0}^{\infty}(1-\delta)^s U(C_{t+s}) \quad (1)$$

where δ is the discount rate. Intergenerational wellbeing is the discounted sum of wellbeing in the current and all future periods. Without the ability to forecast future consumption, there is no way to directly measure V_t.

Arrow et al. (2012) define sustainability as non-declining intergenerational wellbeing $V_{t+s} \geq V_t$. A country's path may be sustainable even if it is investing less than would be optimal given the social discount rate, the utility function, and production function. All that is required for development to be sustainable is that intergenerational wellbeing is not declining.

We cannot directly measure intergenerational wellbeing, but we can measure the social value of capital assets used to produce goods and services. Dasgupta and Mäler (2000) prove that potential intergenerational wellbeing increases if and only if the productive base increases. Conceptually, output (all goods and services) flow from capital stocks according to the production function

$$Y_t = \alpha_t f_t (K_{1t} + K_{2t} + K_{3t} + K) \tag{2}$$

where α_t denotes the level of productivity in period t and K_{it} denotes capital stock of type i.

Individual types of capital have an associated social value in producing wellbeing, as denoted by P_{it}. For assets with no externalities that are sold in a competitive market, the market price is a good approximation of the social value. With prices and quantities, wealth is defined as:

$$W_t = P_{\alpha t}\alpha_t + \sum_i P_{it}K_{it} \tag{3}$$

It is important to note that current prices should always be used as they reflect the current value in production, as determined by the function $f_t (.)$, and social values. This means that wealth in the previous period is defined as

$$W_{t-1} = P_{\alpha t}\alpha_{t-1} + \sum_i P_{it}K_{it-1} \tag{4}$$

If it were possible, we would use future prices rather than the current prices because future prices reflect the production trade-offs and social values that future generations will face. For most assets, however, there is no way for us to know what the future prices will be.

With the above definitions, we can restate the Dasgupta and Mäler (2000) result as saying that the economic development from period t-1 to period t was sustainable if and only if $W_t \geq W_{t-1}$. Note that there is no requirement that the composition of consumption stay the same in future periods. Sustainable development does not imply everyone will consume as much of every good or service as they do now. Similarly, sustainable development does not imply that every form of capital must be sustained. A country that reduces one form of capital and increases another form of capital has experienced sustainable growth if the social value of the capital gain is larger than the social value of the capital loss. To allow for population change, Dasgupta (2004) and Arrow et al. (2003) describe the conditions under which one can restate the Dasgupta and Mäler (2000) result in terms of wealth per capita.

The SNA measure of produced capital (fixed assets) is frequently referred to as national wealth. Produced capital is clearly an important part of the production process, but it is not the most important form of capital. In a production function with only human capital (labour) and produced capital, human capital is generally estimated to have a 60 per cent weight with the remaining 40 per cent attributed to produced capital.[4] Natural resources like oil, coal, natural gas, forests, fisheries and minerals are also important parts of the production process that are not included in the SNA produced capital measure. Arrow et al. (2012) call the sum of all these types of capital comprehensive wealth or inclusive wealth.

In practice, measuring capital stocks is difficult. For example, proven oil reserves increase every year. This is not because nature is producing oil faster than we can extract it. It is because we are inventing technologies for finding and extracting the oil faster than we extract it. So, rather than use the proven reserves as reported in earlier years, we take the current proven reserves and add the extraction estimates for each intervening year to arrive at values for past stocks. Note also that capital can be located in one country, but owned by the citizens of another country. Future returns from the capital asset generally flow to the owner of the asset, regardless of the location.

An even more problematic example is how to measure the stock of human capital. Countries have a large number of worker types as defined by their skills. Within each skill group, there are different expected years of work remaining depending on age and gender. This dramatically increases the number of human capital stock types for which one needs a social value.

---

4   The labour share of national income was constant at about 66 per cent for decades, but has recently declined to about 60 per cent, which suggests that aggregate production has become more capital intensive.

Estimating the prices of social values is even more challenging than measuring the capital stocks. For example, we need an estimate of the discounted lifetime contribution to production for each type of worker. The discount sum of future wages is the most straightforward (though not easy) way to calculate this. Estimating social values for types of natural capital where there is no market is particularly challenging.

Measuring changes in inclusive wealth

Arrow et al. (2012) define comprehensive or inclusive investment as the change in comprehensive or inclusive wealth:

$$\Delta W_t = P_{\alpha t}\Delta\alpha_t + \sum_i P_{it}\Delta K_{it} \tag{5}$$

Note that we are holding the prices fixed so changes in inclusive wealth are either the result of a change in the stock of one or more types of capital or a change in productivity. Capital depreciation and extraction deplete the stock while investment and natural growth (for renewable resources) increase the stock. Kurniawan and Managi (2018) show how to estimate productivity (TFP) in the context of inclusive wealth measurement.

Rather than directly measuring capital stocks as in Arrow et al. (2012) and the Inclusive Wealth Reports (UNU-IHDP & UNEP 2012, 2014, 2018), the World Bank (2011) directly measures comprehensive investment, which it describes as genuine savings, genuine investment or adjusted net savings. In this form, the Dasgupta and Mäler (2000) result is simply $\Delta W_t \geq 0$. Empirically, genuine savings is derived from the SNA measure of gross national savings. The first step is to subtract capital depreciation, called capital consumption of produced assets in the SNA. Then, spending on education is added along with changes in the value of as many types of natural capital as possible.

While the World Bank and Inclusive Wealth Report take different approaches to measuring the same object, they are more similar than they are different. The theoretical grounding of either wealth-based approach is appealing to economists as compared to the host of indices and indicator dashboards.[5]

---

5   The *Inclusive Wealth Report* (UNU-IHDP & UNEP 2014) uses data from 140 countries from 1990 to 2010 to measure inclusive wealth. This is labelled as the 'inclusive wealth index', which is a poor choice. Inclusive wealth is a theoretically grounded comprehensive measurement of wealth and is not an index. Indices are generally ad-hoc combinations of various measures with no theoretical basis for the particular combination chosen.

Empirical evidence of sustainable development in Asia

In this section, I present inclusive wealth measures for several Asian countries and the United States for 1990–2010. Table 3.1 gives the five-year percentage change in three types of capital per capita: produced, natural (forests, minerals, energy) and human (education). The five-year percentage change in productivity is also estimated from BEA and OECD data. The five-year change in GDP per capita is provided for comparison.

Table 3.1. Percentage change in capital stocks and inclusive wealth

Australia				
	1991–95	1996–2000	2001–05	2006–10
Produced capital	10.2%	15.5%	18.9%	19.2%
Natural capital	–6.6%	–7.0%	–8.2%	–13.0%
Human capital	0.7%	0.7%	3.4%	5.3%
Productivity	5.9%	8.1%	3.1%	0.6%
Inclusive wealth	5.5%	8.8%	6.0%	4.0%
GDP	11.1%	14.7%	11.4%	4.8%

China				
	1990–95	1995–2000	2000–05	2005–10
Produced capital	45.7%	56.5%	61.5%	73.4%
Natural capital	–6.6%	–7.4%	–7.7%	–6.8%
Human capital	7.2%	6.0%	4.0%	5.5%
Productivity	38.2%	11.5%	17.8%	11.5%
Inclusive wealth	42.9%	18.4%	27.9%	30.8%
GDP	68.3%	44.7%	54.5%	65.8%

India				
	1990–95	1995–2000	2000–05	2005–10
Produced capital	18.9%	24.5%	32.5%	48.1%
Natural capital	–10.8%	–9.9%	–9.9%	–9.6%
Human capital	1.0%	4.5%	3.4%	2.7%
Productivity	5.7%	13.3%	8.4%	12.0%
Inclusive wealth	5.1%	16.5%	12.8%	20.1%
GDP	16.4%	21.2%	29.5%	39.2%

Indonesia	1990–95	1995–2000	2000–05	2005–10
Produced capital	44.5%	27.0%	15.3%	23.4%
Natural capital	−13.7%	−11.3%	−9.6%	−10.1%
Human capital	3.3%	6.3%	1.8%	4.5%
Productivity	6.0%	−20.1%	8.5%	0.2%
Inclusive wealth	3.7%	−19.5%	7.6%	2.4%
GDP	34.8%	−3.1%	18.3%	25.0%

Japan	1990–95	1995–2000	2000–05	2005–10
Produced capital	17.9%	11.8%	7.0%	4.3%
Natural capital	−2.5%	−0.9%	−3.9%	−1.4%
Human capital	4.2%	2.3%	0.9%	0.1%
Productivity	3.1%	3.4%	4.4%	0.5%
Inclusive wealth	11.5%	8.9%	7.4%	2.1%
GDP	5.3%	3.8%	6.1%	0.5%

Malaysia	1990–95	1995–2000	2000–05	2005–10
Produced capital	52.7%	27.0%	9.7%	13.0%
Natural capital	−16.1%	−17.0%	−17.7%	−16.5%
Human capital	10.5%	5.1%	1.7%	5.4%
Productivity	−1.6%	−7.7%	2.4%	−3.8%
Inclusive wealth	3.7%	−5.8%	1.1%	−1.1%
GDP	38.2%	11.8%	13.1%	14.5%

South Korea	1990–95	1995–2000	2000–05	2005–10
Produced capital	68.7%	40.5%	28.7%	21.5%
Natural capital	0.2%	2.7%	3.8%	1.0%
Human capital	7.9%	4.5%	3.8%	2.4%
Productivity	2.1%	3.6%	4.9%	5.7%
Inclusive wealth	19.2%	16.3%	15.8%	14.4%
GDP	40.7%	25.1%	21.8%	17.6%

United States				
	1990–95	1995–2000	2000–05	2005–10
Produced capital	10.7%	18.6%	17.2%	9.9%
Natural capital	–7.4%	–8.3%	–6.4%	–5.8%
Human capital	–0.3%	0.9%	2.5%	1.5%
Productivity	3.5%	7.3%	8.3%	3.5%
Inclusive wealth	4.4%	10.7%	13.2%	6.5%
GDP	7.8%	16.6%	7.2%	–0.9%

Source. Author's calculations, the UNU-IHDP and UNEP (2014), and OECD statistics

Table 3.1 makes it clear that GDP growth does not necessarily indicate growth in wealth. For example, Indonesia and Malaysia both have periods of GDP growth that occur simultaneously with decreases in inclusive wealth. GDP growth tends to be larger than inclusive wealth growth for most countries. Several countries have five-year GDP growth rates that are 10 or even 20 percentage points higher than the five-year growth rate in inclusive wealth (even with productivity growth included). A counter example is Japan, which has a higher rate of inclusive wealth growth than GDP growth in the four time periods considered.

Our measure of natural capital includes agricultural land, forests, mineral resources, energy resources and fisheries. The costs of global climate change, modelled as a global public bad, increased during the period. Similarly, the ecological services performed by forests and coastal waters have decreased. Across most Asian countries, natural capital has experienced large decreases while produced and human capital have experienced large increases. An exception is South Korea, where natural capital is increasing, driven by renewable natural resources including forests. Those countries with a decline of inclusive wealth in any one of those time periods were simply extracting more from the environment than they were investing in education, roads, housing, production facilities and equipment. For some countries, including the United States, China and India, the per cent reduction in natural capital is declining over time. In other countries, including Australia, the decline in natural capital is accelerating. In Australia's case, this is primarily due to mining.

Conclusion

Wealth accounting allows us to measure the productive base that provides for the wellbeing of future generations. As a theoretically based measure of intergenerational wellbeing, inclusive wealth is the appropriate way to evaluate if economic development is sustainable. The methods for calculating inclusive wealth do not require assumptions about optimality, nor do they require forecasts of future quantities. The methods do, however, require high-quality quantity and price data for a wide variety of capital assets.

Wealth accounting is not going to replace GDP. Flow variables, like GDP, are directly related to current wellbeing. Stock variables, like inclusive wealth, are instead related to potential intergenerational wellbeing. An increase in inclusive wealth implies that future citizens will inherit a larger productive base and will therefore be able to enjoy higher levels of wellbeing. This, however, is only a statement about the potential intergenerational wellbeing, not a claim that wellbeing will definitely be higher.

I encourage government statistical offices to augment their wealth accounts by measuring the value of human and natural capital. Just as firms create annual balance sheets, governments should prepare annual wealth accounts. Citizens need wealth measures to be able to hold their government accountable for the policies it enacts. Without wealth accounting, all citizens can do is look at the usually strong GDP per capita growth rate and hope that it will keep going up indefinitely.

References

Arrow, KJ, Dasgupta, P & Mäler, KG (2003). 'The genuine savings criterion and the value of population', *Economic Theory*, 21(2), 217–25. doi.org/10.1007/s00199-002-0335-2.

Arrow, KJ, Dasgupta, P, Goulder, LH, Mumford, KJ & Oleson, K (2012). 'Sustainability and the measurement of wealth', *Environment and Development Economics*, 17(3), 317–53. doi.org/10.1017/S1355770X12000137.

Barbier, EB (2016). 'Natural capital and wealth in the 21st century', *Eastern Economic Journal*, 43(3), 391–405. doi.org/10.1057/s41302-016-0013-x.

Bond, TN & Lang, K (2014). 'The sad truth about happiness scales', NBER Working Paper, No. 19950, March, www.nber.org/papers/w19950.

Dasgupta, P (2004 (2001)). *Human wellbeing and the natural environment*, 2nd edn. Oxford University Press.

Dasgupta, P & Mäler, KG (2000). 'Net national product, wealth, and social wellbeing', *Environment and Development Economics*, 5(1), 69–93. doi.org/10.1017/S1355770X00000061.

Harper, MJ, Moulton, BR, Rosenthal, S & Wasshausen, DB (2009). 'Integrated GDP-productivity accounts', *American Economic Review Papers and Proceedings*, 99(2), 74–79. doi.org/10.1257/aer.99.2.74.

Hartwick, J (1990). 'Natural resources, national accounting and economic depreciation', *Journal of Public Economics*, 43(3), 291–304. doi.org/10.1016/0047-2727(90)90002-Y.

Kurniawan, R & Managi, S (2018). 'Linking wealth and productivity of natural capital for 140 countries between 1990 and 2014', *Social Indicators Research*, 1–20. doi.org/10.1007/s11205-017-1833-8.

Mumford, KJ (2012). 'Measuring inclusive wealth at the state level in the United States'. In UNU-IHDP & UNEP, *Inclusive Wealth Report 2012: Measuring progress towards sustainability* (pp 69–86). Cambridge University Press.

—— (2016). 'Prosperity, sustainability and the measurement of wealth', *Asia & the Pacific Policy Studies*, 3(2), 226–34. doi.org/10.1002/app5.132.

Stiglitz, J, Sen, A & Fitoussi, J-P (2008). *Report by the Commission on the Measurement of Economic Performance and Social Progress*. Paris.

UNU-IHDP & UNEP (2012). *Inclusive Wealth Report 2012: Measuring progress towards sustainability*. Cambridge University Press.

—— (2014). *Inclusive Wealth Report 2014: Measuring progress towards sustainability*. Cambridge University Press.

—— (2018). *Inclusive Wealth Report 2018: Measuring sustainability and well-being*, wedocs.unep.org/xmlui/handle/20.500.11822/27597.

Weitzman, ML (1976). 'On the welfare significance of national product in a dynamic economy', *The Quarterly Journal of Economics*, 90(1), 156–62. doi.org/10.2307/1886092.

World Bank (2011). *The changing wealth of nations: measuring sustainable development in the new millennium*. Washington DC.

—— (2016). *World development indicators*. Washington DC: World Bank, data.worldbank.org/data-catalog/world-development-indicators.

4

RISING INEQUALITY AMID RAPID GROWTH IN ASIA AND IMPLICATIONS FOR POLICY[1]

Juzhong Zhuang

Introduction

Over the past three decades, developing Asia achieved economic growth and reduced poverty faster than any other region of the world at any time in history. But the bulk of the region's population lives in countries with rising income inequality. This is in contrast with the 'growth with equity' story that marked the transformation of the newly industrialised economies in the 1960s and 1970s, and with recent trends in some other parts of the developing world, particularly Latin America, where income inequality has been narrowing since the 1990s.

Technological change, globalisation, and market-oriented deregulation have driven Asia's rapid growth, but have also had significant distributional implications. These forces tend to favour owners of capital over labour, skilled over unskilled workers, and urban and coastal areas over rural and inland regions. The impacts of these forces have been compounded by

---

1   Views expressed in the paper are those of the author and do not necessarily reflect views and policies of the Asian Development Bank or its Board of Governors or the governments they represent.

various forms of unequal access to opportunity caused by institutional weaknesses and social exclusion. Working together, these have led to a falling share of labour income in total national income, increasing premiums on human capital, growing spatial disparity, and widening wealth inequality – all contributing to rising income inequality.

How should Asian governments respond to rising inequality? The three driving forces of economic growth should not be obstructed even though they cause rising inequality. But it is important for Asian policymakers to deploy policy measures to confront rising inequality, focusing on equalising opportunity, which reduces income inequality. These policies include measures toward creating more high-quality jobs for a wider population, interventions that narrow spatial disparity, fiscal policies that reduce inequality in human capital and that make the tax system effective and fairer, and reforms that strengthen governance, level the playing field, and eliminate social exclusion.

Recent trends of inequality in developing Asia

Many countries in Asia and the Pacific have seen remarkable achievements in growth and poverty reduction in the last three decades. From 1990 to 2017, the average annual growth rate of gross domestic product (GDP) for developing Asia reached 7 per cent in 2011 purchasing power parity (PPP) terms, more than double the 2.8 per cent of Latin America and the Caribbean (Figure 4.1). Much of the growth was driven by the People's Republic of China (PRC) and India – the world's two most populous countries – with annual GDP growth during the period reaching 9.7 per cent and 6.7 per cent, respectively.

The rapid growth has dramatically improved living standards of Asian people and reduced extreme poverty. During 1990–2017, the region's average per capita GDP in 2011 PPP terms increased from $2,423 to $10,725. The proportion of the population living on or below the $1.9-a-day poverty line fell from 53 per cent in 1990 to around 9 per cent in 2013, as over one billion people were lifted out of poverty. Fifteen countries reduced poverty by more than 15 percentage points in the period.

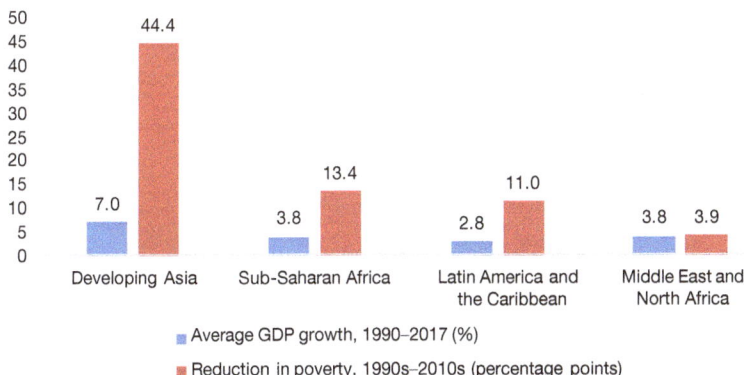

Figure 4.1. Annual GDP growth and cumulative poverty reduction

Source. Asian Development Bank, Asian Development Outlook database; World Bank, World Development Indicators online database; International Monetary Fund, World Economic Outlook October 2017 database (accessed 10 January 2018)

This performance in growth and poverty reduction has, however, been accompanied by rising income inequality in many countries. Of the 30 countries that have comparative data between the 1990s and early 2010s, nine – accounting for more than 80 per cent of developing Asia's population in 2016 – experienced rising inequality (Figure 4.2). The Gini coefficient of per capita expenditure – a common measure of inequality with zero indicating perfect equality and 100 perfect inequality[2] – worsened in the nine economies, including the three most populous countries – the PRC, India, and Indonesia. From the early 1990s to 2013, the Gini increased from 32 to 40 in the PRC, from 32 to 35 in India, and from 31 to 38 in Indonesia. In the PRC, the Gini coefficient has declined slightly since 2008, but the level remains among the highest in Asia (Zhuang & Shi 2016).

Although Asia's inequality levels are generally below those in other developing regions – developing Asia's range of the Gini coefficients is 26– 46 with a median of 37 in 2013, compared with 31–63 and the median of 43 for sub-Saharan Africa, and 40–58 and the median of 47 for Latin America and the Caribbean – inequality declined elsewhere, with the exception of Organisation for Economic Co-operation and Development (OECD) countries (Table 4.1). The majority of OECD countries – with the Gini in the range of 25–47 and the median of 32 – also experienced rising inequality in the last three decades.

---

2   A common measure of inequality, ranging from zero indicating perfect equality and one indicating perfect inequality. For convenience, this note cites the Gini multiplied by 100.

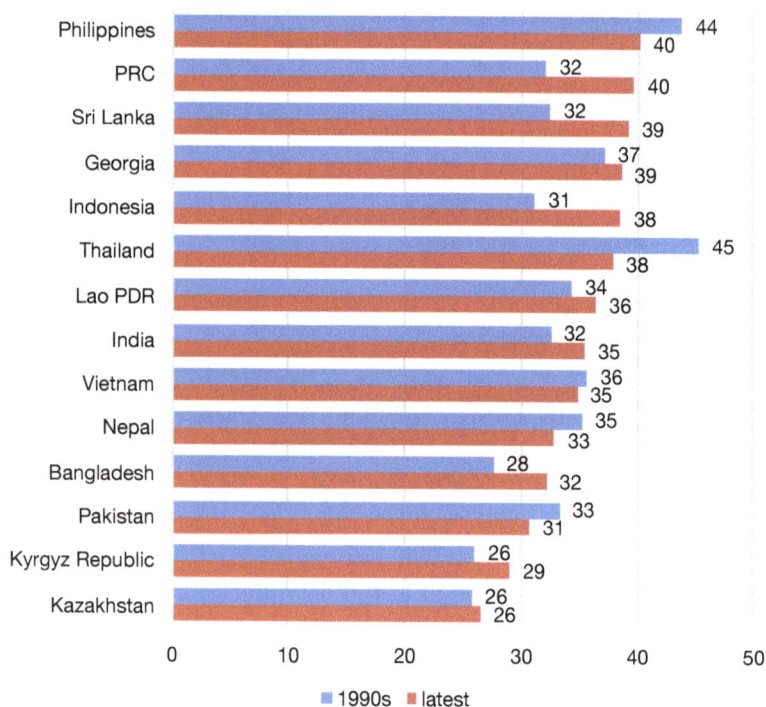

Figure 4.2. Gini coefficient, selected Asian economies, 1990s and 2013 or latest

Source. PovCal Database, World Bank (accessed 11 October 2017)

Table 4.1. Gini coefficients by region

	1981			2013		
	Minimum	Maximum	Median	Minimum	Maximum	Median
Developing Asia	25	55	37	26	46	37
OECD	19	56	31	25	47	32
Latin America and the Caribbean	41	60	49	40	58	47
Middle East and North Africa	29	47	38	28	44	35
Sub-Saharan Africa	32	66	45	31	63	43

Note. The Gini coefficients are based on per capita expenditure for developing Asia and sub-Saharan Africa and per capita disposable income for Latin America and the Caribbean and OECD countries. Income-based Gini coefficients are normally higher than expenditure-based Gini coefficients, and the difference is in the range of 5–10.

Source. PovCal database, World Bank (accessed 11 October 2017)

Inequality of opportunity is also prevalent in developing Asia, and is a crucial factor in widening income inequality (Son 2012). Disparities in the means to raise one's living standards – such as physical assets (e.g. capital and land), human capital (e.g. education and health), and market access (e.g. labour and finance) – are common. Unequal access to public services, especially education and health, is central to generating inequality of opportunity. National household surveys conducted in the mid- to late-2000s revealed facets of diverging opportunities in many developing Asian countries. For instance, school-age children from households in the poorest income quintile were three to five times as likely to be out of primary and secondary school as their peers in the richest quintile in some countries. The situation was even more dire for tertiary education as poorer college-age individuals were 10–20 times more likely not to attend college than their better off peers.

Similarly, infant mortality rates among the poorest households in some countries were double or treble the rates among the richest households. In the most extreme examples, the chance of a poor infant dying at birth was more than 10 times higher than for an infant born to a rich family. With few exceptions, the region's economies have made significant progress toward gender parity in primary and secondary education. Yet high gender disparities in tertiary education remain in South Asia and the Pacific. Inequality of opportunity and of income can lead to a vicious circle, as unequal opportunities create income disparities, which in turn lead to differences in future opportunities for individuals and households.

Why inequality matters

Rising inequality hampers poverty reduction. Each percentage of economic growth will generate a lower rate of poverty reduction when inequality is increasing than when inequality remains unchanged or is decreasing.

Inequality can weaken the basis of growth itself. High and rising inequality can affect growth through a number of economic, social, and political mechanisms. Inequality of wealth and income can lead to a misallocation of human capital. Those with little wealth or low income are unable to invest in human capital, or wealth- and income-enhancing activities, and will remain poor. In principle they may be able to borrow to finance investment. But imperfect financial markets, coupled with other market failures, often heavily constrain their ability to borrow and invest.

Widening inequality – leaving more people at the top and bottom of the ladder – can mean a hollowing out of the middle class. It has been argued that growth driven by and benefiting a middle class is more likely to be sustained – both economically, to the extent that the rent seeking and corruption associated with highly concentrated gains to growth are avoided, and politically, to the extent that conflict and horizontal inequalities between racial and ethnic groups are easier to manage.

In fact, there is a broad consensus among researchers on the link between inequality and the quality of institutions. Along several dimensions, ranging from political stability, through institutional stability, to property rights, the negative impact of inequality on institutional quality seems to be well established, although the two-way causality is also widely recognised (Zhuang et al. 2010; Nye 2014). At the same time, there is also a literature on the effect of inequality on crime and violence and, through that, on the investment climate (Fajnzylber et al. 2002; Ozler & Demombynes 2002).

Finally, greater inequality may lead to a political backlash and growing pressure for governments to enact populist policy measures. In response to rising demands, the political process may favour policies that, in the short term, would benefit the lower end of income distribution, but which in the long run could hold back efficiency and growth. Under such conditions, the interests of the political system diverge from the interests of the economy as a whole. This is a widespread concern in developing and developed countries alike.

Asian policymakers are becoming more concerned about inequality. In an informal web-based survey of Asian policymakers,[3] about two-thirds of the respondents indicated that the level of income inequality is high or very high and that it has increased from 10 years ago; three-quarters of the respondents indicated that the level of concern over inequality among policymakers has increased; almost all the respondents thought that it is important or very important to have policies in place to prevent rises in inequality in order to maintain stability and sustain growth; and more than half believed that success in reducing poverty was insufficient to justify widening inequality.

---

3   The survey was carried out by Asian Development Bank (ADB) in January–February 2012. From key government agencies in 25 of the ADB's developing member countries, 504 respondents registered their opinions.

Asian governments are responding to this concern, which is increasingly being addressed through development plans across the region that include explicit goals to make growth more inclusive. In India, the government made an explicit commitment to inclusive growth in its recent successive five-year plans. In the PRC, the authorities set about building a harmonious society, scientific development, and realising the Chinese dream as the development goals and have committed to making growth inclusive. In Indonesia, Malaysia and the Philippines, inclusive growth or development is at the heart of their current medium-term development strategies.

The distinction between inequality of opportunity and inequality of outcome is important in guiding public policy. Inequality of opportunity – access to education, health, public services or jobs – often arises from differences in individual circumstances that are outside the control of individuals – such as gender, ethnic origin, parental education or birth location. Such inequality largely reflects institutional weaknesses and social exclusion, and should be the target of public policy. On the other hand, given an individual's circumstances, what the individual chooses for effort in the labour market or in education will also influence his or her outcomes – such as income or consumption. Inequality of outcomes arising from differences in individual effort reflects and reinforces the market-based incentives that are needed to foster innovation and growth. This distinction is something of which the general public and policymakers in Asia are aware, as shown by the results from the World Values Survey (2005) and the Asian Development Bank's (ADB) web-based survey of Asian policy makers (ADB 2012).[4]

---

4   The 2005 World Values Survey asked representative samples of people in 69 countries to locate their views on a scale of 1 to 10, with 1 meaning 'incomes should be made more equal' and 10 meaning 'we need larger income differences as incentives'. The Asian responses are more skewed toward 10 – about 63 per cent of the responses are in the 6–10 range – although there is still significant weight in the lower value responses. In comparison, the OECD responses are spread more evenly over the 10 categories. Results from ADB's web-based survey indicate that about 60 per cent of the respondents agree or strongly agree with the statement that it is more important to reduce inequality of opportunity (such as access to education, health and employment services) than to reduce inequality of income.

What drives Asia's rising income inequality?

Conceptual discussion

Total income of a household is the sum of its income derived from labour and that derived from capital:

$$Income = W\,L + R\,K \tag{1}$$

Capital income is the product of the different types of capital assets (K) owned by the household and their respective rates of return (R). For a typical household, capital assets consist mostly of housing, land, factories and machinery, and financial assets. Labour income – which includes returns to human capital – is the product of the different types of labour assets (L) and their respective wage rates (W). The return to human capital is reflected in the skill premium; that is, the more educated and skilled labourer earns higher wages. K, R, L, and W can all be considered as vectors. Income inequality estimates are usually based on per capita household income (where H is the total number of households), that is:

$$\frac{Income}{H} = W\left(\frac{L}{H}\right) + R\left(\frac{K}{H}\right) \tag{2}$$

Therefore, inequality in per capita household income is the result of inequality in per capita labour income $(L\,W/H)$, inequality in per capita capital income $(K\,R/H)$ and the relative importance of labour and (non-human) capital incomes $(WL\,Income)$ and $RK/Income$, respectively) in total household income.[5] Changes in income inequality can be thought of as resulting from a combination of changes in the distributions of assets, changes in the relative returns to these assets, and changes in the relative importance of labour and capital incomes in total household income.

In any society, the distribution of non-human capital reflects its ownership structure, while the distribution of human capital is determined mostly by inequality in access to education and health services. Over time, many factors shape these distributions, including initial distributions, household savings behaviour and investment decisions, differences in individual

---

5   Lerman and Yitzhaki (1985) decompose the Gini coefficient into the contributions by income source. Each source's contribution to overall inequality is the product of its Gini coefficient, its share in total income, and its correlation with the rank of total income.

effort and entrepreneurship, political economy factors (such as pressures for land redistribution, taxation on wealth, and public spending on human capital), the quality of governance and institutions, and demographics.

Changes in the relative returns to assets reflect demand and supply conditions in the marketplace and how efficiently the market works – for instance, the presence or absence of monopoly or discrimination against particular population groups (such as females or rural residents), and political economy factors (such as labour market institutions and taxation on labour and capital incomes).

Finally, changes in the relative importance of labour and capital incomes in total household income are determined by the relative changes in returns to labour and capital and in the capital–labour ratio. These are in turn determined by technological advances and the bias of technical progress, the relative bargaining positions of labour and capital, political economy factors such as labour market institutions (minimum wages, collective bargaining and employment protection), taxation, and the presence or absence of market distortions.

Within this framework, income inequality increases if changes in relative returns to assets or in the distribution of assets, or in the relative importance of labour and capital incomes in total income, favour the better-off households. There are many ways in which this could happen.

First, wage rates could increase faster for better educated and skilled workers than for the less educated and skilled. There is a large literature showing that globalisation and technological progress may have increased the demand for skilled workers relative to that for unskilled workers in many developing countries, leading to an increasing skill premium (ADB 2012). In the case of the PRC, the market-oriented reforms introduced after 1979 dismantled the fixed-wage system that existed under central planning and made wages more reflective of workers' skills and educational attainments and of market demand and supply conditions, and may have also contributed to the increase in the skill premium.

Second, the differential in the returns to capital and in wage rates between richer coastal and urban areas and the poorer interior and rural areas could increase as growth accelerated, leading to increasing spatial inequality. This is because coastal regions are closer to trade routes and world markets than interior regions; and, because cities have better infrastructure than rural areas, they are more likely to attract investment and new technologies, especially during the initial phase of growth take-off (Lewis 1954). All these factors could lead to greater increases in productivity, wages and returns to capital assets in the favoured areas. In the PRC, for example, land and housing prices have increased much faster in coastal areas and cities than in inland provinces and rural areas in the last 30 years or so.

Third, capital income could increase faster than labour income. This would lead to a rising share of capital income in total household income (which tends to be less equally distributed and mostly earned by richer households) and a declining share of labour income (which tends to be more equally distributed and more important for poorer households). This occurs when total income grows faster than total labour income, leaving a larger share of income accruing to capital.[6] It has been suggested that technological progress, especially the adoption of information and communications technology (ICT) and automation, has reduced the demand for labour relative to that for capital (as shown by a declining employment elasticity of growth in recent decades), thus favouring capital. In some countries, the large pool of rural surplus labour has also put downward pressure on urban wage rates (until recently in the case of the PRC).

Fourth, increasing inequality in asset distribution can also lead to an increase in income inequality. Inequality in human capital could increase if wealthier households invest more in education and health than poorer households. Inequality in capital assets could increase if wealthier households save more, if they receive higher returns to capital due to economies of scale or if they have lower fertility rates than less wealthy households.

In addition to these major drivers, there are other reasons why income inequality could increase. One is increases in corruption and rent-seeking, if better off households are more likely to engage in such activities. Another source is the remittances sent home (mostly in rural areas) by migrant workers working in urban areas, which may increase inequality in rural areas but nevertheless reduce urban–rural income gaps.

---

6   Alternatively, the share of labour income can decline and that of capital increase when the rate of return to capital grows faster, or decreases more slowly, than the output–capital ratio. It is easy to show that the capital–output ratio equals the ratio of the savings rate (s) to the growth rate of the capital stock. In a steady state, the latter equals the growth rate of output (g), which implies that capital–income share is the ratio of the product of the rate of return to capital times the savings rate (r s) to the growth rate (g). This means that, assuming a constant savings rate, capital–income share will increase as the gap between r and g increases. And likewise, assuming a constant ratio (r/g), a higher saving rate will lead to a higher capital share.

Empirical evidence

Technological progress, globalisation, and market-oriented deregulation have been the key drivers of developing Asia's rapid growth in the last several decades – but they have also had huge distributional implications. Together, they have favoured skilled over unskilled labour, leading to a rising skill premium; capital over labour, leading to a rising share of capital income; and urban and coastal areas over rural and inland regions, leading to rising spatial inequality. These forces can explain a large part of the movements in income distribution and inequality in many countries in Asia. In the PRC, evidence shows that rising income inequality has also led to rising wealth inequality, which in turn increases income inequality.

Rising skill premiums

There is significant global evidence that the rates of return to progressively higher levels of education have been trending upward in recent years. In OECD countries, for instance, those who do not complete an upper secondary education could earn an average of 23 per cent less than their counterparts who do. A person with a tertiary education can expect to earn over 50 per cent more than a person with an upper secondary or post-secondary non-tertiary education (OECD 2011).

In Asia, empirical studies find that the returns from education increase with educational attainment and that the relationship has been getting steeper over time. An ADB study (2007) found that from the mid-1990s to mid-2000s, real wages in India and the Philippines grew much faster for wage earners with tertiary or higher education than for those with lower educational attainment, leading to wider wage differentials. The same study also found that education is the single-most important factor among those variables that were included in analysing wage inequality. In the case of India, the Gini coefficient of wages increased from 40.5 in 1993 to 47.2 in 2004. Half the increase can be explained by individual characteristics. Of this explained increase, about 50 per cent is accounted for by education.

Many other studies have provided direct or indirect evidence of rising skill and/or education premiums in developing Asia. Son (2010) found that education increases individuals' employability in the Philippines. A study on India, the Philippines and Thailand found that the rate of return to college education rose relative to that of secondary education between the mid-1990s and mid-2000s (Mehta et al. 2011). This rise was related to the expansion of high-skill service jobs that, while they employed only 7–11 per cent of the labour force, contributed 40–70 per cent of the rate of return to college education.

A World Bank study (World Bank 2012) reported that the tertiary education premium[7] stood at 90 per cent for Cambodia (2007), 60 per cent for the PRC (2005), 84 per cent for Indonesia (2007), 70 per cent for Mongolia (2007), 70 per cent for the Philippines (2006), 120 per cent for Thailand (2004) and 55 per cent for Vietnam (2006). In Cambodia, the PRC, Mongolia and Vietnam, the premium has increased in recent years across sectors. The tertiary education premium increased in Indonesia in the manufacturing sector and in the Philippines in the services sector.

Household survey data help reveal patterns of income inequality due to educational attainment (in this case, of the household head) (Figure 4.3). First, education inequality almost always accounts for more than 20 per cent of total income inequality. Second, the share of total income inequality explained by educational inequality has by and large been on the increase. The share of inequality accounted for by differences in educational attainment increased in all the countries during the periods reviewed, with the increase most significant in the PRC, from 8.1 per cent in 1995 to 26.5 per cent in 2007.

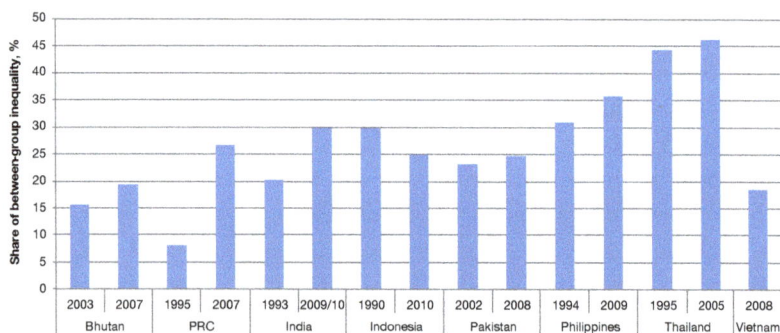

Figure 4.3. Income inequality decomposition by educational attainment

PRC = People's Republic of China.

Note. Estimates are based on per-capita expenditure in nominal terms, except for the PRC which is based on income. The decomposition is based on GE(0), which is a special form of the generalised entropy index.

Source. The author's estimates using household survey data from ADB

---

7   Tertiary education premium refers to the wage premium for workers with at least tertiary education compared with workers with a lower level of education.

As in the rest of the world, developing Asia is facing strong upward pressure on the wage gap between skilled and unskilled labour. Is this because of skill-biased technological progress? There are empirical difficulties in isolating this factor because the wage premium depends on both demand-and supply-side factors. Unsurprisingly, analysts have come down on both sides of the explanation.[8] To the extent that skill-biased technological change happens, its impact can be transmitted through globalisation. It is unlikely that policymakers can reverse this trend, nor should they want to, since technological progress is delivering higher levels of productivity and growth in the economy. The answer, rather, is to address inequality in human capital itself.

Labour's falling share of total income

In the last several decades, the income share of labour has been on the decline and that of capital on the rise in many countries around the world. In the United States, for example, the labour-income share in industry declined from 65 per cent in 1992 to 52.4 per cent in 2009. Similarly, in Germany, the labour-income share of industry peaked at 79.5 per cent in 1993 from the rise that started in the mid-1980s, declining since then.

A declining labour-income share means that the growth of real wage rates lags behind growth of labour productivity. A number of contributing factors have been identified in the context of the developed world. The first is that technological change, especially connected with improvements in information and communication technologies and automation, has raised the productivity of and return to capital relative to labour. The second is the decrease in the bargaining power of labour, due to changing labour market policies and declining union membership in these countries. The third is increased globalisation and trade openness, which led to migration of relatively more labour-intensive sectors from advanced economies to emerging economies – with the sectors remaining in the

---

8   Acemoglu (2002) noted that, for the late-twentieth century, there has been a rise in returns to education and a decrease in low-skill wages, despite an increase in the supply of college graduates, which suggests that supply has not kept up with demand for high-skilled labour. Studies have also argued for evidence of skill-biased technological change in developing countries (Goldberg & Pavcnik 2007; Robbins 1996; Sanchez-Paramo & Schady 2003; and Attanasio, Goldberg & Pavcnik 2004 for Latin America; Hsieh & Woo 2005 for Hong Kong, China; and Kijima 2006 for India). However, Card and DiNardo (2002) pointed out that wage inequality stabilised in the United States despite continuing developments in computer technology. They also argued that skill-biased technological change does not fully explain wage gaps across genders, and racial and demographic structures. The debate between competing explanations for the United States is ongoing (see Autor, Katz & Kearney 2008; Marquis, Trehan & Tantivong 2011).

advanced economies being relatively less labour-intensive and having a lower average share of labour income (Jacobson & Occhino 2012; Arpaia et al. 2009). It has also been noted that globalisation and trade openness increase the elasticity of labour demand, which also weakens labour's bargaining position (Rodrik 1997; Harrison 2002).

Empirical evidence suggests that Asia is following this trend – all the economies in Figure 4.4 saw declines in labour-income shares during the mid-1990s to mid-2000s. What are the causes of these declines? Technological progress in the region appears to have been labour-saving and capital-using. Partly, this can be explained by a high level of capital accumulation in many Asian countries (Felipe 2009). As a result, the wage employment elasticity of growth[9] has been on the decline in many countries in recent years – for example, in the PRC from 0.44 in 1991–2001 to 0.28 in 2001–11 and in India from 0.53 to 0.41 for the same period. This decline means that each percentage of employment growth now requires a higher percentage of output growth than in the past – a phenomenon sometimes referred to as 'jobless growth' (ADB 2012).

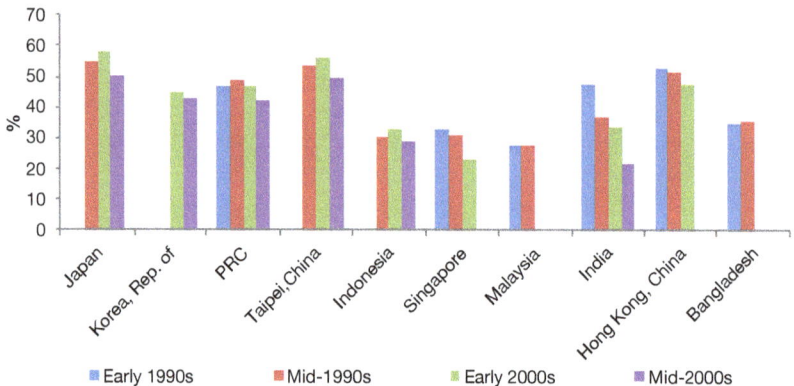

Figure 4.4. Share of labour income in industrial value added, selected Asian economies

Note. Early 1990s (1990–92), mid-1990s (1994–96), early 2000s (2000–02), and mid-2000s (2004–06) for the PRC; India; Singapore; Malaysia; India; Hong Kong, China; and Bangladesh.

Source. OECD.Stat database (OECD 2018) for Japan; Republic of Korea; Taipei, China; and Indonesia (accessed 1 March 2012); Felipe & Sipin (2004) for Singapore; Malaysia; Hong Kong, China; and Bangladesh; Bai & Qian (2009) for the PRC; and Felipe & Kumar (2010) for India's organised manufacturing sector

---

9   Wage employment refers to wage-earning employment, mostly in the formal sector. Wage employment elasticity is the ratio of employment growth to GDP growth between two periods. It thus measures the amount of employment growth required to generate each percentage point of GDP growth.

A declining employment elasticity of growth implies increases in labour productivity. Annual growth of manufacturing labour productivity in 2000–08 reached 6.7 per cent in the PRC and 5.5 per cent in Malaysia, and was in the range of 3–4 per cent in Indonesia, Pakistan, the Philippines, Thailand and Vietnam (Asian Productivity Organization 2011).

That labour productivity is increasing but labour income share is declining implies that real wage growth has lagged behind labour productivity growth, partly because of the presence of a large pool of surplus rural labour in many countries associated with their dual-economy structure. The surplus labour pool weakens the bargaining power of labour and depresses wages in the non-agriculture sectors, contributing to declines in the labour-income share when globalisation and market-oriented reform led to rapid growth. In India, for instance, average annual growth of labour productivity was 7.4 per cent in 1990–2007, while average annual real wage growth was only 2 per cent. In the case of the PRC, Zhuang (1996) showed that if the labour market had been fully liberalised and controls over labour transfer from rural to urban areas fully relaxed in the early 1980s, urban wage rates would have fallen, and the labour-income share of the urban sector would have decreased by half. A lower share of income going to labour and a higher share of income going to capital tends to increase inequality, because capital income is mostly earned by richer households and more unequally distributed than income from basic wage labour.

Increasing spatial inequality

As the distribution of economic activity is structured geographically – high concentrations and incomes in some locations, and low on both counts in others – so are the distribution of income and its evolution. Some locations have natural advantages, like fertile soil for agriculture or proximity to a coastline for trade.[10] Economic analysis has also highlighted the role of agglomeration benefits, where once concentration starts because of natural advantages or because of advantages conferred by infrastructure, there is a self-perpetuating process of increasing concentration (Krugman 2008).

The increasing rural–urban income gap is a significant contributor to inequality in several Asian countries (Figure 4.5), especially the PRC (around 45 per cent).

---

10   Several decades ago, Nobel laureate in economics Arthur Lewis pointed out the tendency of the development process to be inegalitarian: 'Development must be inegalitarian because it does not start in every part of the economy at the same time … There may be one such enclave in an economy, or several; but at the start, development enclaves include only a small minority of the population' (Lewis 1976).

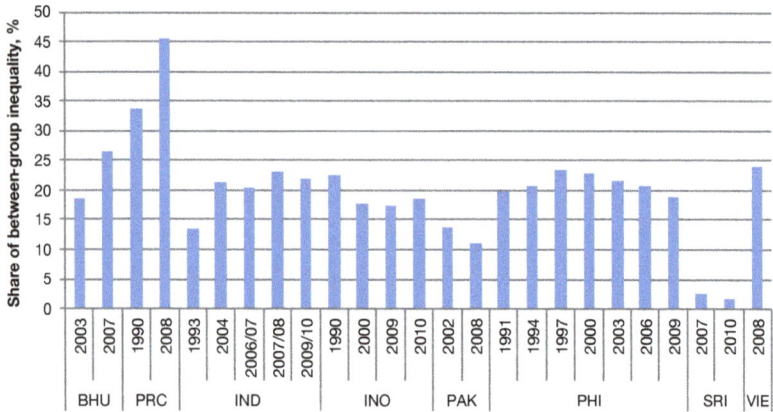

Figure 4.5. Income inequality decomposition, urban/rural

BHU = Bhutan, IND = India, INO = Indonesia, PAK = Pakistan, PHI = Philippines, PRC = People's Republic of China, SRI = Sri Lanka, VIE = Vietnam.

Note. Estimates are based on per-capita expenditure in nominal terms. Decomposition is based on GE(0), which is a special form of the generalised entropy index.

Source. The author's estimates using household survey data from the ADB

The possibility of rising inequality due to urbanisation as part of the development process was first pointed out by Kuznets (1955). The mechanism that he highlighted in his contribution starts with a two-sector model with the population divided between a low mean income, low inequality sector (rural/agriculture) and a high mean income, high inequality sector (urban/industrial). In this model, the drivers of inequality are changes in inequality within the two sectors, a widening of the gap between average incomes in the two sectors, and a shift of population from agriculture in the rural sector to industry in the urban sector – or the process of urbanisation.

Inequality changes within the two sectors are most likely affected by the same factors discussed in the previous sections, particularly the widening wage premium for skills, and the regional disparity (to be discussed in the next section). To the extent that the urban labour force has a higher level of human capital than the rural labour force, this factor would also tend to widen the rural–urban gap in average incomes. Perhaps the strongest driver of that gap, however, is the cumulative force of agglomeration economies and its impact on productivity (de Groot et al. 2008). For whatever combination of reasons, the rural–urban income gap in Asia has been widening in the last two decades, and it has been a driving force of rising inequality in the PRC (Figure 4.6). Thus the first two factors – change in inequality within the two sectors and a widening of the gap in the average income between the two sectors – are likely to put upward pressure on inequality in Asian countries.

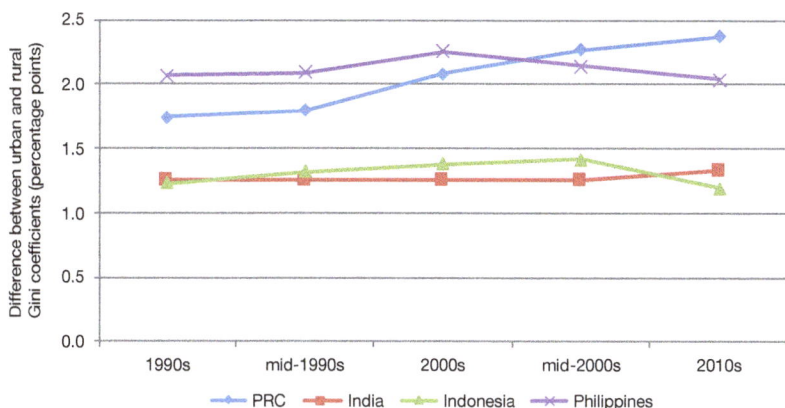

Figure 4.6. Urban–rural income gaps in selected Asian economies, 1990s–2010s

Note. Figures are for the closest available year. Missing data in India for the mid-1990s and 2000s are assumed to be the same as the closest five-year period.

Source. The author's estimates using PovcalNet (accessed 9 March 2012)

What about the third factor? As is well known, urbanisation in Asia has been rapid. Kuznets explored this with the aid of a numerical example, which showed increasing inequality to start with as urbanisation begins, followed by a decrease at the later stages. Anand and Kanbur (1993) showed that if there is no inequality within the two sectors, with the only difference between them being because of the higher income in the urban area, then inequality will indeed follow an inverse U-shape, so that this driver will tend to raise inequality in the early stages of urbanisation. Further, if urban inequality is higher than rural inequality, this effect will be reinforced. Kanbur and Zhuang (2013) find that, during the period from the early 1990s to the late 2000s, urbanisation can explain about 54 per cent of the increase in inequality in Indonesia and 14 per cent in India, but helped reduce inequality in the PRC.

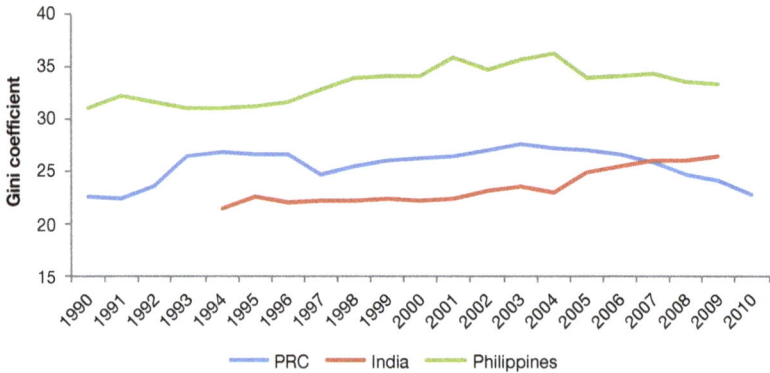

Figure 4.7. Inequalities in provincial per capita incomes in selected Asian economies, 1990–2010

Note. Gini coefficients are weighted by group population.

Source. The author's estimates using province-level data for the PRC and the Philippines from the CEIC database (accessed 5 March 2012) and data for India from the Ministry of Statistics and Programme Implementation (accessed 5 March 2012)

Regional inequality has also been a key contributor to total inequality in many Asian countries, particularly in the PRC and India (Figure 4.7). Notably for the PRC, in 1990–2003, regional inequality increased more or less concurrently with overall inequality.

In the PRC, there appears to be a general consensus that increased openness contributed to sharpening income disparities between coastal and interior regions. As Lin (2005) noted, an important feature of the country's global integration is the depth of concentration of international trade along the east coast – which has far lower transport costs to the country's major markets such as Hong Kong, China; Europe; Japan; and the United States. Since 2003, the PRC's regional inequality has declined somewhat. This has been partly attributed to the government's Great Western Development Strategy (Fan et al. 2011).

In India, coastal states have also fared better than inland states, although here a set of compounding factors including initial level of human capital and public infrastructure is also important (Kanbur et al. 2007). New private sector industrial investments typically take place in existing industrial and coastal districts to reduce costs, and overall investments have become more concentrated.

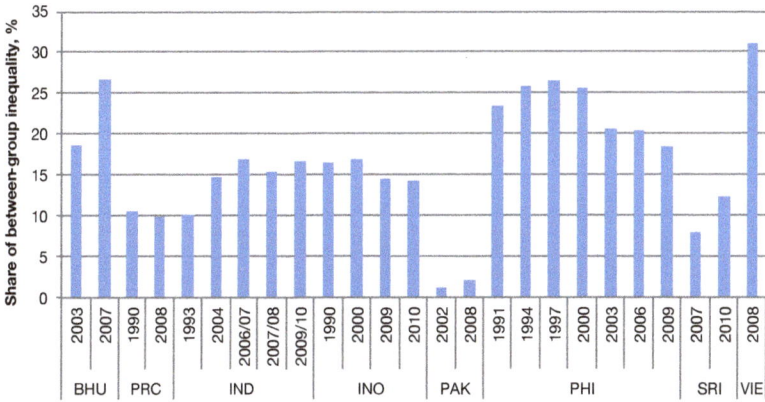

Figure 4.8. Income inequality decomposition, province/region

BHU = Bhutan, PRC = People's Republic of China, IND = India, INO = Indonesia,
PAK = Pakistan, PHI = Philippines, SRI = Sri Lanka, VIE = Vietnam.

Note. Estimates are based on per-capita expenditure in nominal terms. Decomposition
is based on GE(0), which is a special form of the generalised entropy index.

Source. The author's estimates using household survey data

More generally, the interplay between market-oriented reforms and
economies of agglomeration has given certain regions within countries
an edge when it comes to economic growth. Indeed, this interplay has
been linked to increasing inequality in South-East Asia and East Asia's
middle-income economies (Gill & Kharas 2007). Figure 4.8 provides
decomposition results for regional inequality in selected Asian countries.
Between-region inequality can explain 20–30 per cent of the national
inequality in the late 2000s in Bhutan, the Philippines and Vietnam, and
10–15 per cent in the PRC, Indonesia, India, and Sri Lanka.

Combining the two components of spatial inequality and calculating the
fraction of total inequality explained by rural–urban and interregional
(provinces or states) divides, we see a share of more than half for the PRC
(Figure 4.9).

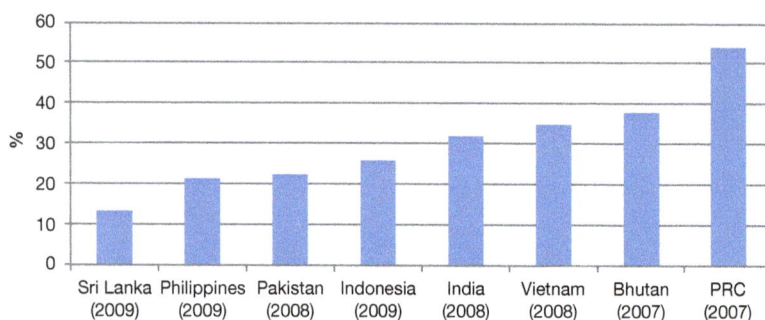

Figure 4.9. Combined contribution of spatial inequality to overall inequality in selected Asian countries

Note. Spatial inequality covers both between-region and urban–rural inequality. The estimation involves dividing all sample households into groups classified by both region and urban–rural. For example, if a country has 20 provinces, the total groups will be 40 (20 urban and 20 rural). The between-group inequality is the combined spatial inequality.

Source. The author's estimates using household survey data

In sum, the widening gaps between provinces and states, on the one hand, and between urban and rural areas, on the other, provide and will provide the geographic driver of inequality in Asia. These divides are important in themselves and because they account for a significant proportion of observed inequality in Asian countries. The driver of inequality in the spatial dimension is the interaction between new opportunities through trade, technology and market-oriented reform, interacting with the structure of geography and infrastructure. The rise in spatial inequality is not a reason to reverse openness and technological progress, or stop the reform process, but rather to reorient infrastructure investment to lagging regions, and to remove barriers to migration to the fast-growing regions.

Widening wealth inequality

Wealth distribution is usually more unequal than income distribution. Rising wealth inequality has likely also been a major contributor to the rising income inequality in the PRC, although it has not been studied as extensively as income inequality and other income inequality drivers, because of limited data. A recent study by Li and Wan (2015) finds that between 2002 and 2010, per capita household wealth (including land, housing, financial assets and other physical capital) increased by 4.1 times, and its Gini coefficient increased from 53.8 to 73.9. A major contributing factor to the rising wealth distribution has been rising housing prices.

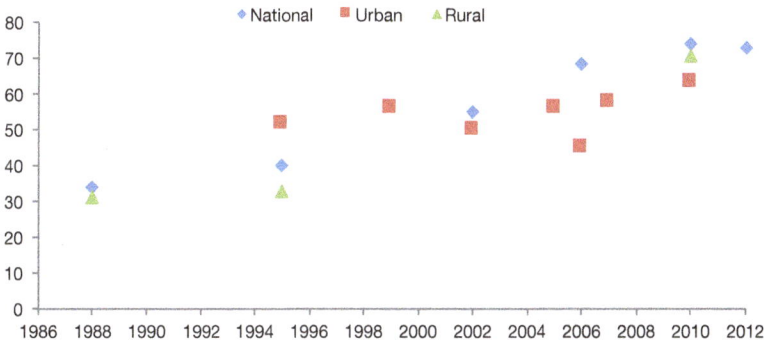

Figure 4.10. Gini coefficient of per capita net household wealth, PRC, 1988–2012

Source. Li & Wan (2015)

Figure 4.10 plots various estimates of the Gini coefficient of per capita net household wealth from 1988 to 2012 for the entire PRC, urban PRC and rural PRC. It shows that wealth distribution has become more and more unequal in the PRC. For the PRC as a whole, the wealth Gini coefficient increased from 34 in 1988 to 73 in 2012. For urban PRC, it increased from about 50 in the mid-1990s to 63 in 2010. For rural PRC, it increased from 31 in 1988 to 71 in 2010.

How to respond to rising inequality – promoting inclusive growth

Because the forces behind rising inequality are also the engines of productivity and income growth, policymakers should not hinder their progress. A distinction needs to be made between the income differences that arise as economies and individuals take advantage of the new opportunities of technology, trade and efficiency-enhancing reforms; and those that are generated by unequal access to market opportunities and public services. This latter source of inequality requires a policy response because it is magnified by the driving forces of growth, leads to inefficiency and undermines the sustainability of growth.

Based on these considerations, Zhuang and Ali (2010) propose an inclusive growth strategy to respond to rising income inequality in Asia. They define inclusive growth as 'growth with equality of opportunity', argue that an inclusive growth strategy should focus on both expanding economic opportunity and ensuring equal access to it, and that it should have the following policy pillars:

- sustaining robust economic growth. A large percentage of people in Asia are employed in the informal sector, and tens of millions of workers are set to join the region's labour force each year in the coming decades. Robust economic growth is needed for job creation. But to be inclusive, growth must provide decent, productive jobs for a wide spectrum of the population and expand economic opportunity for all
- promoting social inclusion. Every person must have equal access to opportunity. In many Asian economies, large portions of populations cannot benefit from economic opportunity created by growth for reasons beyond their control. Ensuring equal access to opportunity requires, on the one hand, investing in education and health care, especially for the disadvantaged, to enhance human capacities; and on the other hand, correcting market and institutional failures and eliminating social exclusion to level the playing field
- developing social safety nets. Programs are needed to mitigate the risks and vulnerabilities associated with transitory shocks to livelihoods that often are caused by ill health, economic crises, industrial restructuring, or natural disaster. Programs that cater to the special needs of the disadvantaged and chronically poor also are needed to prevent poverty
- mobilising more fiscal revenues. Greater spending on education and health and social protection programs requires Asian governments to mobilise more fiscal revenues to ensure fiscal sustainability. In many Asian countries, there is room for greater revenue mobilisation by improving tax administration and introducing taxes that are inherently progressive – such as those on capital gains, properties, and inheritance – that also help to reduce wealth inequality
- promoting good governance and sound institutions.

Each of the above pillars and their implementation must be supported by good governance and sound institutions.

Creating productive jobs through robust economic growth

For the benefits of economic growth to be widespread, it must generate ample productive employment – the most important opportunity for human beings. Greater job creation will increase labour demand and hence labour's share in national income. Job creation, therefore, should be at the core of any country's inclusive growth strategy and at the top of its policy agenda. Achieving this goal in Asia remains a daunting task. An ADB Institute study (ADBI 2014) looked at the challenge of job creation in 12 Asian countries including China, India and 10 Association of Southeast Asian Nations (ASEAN) members, and found that more than half of their employment, amounting to 800 million people in total, can be classified as vulnerable under the International Labour Organization (ILO) definition. The study also showed that, between 2020–30, the combined labour force of these countries will expand by more than 10 million workers per year.

To create more jobs, Asian countries must maintain enabling environments for business investment and private entrepreneurship by eliminating impediments due to failures of markets, institutions and policies. This requires investment in physical infrastructure and human capital, development of institutional capacity, maintaining macroeconomic stability, adopting market-friendly policies, protection of property rights, and enforcement of the rule of law. In setting policy priorities, governments must identify the binding constraints to growth and target their efforts and resources to ease them. Governments should also pay attention not only to the pace of economic growth, but also to its pattern to ensure that it is broadly based (Ianchovichina & Lundstrom 2009).

High growth will have to be driven by dynamic private sectors. But to attain full employment, the role of government will also be critical. Felipe (2009) proposes five sets of government policies to achieve full employment of the labour force. First, governments must redress the neglect of agriculture. Second, they should target high-employment public-investment projects in basic infrastructure such as energy, transport, and urban services. Third, they should collaborate with the private sector on policies to accelerate industrialisation and structural transformation. Fourth, governments should gear fiscal and monetary policies to the achievement of full employment. Fifth, they should devise job guarantee programs to ensure full employment with price stability.

Broadening opportunities by investing in education and health

An effective way to reduce inequality and promote social inclusion is to enhance human capabilities, especially those of disadvantaged groups, by investing in education, health care, and other basic public services. Education improves labour productivity, facilitates technological innovation, increases return on capital, and helps improve health outcomes. Empirical studies find that basic education enables farmers to switch from traditional to more productive methods, and from farming to other more rewarding professions (Brooks et al. 2010). Similarly, good health can improve growth by boosting accumulation of human capital. The large gaps in education attainment and health indicators for many Asian countries compared with those of developed countries as well as differences within the region suggest Asian countries have much to do.

Governments – both central and local – have a critical role to play in investing in education and health because these services are public goods and have a strong external impact. In 2010, public spending on education was about 3 per cent of GDP for developing Asia as a whole, far less than the 5.5 per cent for Latin America and the Caribbean and 5.3 per cent for OECD countries; public spending on health was 2.4 per cent of GDP for developing Asia, compared with 3.8 per cent for Latin America and the Caribbean and 8.1 per cent for OECD countries (ADB 2014). Although public spending on education and health has increased in developing Asia in recent years, the gaps remain large.

In addition to providing adequate funding, governments should also ensure strong institutional capacity, sound policy frameworks, and good governance of health and education services. Governments also need to allocate resources equitably, such as among primary, secondary and tertiary schools and between primary health care facilities in rural areas, tertiary hospitals in cities, and prevention and treatment programs. Public investment must be complemented by supply-side policies to ensure the efficiency and quality of public services and demand-side policies to avoid moral hazard behaviour and waste. More innovative delivery mechanisms, such as the use of conditional cash transfers, non-government organisations in services contracting, and vouchers and contract teachers in delivering basic education services, can be explored to ensure that poor and disadvantaged groups are not excluded in accessing public services (Brooks et al. 2010).

Preventing poverty with social safety nets

Inclusive growth also requires social safety nets that mitigate the effects of external and transitory livelihood shocks and meet the minimum needs of the chronically poor. Exposure to such risks can have a profound and long-lasting impact on human wellbeing. Social safety nets not only help the poor and vulnerable cope with the above risks, they can also play a role in improving human capital in the long run, which makes opportunities more accessible to those with limited assets and capabilities (Brooks et al. 2010). In 2010, public spending on social protection was 6.2 per cent of GDP for developing Asia as a whole, compared with 12 per cent for Latin America and the Caribbean and 20 per cent for OECD countries.

Social safety nets come in a variety of forms. Labour market policies and programs aim to reduce risks associated with unemployment, underemployment, or low wages that result from inappropriate skills in the workforce or poorly functioning labour markets. A range of social-insurance programs, such as pensions and health or unemployment insurance, cushion risks associated with unemployment, ill health, disability, work-related injuries and old age. Social-assistance schemes such as welfare programs, social services, and cash or in-kind transfers are aimed at assisting single-parent households, victims of natural disasters or civil conflicts, the disabled, and other vulnerable groups. Other programs promote healthy and productive development of children by providing services such as early childhood development, school meals, scholarships, free or subsidised health care for mothers and children, and family allowances or credit (Ali & Zhuang 2007). A growing body of empirical evidence suggests that social-protection schemes have significant impacts on poverty, inequality and human development (Skoufias 2001; Soares et al. 2006).

Targeting social protection programs toward the poor is a key issue for many Asian countries. Affordability is often raised as an issue when a country tries to expand safety nets. Yet studies assert that the costs of basic universal social protection are not beyond the reach of most developing countries (Ortiz & Yablonski 2010). The United Nations Department of Economic and Social Affairs estimates that a universal social-pension scheme designed to keep the elderly above the $1-a-day poverty line costs less than 0.5 per cent of GDP in most countries (UN 2007). Another study by the ILO argues that virtually all countries can afford some form of basic social security (ILO 2008). Affordability, therefore, may depend on a country's willingness to finance social-protection schemes.

Mobilising more fiscal revenues through tax reforms

To increase public spending on education, health and social protection to enhance inclusion, and at the same time to ensure fiscal sustainability, Asia needs to expand and strengthen its fiscal revenue base. In 2010, total fiscal revenue as percentage of GDP was about 20 per cent for developing Asia, compared with 25 per cent in Latin America and more than 28 per cent for OECD (ADB 2014). Many governments in the region have made efforts to increase fiscal revenues through tax reforms, but more needs to be done.

Greater mobilisation of fiscal revenues requires exploring a range of options, including broadening the base for personal income tax and value-added tax (VAT), enlarging corrective taxes and nontax revenues, and introducing naturally progressive taxes on property, capital gains and inheritance. Broadening the base for personal income tax and VAT offers scope for raising more revenues by reducing various exemptions, deductions and tax incentives. For some Asian countries, lowering income thresholds for the higher tax rates can generate increased personal income tax revenues. Expanding VAT – or introducing one where it does not exist – generates revenue efficiently. Using additional revenues from VAT for public social spending can make this regressive tax progressive on balance. Corrective taxes and nontax revenues can promote efficiency and equity while raising revenue. Taxing property, capital gains and inheritance can make the tax structure more progressive and equitable.

Strengthening governance and institutions

Promoting good governance and sound institutions has been a key focus in development policy discussions in recent years and should also be a critical component of an inclusive growth strategy. Poor governance and weak institutions lead to unequal access to opportunities and public services, allow corruption and rent-seeking activities to prevail, and create social exclusion and injustice, all of which contribute to inequality. Good governance and sound institutions have intrinsic and instrumental value as they are a key precondition for sustained economic growth and prosperity (Acemoglu & Robinson 2012).

Asian countries have made significant progress in strengthening governance and institutions in recent years. Going forward, a tailored approach to governance reform can be followed to maximise development impact. As development goals in themselves, all dimensions of governance should be pursued. But the stage dependency of the governance–development nexus calls for prioritisation. Policymakers need to focus their efforts on the particular governance deficiencies that hold their country back from its next stage of development. Growth-supporting aspects of governance take centre stage for low-income economies. Strengthening government effectiveness, improving regulatory quality and rule of law, and scaling up control of corruption provide entry points to wider governance reform.

For middle-income economies, maintaining an environment supportive of growth is important, but policy must also respond to the rising aspirations of the populace. As their incomes improve and access to technology expands, citizens will demand greater say in national affairs. Moving to even higher income entails improving governance quality with respect to participation and accountability.

It is encouraging that more and more developing Asian countries are embracing the concept of inclusive growth, with an increasing number of countries – including the PRC, India and many South-East Asian countries – placing inclusive growth at the heart of their development policy, as reflected in their recent medium-term development plans. Indeed, the entire development community is embracing the concept of inclusive growth. These developments will go a long way toward reducing poverty and inequality and making the world a more equitable place.

References

Acemoglu, D (2002). 'Technical change, inequality and the labor market', *Journal of Economic Literature*, 40, 7–72. doi.org/10.1257/jel.40.1.7.

Acemoglu, D & Robinson, JA (2012). *Why nations fail.* New York: Crown Publishers.

Ali, I & Zhuang, J (2007). *Inclusive growth toward a prosperous Asia: policy implications*, ERD Working Paper Series, No. 97. Manila: Asian Development Bank.

Anand, S & Kanbur, R (1993). 'Inequality and development: A critique', *Journal of Development Economics*, 41(1), 19–43. doi.org/10.1016/0304-3878(93)90035-L.

Arpaia, A, Perez, E & Pichelmann, K (2009). *Understanding labour income share dynamics in Europe*, MPR.000A Paper 15649. Germany: University Library of Munich.

Asian Development Bank (ADB) (2007). *Key indicators for Asia and the Pacific 2007*. Manila.

—— (2012). *Asian development outlook 2012*. Manila.

—— (2013). *Asian development outlook 2013 update*. Manila.

—— (2014). *Asian development outlook 2014*. Manila.

Asian Development Bank Institute (ADBI) (2014). *ASEAN, PRC, and India: The great transformation*. Tokyo.

Asian Productivity Organization (APO) (2011). *APO productivity databook 2011*. Tokyo: Keio University Press, Inc.

Attanasio, O, Goldberg, PK & Pavcnik, N (2004). 'Trade reforms and wage inequality in Colombia', *Journal of Development Economics*, 74(2), 331–66. doi.org/10.1016/j.jdeveco.2003.07.001.

Autor, DH, Katz, LF & Kearney, MS (2008). 'Trends in US wage inequality: Revising the revisionists', *The Review of Economics and Statistics*, 90(2), 300–23. doi.org/10.1162/rest.90.2.300.

Bai, C-E & Qian, Z (2009). *Factor income distribution: The story behind the statistics*. People's Republic of China: Tsinghua University.

Brooks, DH, Hasan, R, Lee, JW, Son, HH & Zhuang, J (2010). *Closing development gaps: Challenges and policy options*, No. 209, ADB Economics Working Paper Series. Manila: Asian Development Bank.

Card, D & DiNardo, JE (2002). 'Skill-biased technological change and rising wage inequality: Some problems and puzzles', *Journal of Labor Economics*, 20(4), 733–83. doi.org/10.1086/342055.

de Groot, HLF, Poot, J & Smit, MJ (2008). *Agglomeration externalities, innovation and regional growth: Theoretical perspectives and meta-analysis*, Working Paper in Economics, 01/08. Hamilton, New Zealand: University of Waikato.

Fajnzylber, P, Lederman, D & Loayza, N (2002). 'Inequality and violent crime', *Journal of Law and Economics*, 45(1), 1–40. doi.org/10.1086/338347.

Fan, S, Kanbur, R & Zhang, X (2011). 'China's regional disparities: Experience and policy', *Review of Development Finance*, 1(1), 47–56. doi.org/10.1016/j.rdf.2010.10.001.

Felipe, J (2009). *Inclusive growth, full employment and structural change: Implications and policies for developing Asia*. London: Anthem Press.

Felipe, J & Kumar, U (2010). *Technical change in India's organized manufacturing sector*, Levy Economics Institute of Bard College Working Paper, No. 626. New York. doi.org/10.2139/ssrn.1691695.

Felipe, J & Sipin, GC (2004). *Competitiveness, income distribution, and growth in the Philippines: What does the long-run evidence show*, ERD Working Paper?, No. 53. Manila: ADB.

Gill, I & Kharas, H (2007). *An East Asian renaissance: Ideas for economic growth*. Washington, DC: World Bank. doi.org/10.1596/978-0-8213-6747-6.

Goldberg, PK & Pavcnik, N (2007). 'Distributional effects of globalization in developing countries', *Journal of Economic Literature*, 45(1), 39–82. doi.org/10.1257/jel.45.1.39.

Harrison, AE (2002). *Has globalization eroded labor's share? Some cross-country evidence*, MPRA Paper, No. 39649, mpra.ub.uni-muenchen.de/39649/1/MPRA_paper_39649.pdf.

Hsieh, C-T, & Woo, KT (2005). 'The impact of outsourcing to China on Hong Kong's labor market', *American Economic Review*, 95, 1673–87. doi.org/10.1257/000282805775014272.

Ianchovichina, E & Lundstrom, S (2009). 'What is inclusive growth? A note supporting the diagnostic facility for shared growth', siteresources.worldbank.org/INTDEBTDEPT/Resources/468980-1218567884549/WhatIsInclusiveGrowth20081230.pdf.

International Labour Organization (ILO). (2008). *Can low-income countries afford basic social security?*, Social Security Policy Briefings Paper, 3. Geneva: ILO.

Jacobson, M & Occhino, F (2012). 'Behind the decline in labor's share of income', *Economic Trends*. Federal Reserve Bank of Cleveland.

Kanbur, R, Gajwani, K & Zhang, X (2007). 'Comparing the evolution of spatial inequality in China and India: A fifty-year perspective', *Annual World Bank Conference on Development Economics* (pp 155–77).

Kanbur, R & Zhuang, J (2013). 'Urbanization and inequality', *Asian Development Review*, 30(1). doi.org/10.1162/ADEV_a_00006.

Kijima, Y (2006). 'Why did wage inequality increase? Evidence from urban India 1983–99', *Journal of Development Economics*, 81, 97–117. doi.org/10.1016/j.jdeveco.2005.04.008.

Krugman, P (2008). 'The increasing returns revolution in trade and geography', lecture delivered at Aula Magna, Stockholm University, 8 December, www.nobelprize.org/uploads/2018/06/krugman_lecture.pdf.

Kuznets, S (1955). 'Economic growth and income inequality', *American Economic Review*, 45, 1–28.

Lerman, RI & Yitzhaki, S (1985). 'Income inequality effects by income source: A new approach and applications to the United States', *Review of Economics and Statistics* 67(1), 151–56. doi.org/10.2307/1928447.

Lewis, WA (1954). 'Economic development with unlimited supplies of labour', *The Manchester School*, 22(2), 139–91. doi.org/10.1111/j.1467-9957.1954. tb00021.x.

—— (1976). 'Development and distribution'. In A Cairncross & M Puri (eds), *Employment, income distribution and development strategy: Problems of the developing countries (Essays in honour of HW Singer)* (pp 26–42). New York: Holmes & Meier Publishers, Inc. doi.org/10.1007/978-1-349-81529-6.

Li, S & Wan, H (2015). 'Evolution of wealth inequality in China', *China Economic Journal*, 8(3), 264–87. doi.org/10.1080/17538963.2015.1110338.

Lin, S (2005). 'International trade, location and wage inequality in China'. In R Kanbur & AJ Venables (eds), *Spatial inequality and development* (pp 260–91). Oxford University Press.

Marquis, MH, Trehan, B & Tantivong, W (2011). *The wage premium puzzle and the quality of human capital*, Working Paper 2011–06. Federal Reserve Bank of San Francisco.

Mehta, A, Felipe, J, Quising, P & Camingue, S (2011). *Where have all the educated workers gone? Services and wage inequality in three Asian economies*, Working Paper, University of California – Santa Barbara, Global & International Studies Program.

Nye, JVC (2014). 'Institutions and economic inequality in Asia: Disentangling policy and political structure'. In R Kanbur, G Rhee & J Zhuang (eds), *Inequality in Asia and the Pacific: Trends, drivers and policy implications* (pp 156–72). London: Routledge and Manila: ADB.

Organisation for Economic Co-operation and Development (OECD) (2011). *Education at a glance 2011: OECD indicators*. Paris.

—— (2018). OECD.Stat database, stats.oecd.org.

Ortiz, I & Yablonski, J (2010). 'Investing in people: Social protection for all'. In SW Handayani (ed.), *Enhancing social protection in Asia and the Pacific: Proceedings of the regional workshop* (pp 36–56). Manila: Asian Development Bank.

Ozler, B & Demombynes, G (2002). *Crime and local inequality in South Africa*, World Bank Policy Research Working Paper, No. 2925. Washington DC: World Bank.

Robbins, DJ (1996). *Evidence on trade and wages in the developing world*, OECD Technical Paper, No. 119. Paris.

Rodrik, D (1997). *Trade, social insurance, and the limits to globalization*, NBER Working Papers, 5905. National Bureau of Economic Research, Inc. doi.org/10.3386/w5905.

Sanchez-Paramo, C & Schady, NR (2003). *Off and running? Technology, trade, and the rising demand for skilled workers in Latin America*, World Bank Policy Research Working Paper, 3015. Washington, DC: World Bank. doi.org/10.1596/1813-9450-3015.

Skoufias, E (2001). *PROGRESA and its impact on human capital and welfare of households in rural Mexico: A synthesis of the results of an evaluation by IFPRI.* Washington, DC: International Food Policy Research Institute.

Soares, FV, Soares, S, Medeiros, M & Osório, RG (2006). *Cash transfer programmes in Brazil: Impacts on poverty and inequality*, IPC Working Paper, No. 21. Brasilia: International Poverty Centre.

Son, HH (2010). 'Growth, inequality, and the labor market: The Philippines'. In J Zhuang (ed.), *Poverty, inequality, and inclusive growth: Measurement, policy issues, and country studies* (pp 58–78). London: Anthem Press and Manila: ADB.

—— (2012). *Inequality of human opportunities in developing Asia*, ADB Economics, Working Paper No. 328. Asian Development Bank. Manila.

United Nations (UN) (2007). *Development in an ageing world: World Economic and social survey 2007.* New York: United Nations.

World Bank (2012). *Is higher education meeting its promises? Putting higher education to work: Skills and research for growth in East Asia*, East Asia and Pacific Regional Report. Washington, DC.

World Values Survey (2005). www.worldvaluessurvey.org/WVSDocumentation WV5.jsp.

Zhuang, J (1996). 'Estimating distortions in the Chinese economy: A general equilibrium approach', *Economica*, 63(252), 543–68. doi.org/10.2307/2554995.

—— (ed.) (2010). *Poverty, inequality, and inclusive growth: Measurement, policy issues, and country studies*. London: Anthem Press and Manila: ADB.

Zhuang, J & Ali, I (2010). 'Poverty, inequality and inclusive growth in Asia'. In J Zhuang (ed.), *Poverty, inequality, and inclusive growth: Measurement, policy issues, and country studies* (pp 1–32). London: Anthem Press and Manila: ADB.

Zhuang, J, de Dios, E & Lagman-Martin, A (2010). 'Governance and institutional quality and the links with growth and inequality: How Asia fares'. In J Zhuang (ed.), *Poverty, inequality, and inclusive growth: Measurement, policy issues, and country studies* (pp 268–320). London: Anthem Press and Manila: ADB.

Zhuang, J & Shi, L (2016). *Understanding recent trends of income inequality in the People's Republic of China*, ADB Economics Working Paper Series, No. 489. Manila, ADB.

5

OPENNESS AND INCLUSIVE GROWTH IN SOUTH-EAST ASIA

Aekapol Chongvilaivan

Introduction

Openness – the extent to which a country is exposed to trade in goods, services and foreign investment – played a pivotal role in fast-growing South-East Asian economies in the 1980s–2000s. It has transformed many countries, such as Indonesia, Malaysia and Thailand, from low- to upper middle-income statuses (ADB 1997; Lloyd & MacLaren 2000). Notwithstanding South-East Asia's exceptional economic performance in terms of rapid economic growth, rising income per capita, improving standards of living and persistent poverty reduction in the past decades, it is increasingly apparent that the region's economic development is uneven. The Association of Southeast Asian Nations (ASEAN) Economic Community (AEC) recognises the income divides between and within its member countries as a critical development agenda.

The effects of openness on inequality or inclusive growth in developing countries are, however, complex. Different initial conditions and policy reforms mean that unskilled labour or the poor may or may not fall out of the race toward liberalisation.[1] The standard trade theory suggests that

---

1   Jaumotte et al. (2013) provide a comprehensive empirical analysis on this issue.

openness in developing countries brings about reallocation of resources from relatively inefficient capital- and skill-intensive production towards more efficient sectors that make use of the production factors with which developing countries are well endowed; for example, unskilled labour and land. In principle, trade and investment liberalisation is expected to deliver an upward shift in relative demand for unskilled workers, thereby mitigating inequality. On the contrary, a path toward more openness is typically followed by domestic policy changes that exacerbate inequality. For instance, proliferating free trade agreements in ASEAN have often touched upon clauses and provisions related to enhancing movement of skilled labour, which is naturally more mobile, and thus further liberalisation may be in favour of skilled rather than unskilled labour. Likewise, the establishment of industrial parks to build up competitiveness of some sectors, like automotive and electronics sectors, and to make South-East Asian countries attractive to foreign investors has, by and large, concentrated on locations where capital and infrastructure are abundant.

Given the complex interplay between openness and inclusive growth, this paper aims to empirically investigate the redistributive effects of trade and financial openness in the context of South-East Asian economies. The empirical estimates yield the following main findings. First, consistent with the literature in the context of South-East Asia, trade openness has insignificant impacts on inequality in aggregate. But when measures of trade openness are broken down into export and import components, this paper finds exports and imports have opposing effects on inequality. While export openness mitigates inequality, more exposure to imports results in higher inequality. One policy implication of this finding is that export promotion policy could be the effective impetus for South-East Asian governments to address the issues of rising inequality and put in place inclusive growth. Additionally, financial liberalisation, measured by the ratio of foreign assets to gross domestic product (GDP), helps reduce inequality. This result suggests that freer flows of cross-border capital may provide the poor with greater access to financial resources and economic opportunity.

The following sections investigate the current status of inequality in South-East Asia and explore the possible theoretical linkages between openness and inequality, define the notions of openness and inequality, detail the methodology, and present the main empirical results.

Inclusive growth in South-East Asian countries

Current status of inequality

Table 5.1. Current levels of income inequality in South-East Asia

Country	Year	Gini coeffcient (%)	MLD[b]
Cambodia	2012	30.76	15.11
India[a]	2011	39.01	25.03
Indonesia	2013	43.11	30.48
Lao PDR	2012	37.89	23.58
Malaysia	2009	46.26	37.18
Philippines	2012	43.04	30.58
PRC[a]	2013	36.69	22.63
Thailand	2013	37.85	23.45
Vietnam	2014	37.59	23.81

Note. a) Data are based on income distribution in urban areas; b) MLD = mean log deviation. This is an index of inequality, given by the mean across the population of the log of the overall mean divided by individual income.

Source. PovcalNet, the World Bank

Table 5.1 reports two conventional measures of income inequality, including Gini coefficients and mean log deviation (MLD).[2] Among the South-East Asian countries, Malaysia's income distribution is the most uneven with all three indices taking the highest values: 46.26 per cent for the Gini coefficient and 37.18 for MLD. Indonesia, Lao PDR, the Philippines, Thailand, and Vietnam experience somewhat lower degrees of income inequality than Malaysia, with Gini coefficients between 37 and 44 per cent and MLDs between 23–30. Interestingly, the situations of widening income inequality in these middle-income countries are noticeably inferior to those in the fast-growing emerging economies, such

---

2   The Gini coefficient captures dispersion of income distribution and ranges between nil and unity. The nil value represents perfect equality whereby individuals have the same income, while the value of unity implies perfect inequality whereby only one person takes up all income. The quintile ratio is defined as the ratio of total income of the richest 20 per cent to that of the poorest 20 per cent, and therefore the higher values of quintile ratios mean more uneven income distribution. Last, MLD can be calculated by the mean across the population of the log of the overall mean divided by individual income. In the same manner as the Gini coefficients and quintile ratios, the higher values of MLD can be interpreted as greater income inequality.

as the People's Republic of China (PRC) and India. Cambodia seems to be at the forefront of lowering income inequality, with measures that are noticeably lower than those of Indonesia, Lao PDR, Malaysia, the Philippines, Thailand, and Vietnam. As shown in Table 5.1, in Cambodia, the measures of income disparities are about 30.76 per cent for the Gini coefficients and 15.11 for MLD. A comparison with neighbouring Asian countries underlines that income inequality in Cambodia is the lowest among South-East Asian countries and lower than that in PRC and India.

Is growth in South-East Asia inclusive?

One way to examine whether growth is inclusive is to explore whether economic progress in terms of increasing income, poverty reduction, and improved standards of living have translated into reduced inequality (ADB 2012). The accelerated poverty reduction accompanied by rising income inequality is particularly discernible in Indonesia and Lao PDR (Figure 5.1). This pattern also prevails to a lesser extent in the Philippines. In Cambodia, Malaysia and Thailand, the substantial plunges in poverty have been coupled with slight drops in income inequality since the 1980s, notwithstanding some spikes in the aftermath of the Asian financial crisis for Cambodia and Thailand and in the run-up to the global financial crisis in 2008–09 for Malaysia. This pattern of change implies that in some countries such as Lao PDR, Indonesia and the Philippines, the region's rising inequality is driven primarily by the extent to which incomes of the rich surge at a faster pace than those of the poor. This is in contrast to other regions, like sub-Saharan Africa and South America, where the rich exclusively benefit from economic growth while the poor remain poor, if not even poorer. In the context of South-East Asia, this suggests there is scope for more inclusive gains from swift economic development.

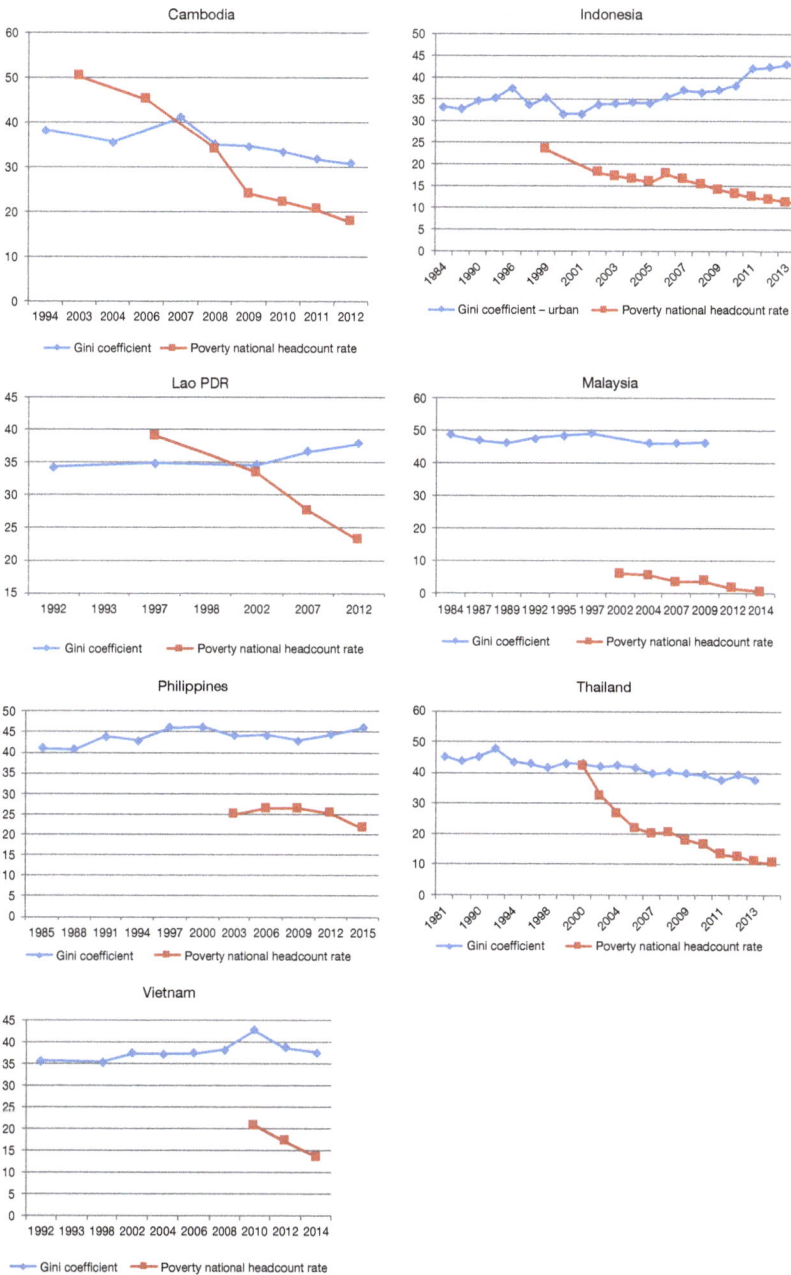

Figure 5.1. Gini coefficients and poverty headcount ratios in South-East Asia (per cent)

Source. PovcalNet and World Development Indicators (WDI), the World Bank

Pace and direction of change in income inequality can also be observed in Figure 5.1. In Cambodia, the Gini coefficients persistently soared since 1994, but have slowed since 2007. The trend in Indonesia, in contrast, is more variable. Income inequality gradually escalated from the late 1980s, but the aftermath of the Asian financial crisis witnessed a sudden plunge in income inequality even though it soon bounced back and rose rapidly after 2002, reaching the unprecedented high level of 42.15 per cent in 2011. In Lao PDR, even though the Asian financial crisis resulted in a modest decrease in income inequality during 1997–2002, the Gini coefficients have markedly increased from 30.43 per cent to 34.91 per cent in 1992–97 and from 32.63 per cent to 36.74 per cent in 2002–08. Malaysia exhibited the same pace and direction. The Gini coefficients gradually escalated during the late 1980s, followed by a drop in the aftermath of the Asian financial crisis during 1997–2004 and a widening trend in the run-up to the global financial crisis in 2009. In the Philippines, income inequality substantially deteriorated during 1985–97; nevertheless, the trend of rising inequality reversed thereafter. In the aftermath of the Asian financial crisis, the Philippines managed to achieve a consistent drop in the Gini coefficients. Income inequality in Thailand has reduced modestly since the 1990s, notwithstanding a considerable spike in the aftermath of the Asian financial crisis in 1998–2000. Lastly, inequality in Vietnam was relatively unchanged during 1992–2008. The Gini coefficients picked up insignificantly during 1992–2004, followed by a modest decline in 2004–08.

Inequality–openness nexus

Trade openness

Another cause of rises in economic inequality in South-East Asia pivots around the consequences of policies that advocate trade liberalisation. The past three decades witnessed remarkable reductions of tariff rates and non-tariff barriers such as quotas and anti-dumping duties on top of unprecedented increases in openness and exports. As noted by Milanovic (2005) and Wade (2004), most studies in developing countries find that the effects of trade liberalisation on inequality are statistically insignificant.

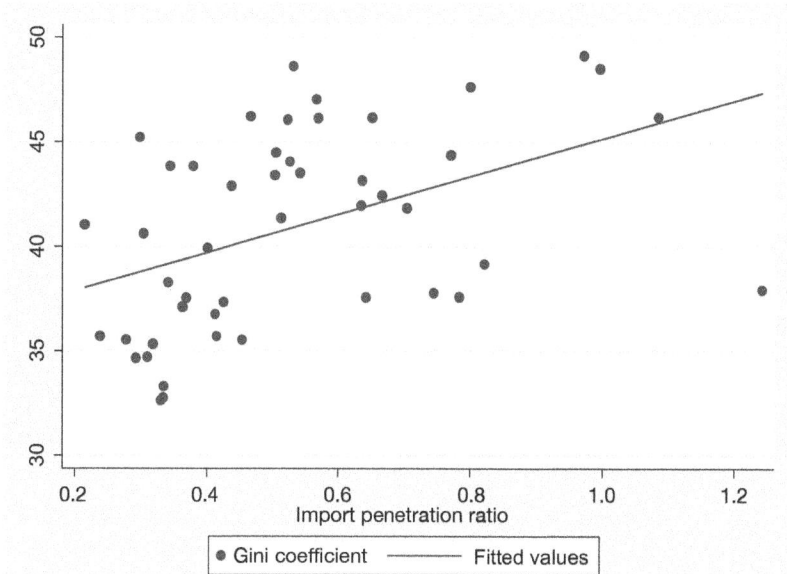

Figure 5.2. Income inequality and trade openness in South-East Asia

Note. Country samples include: Cambodia, Indonesia, Lao PDR, Malaysia, the Philippines, Thailand and Vietnam, in various years.

Source. Author's calculation based on the World Bank's PovcalNet and WDI

Figure 5.2 presents preliminary evidence that trade openness in South-East Asia may lead to aggravating inequality. As before, the Gini coefficient is utilised as a measure of inequality. A conventional measure of import penetration is employed as a proxy of trade openness (see, for instance, Bernard et al. 2006). This measure essentially captures the proportion of domestic demands that are satisfied by imports and is traditionally interpreted as indicating trade openness. The index of import penetration (*MPEN*) can be expressed as:

$$MPEN_i = \frac{M_i}{M_i + Y_i - X_i} \tag{1}$$

where M_i is total imports of country i; Y_i is GDP of country ; and X_i is total exports of country i. All variables are retrieved from the World Bank's World Development Indicators (WDI) and are reported at the constant price of the year 2000.

Trade liberalisation produces an unfavourable distributive impact on inequality in ASEAN. The positive correlation between trade penetration and the Gini coefficients is in contrast with the exposition by the standard trade theory that developing countries stand in good stead to bridge the disparities as they reallocate resources toward labour-intensive and unskilled production, thereby shifting the relative demand for unskilled labour. This empirical exercise underlines that the linkage between trade openness and inequality is not straightforward. Even in developing South-East Asian countries, where unskilled workers are abundant, gains from trade are more pronounced for the high-income group than the low-income one.

Financial openness

As with trade liberalisation, the effects of financial-sector development as substantiating cross-border movement of capital remain controversial (Agenor 2002; Fallon & Lucas 2002). On the one hand, domestic financial deregulation helps perk up resource allocation and returns on financial assets by channelling capital to the most efficient uses. The rises in income accrued by the holders of financial assets could potentially be redistributed to put forward equitable economic development. Financial-sector development, on the other hand, can exacerbate the distribution of income in developing countries in various ways. First, the appreciation of domestic currencies because of an enormous influx of capital inflows may divert resources away from low skill-intensive sectors and trigger a plunge in demands for unskilled workers (Taylor 2000). Second, undue development toward a free capital market puts countries at risk of financial crises in which the poor are the most affected. The 1997 Asian financial crisis offers an exceptional example of how the gratuitous, impulsive liberalisation of financial sectors ultimately propelled millions of the poor into poverty, thereby widening inequality in South-East Asia. Finally, it has been widely perceived that the problems of incomplete information, herd behaviour, weak supervision, excessive speculation and inadequate institutional infrastructure plague the well-functioning liberalised international financial system, and thus the real effects of financial market reforms on inequality are overestimated, if not adverse.

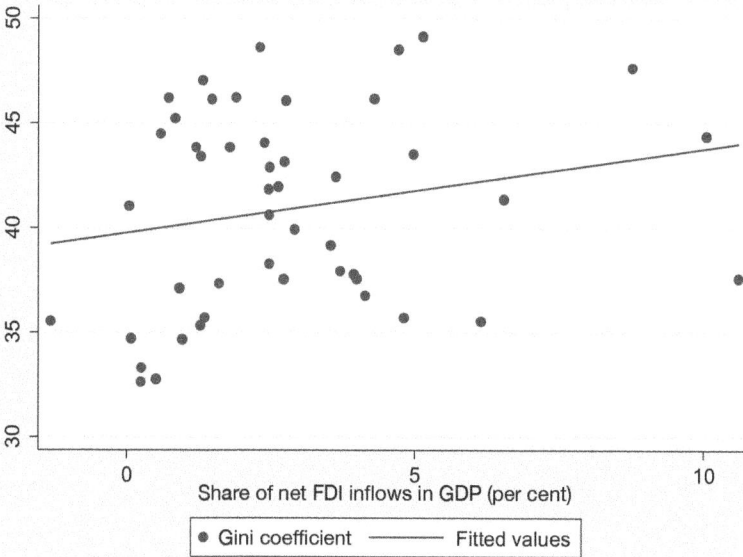

Figure 5.3. Income inequality and financial sector development in South-East Asia

Note. Country samples include: Cambodia, Indonesia, Lao PDR, Malaysia, the Philippines, Thailand and Vietnam, in various years.

Source. Author's calculation based on the World Bank's PovcalNet and WDI

Figure 5.3 portrays a scattered plot of the Gini coefficients and the shares of foreign direct investment (FDI) inflows into South-East Asian countries in GDP as a proxy of financial-sector development. The share of FDI inflows in GDP are positively correlated with the Gini coefficients, suggesting that financial-market development and liberalisation have been a catalyst for rising income inequality in South-East Asia. The worsening distributive effects associated with financial-sector liberalisation can be explained by the fact that the high-income groups, which typically own financial assets, stand to take in the upside gains in terms of higher rates of return on financial assets while the poor tend to bear the downside losses in terms of destabilising speculation and crises, a downward shift of relative demand for unskilled labour as a consequence of resource reallocation and the ensuing caveats to and incompleteness of financial reforms.

Empirics

To empirically investigate the linkages between openness and inequality in South-East Asian countries, this section develops a simple econometric model that relates the Gini coefficients to measures of trade and financial openness, in addition to other control variables. As in International Monetary Fund (IMF) (2007), the econometric specification can be loosely written as:

$$\ln(\ Gini_{it}) = \alpha_0 + \alpha_1 \ln(\ TRADE_{it}) + \alpha_2 \ln(\ FINANCE_{it}) + \mathbf{x}'_{it}\boldsymbol{\beta} + u_{it} \qquad (2)$$

where the subscripts i and t represent a country $i = 1,\ldots, N$ and the time period $t = 1,\ldots, T$, respectively. Trade liberalisation, $TRADE_{it}$, is measured by the ratio of exports and imports to GDP. As discussed later in this section, it can be further portioned into the ratio of exports and the ratio of imports to GDP to see how exports and imports may have contrasting effects on inequality. There are two proxies of financial liberalisation, $FINANCE_{it}$. One is the ratio of foreign assets to GDP, and the other is the ratio of inward FDI stocks to GDP. In addition to the key variables of trade and financial liberalisation, the econometric specifications also control for four country-specific characteristics in the vector $\mathbf{x}_{it}$. The first is labour productivity measured by the ratio of value added to total employment. The other three control variables are the employment shares in agriculture, industry and service sectors. The empirical model (3) is estimated by the standard ordinary least squares (OLS), with the heteroskedasticity-robust estimators. It should also be highlighted that all dependent and independent variables enter the model in terms of natural logarithm to yield more amenable OLS estimates.

Table 5.2. Summary of statistics

Variables	Obs.	Mean	SD	Min	Max
Gini coefficient	57	40.71	4.82	30.43	49.15
Ratio of trade to GDP	55	1.09	0.46	0.46	2.29
Ratio of exports to GDP	55	0.55	0.24	0.23	1.21
Ratio of imports to GDP	55	0.54	0.23	0.20	1.08
Ratio of foreign assets to GDP	50	0.19	0.12	0.01	0.51
Ratio of inward FDI to GDP	50	3.07	2.42	0.07	10.52
Labour productivity	52	9,503.9	5,293.7	2,567	24,059

Variables	Obs.	Mean	SD	Min	Max
Agriculture employment share (per cent)	46	43.77	14.41	13.5	72.2
Industry employment share (per cent)	46	18.75	5.79	8.3	33.7
Service employment share (per cent)	46	37.45	9.99	19.2	59.5

Note. Labour productivity is proxied by the ratio of value added to total employment.

Source. Author's calculation based on the World Bank's PovcalNet and WDI databases

Now that the objective is to examine the effects of structural drivers on inequality in South-East Asia, the dataset involves seven South-East Asian countries including Cambodia, Indonesia, Lao PDR, Malaysia, the Philippines, Thailand, and Vietnam. The empirical estimates should be interpreted as correlation, rather than causality. In addition, different countries have growth of domestic product, increasing employment and reducing poverty. Therefore, the empirical results in this paper do not necessarily suggest policies for reducing income inequality. It retrieves the information on the Gini coefficients from the World Bank's PovcalNet database, and the data for the independent variables are extracted from the World Bank's World Development Indicators (WDI). Table 5.2 summarises key statistics of the dataset.

Empirical results

Table 5.3 presents the estimation results. The first column (Model 1) is the regression of the Gini coefficients on the ratio of exports and imports to GDP, in addition to other control variables. The second column (Model 2) puts emphasis on the variables of financial liberalisation by regressing the Gini coefficients on the ratios of foreign assets to GDP and the ratios of inward FDI to GDP, with other control variables. The third column (Model 3) puts together the variables of trade and financial liberalisation. The fourth and fifth columns (models 4 and 5) perturbed the specification by breaking down the variable of trade liberalisation into the ratios of exports to GDP and the ratios of imports to GDP to account for the possibilities that exports and imports may have impacts on inequality in diverse ways. The main findings are recapitulated below.

Table 5.3. Determinants of the Gini coefficients in South-East Asia

Dependent variable: Natural logarithm of the Gini coefficients					
Variable	Model 1	Model 2	Model 3	Model 4	Model 5
Trade liberalisation:					
Ratio of trade to GDP	.007 (.060)	— —	.041 (.097)	— —	— —
Ratio of exports to GDP	— —	— —	— —	−.480*** (.103)	−.554*** (.096)
Ratio of imports to GDP	— —	— —	— —	.449*** (.097)	.501*** (.096)
Financial liberalisation:					
Ratio of foreign assets to GDP	— —	−.048** (.018)	−.055** (.026)	— —	−.006 (.023)
Ratio of inward FDI to GDP	— —	.037** (.014)	.032* (.017)	— —	.023* (.013)
Control variables:					
Labour productivity	.072 (.047)	.116*** (.040)	.118*** (.042)	.121*** (.042)	.161*** (.042)
Agriculture employment share	−.068 (.118)	−.077 (.093)	−.045 (.132)	.058 (.097)	.086 (.105)
Industry employment share	.021 (.109)	−.037 (.085)	−.042 (.090)	.056 (.081)	.056 (.069)
Service employment share	−.059 (.142)	−.021 (.120)	.012 (.170)	.188** (.091)	.209** (.096)
Constant	3.47*** (.959)	3.01*** (.792)	2.75** (1.11)	1.56* (.899)	.985 (.942)
No. of observations	46	39	39	46	39
R-squared	.251	.400	.402	.577	.679
F-statistics	2.95**	7.74***	5.69***	9.68***	13.36***

Note. a) *, **, *** denote at the 10, 5 and 1 per cent levels, respectively; b) Heteroskedasticity-robust standard errors in parentheses; c) All explanatory variables are in natural logarithm; d) All specifications are estimated by ordinary least squares (OLS); e) Selected South-East Asian countries include: Cambodia, Indonesia, Lao PDR, Malaysia, the Philippines, Thailand and Vietnam.

Source. Author's calculation based on the World Bank's PovcalNet and WDI databases

First, although the coefficients of the ratio of exports and imports to GDP appear to be statistically insignificant, the partition of the trade openness index into the ratio of exports and the ratio of imports to GDP strongly indicates that an expansion of exports as a result of trade liberalisation helps mitigate inequality in South-East Asia, while an influx of imports puts upward pressure on inequality. As shown in Table 5.3, the coefficients of the ratio of exports to GDP are positive and statistically significant at the 1 per cent level in both models 4 and 5. In contrast, the coefficients of the ratio of imports to GDP turn out to be negative and statistically significant at the 1 per cent level. The fact that the impacts of exports and imports on inequality work in opposite directions may explain why the overall impacts of trade liberalisation captured by the ratio of exports and imports to GDP are insignificant. This may also suggest that in the South-East Asian context, exports are associated with skill-intensive production, thereby benefiting skilled workforces in the higher income groups. This is possible given the fact that the key export products from these countries are electronics, and electrical and automotive products, which are typically more skill-intensive to produce. Imports such as equipment and machinery could supplement productivity of unskilled labour and boost wages of the lower income groups, thereby reducing income inequality.

Second, financial liberalisation, which boosts the cross-border capital flows of foreign assets, seems to help bring down inequality. Although the statistical significance is somewhat sensitive in Model 5, the coefficients of the ratio of foreign assets to GDP appear to be negative in all estimations. This suggests that greater financial liberalisation provides greater access to financial resources and opportunities for the poor.

Third, consistent with ADB (2012) and IMF (2007), an increase in inward FDI from advanced economies critically fuels rising inequality in South-East Asia. As portrayed in Table 5.3, the coefficients of the ratio of inward FDI to GDP are positive and statistically significant in all specifications. The positive effects of inward FDI on inequality are, however, not surprising. In the context of South-East Asia, most foreign investments and capital resources are directed toward skill-intensive industries such as automotive and electronics industries, thereby shifting labour demands away from unskilled toward skilled workers. The widening gap between skilled and unskilled wages because of inward FDI is eventually translated into escalating unevenness of income distribution.

Fourth, labour productivity may also be a source of inequality in South-East Asia. The coefficients of labour productivity are positive and statistically significant in all specifications (except Model 1), suggesting that the countries with higher labour productivity in terms of value added per worker tend to be characterised by more unevenness of income distribution. This evidence can be explained by that fact that higher labour productivity is associated with high-tech capital accumulation and technology advancement, which in turn bolster up the premium for skilled workers and capital. Since unskilled workers take up a larger share of population in South-East Asia, higher labour productivity leads to more uneven income disparities.

Last, developing South-East Asia's expansion of industry and service sectors, together with the downsizing agricultural sector, has implications for rising inequality. As shown in Table 5.3, the coefficients of the service employment share appear to be positive and statistically significant at the 5 per cent level in models 4 and 5, even though the employment shares in the agriculture and industry sectors do not produce statistically significant estimates. This posits that the burgeoning service sector in South-East Asia exacerbates income inequality. An explanation perhaps rests with labour market rigidity whereby labour is hindered in moving away from low-return activities in the agriculture sector to high-return service activities (Topalova 2007).

It should also be underlined that the empirical exercise in this section is subject to several caveats. Limitations of the Gini coefficient data impose somewhat critical constraints on the sample size and consistency of the dataset. Limited data availability confines the control variables only to labour productivity and employment shares across sectors and may cause estimation biases arising from the omitted variables. Additionally, the limited scope of this section leaves several econometric issues unaddressed, such as endogeneity biases, in addition to country- and time-specific effects. Therefore, the empirical results discussed in this section should be considered to be tentative.

Conclusion

This paper empirically investigates the correlation between trade openness and income inequality using the country-level information of seven South-East Asian countries including Cambodia, Indonesia, Lao PDR, Malaysia, the Philippines, Thailand and Vietnam. The empirical estimates point to consistency with the existing literature that trade openness measured as a share of exports and imports in GDP has a statistically insignificant relationship with income inequality. We find an interesting result that exports and imports, individually, contribute to income inequality in opposite directions. Imports are positively correlated with income inequality whereas exports seem to help reduce income inequality. Therefore, the empirical exercise in this paper offers an alternative explanation of the insignificant correlation between trade openness and income inequality as in the existing literature in the context of South-East Asia.

Like any research study, this paper is not without limitations. First, there is interplay between exports and imports particularly in the context of South-East Asian countries. The prevalence of supply chains and outsourcing activities in South-East Asian countries implies that countries import for re-exports, and there is a strong correlation between exports and imports. Hence, it is indispensable to look into more detailed exporting and importing activities in the context of supply chains. Second, while this paper focuses on a country-level analysis, the nexus among trade openness, financial openness, and income inequality depends critically on industrial structures, country- and time-specific contexts, and policy goals. Therefore, it would be interesting to further investigate these results using more disaggregated data at the sector, industry, and firm levels. Lastly, there are many other indicators of income inequality, such as the relative share of the 10 per cent highest and lowest income of the population, among many others. The use of alternative measures for income inequality will help confirm robustness of the findings. Due to the limited scope of this paper, we leave these pending issues and inquiries for future research to shed light on them.

References

Agenor, P-R (2002). *Does globalization hurt the poor?*, World Bank Working Paper, No. 2922. Washington: The World Bank. doi.org/10.1596/1813-9450-2922.

Asian Development Bank (ADB) (1997). *Emerging Asia: Changes and challenges*. Manila: Asian Development Bank.

—— (2012). *Asian development outlook 2012*. Manila: Asian Development Bank.

Bernard, AB, Jensen, JB & Schott, PK (2006). 'Survival of the best fit: Exposure to low-wage countries and the (uneven) growth of US manufacturing plants', *Journal of International Economics*, 68(1), 219–37. doi.org/10.1016/j.jinteco.2005.06.002.

Fallon, PR & Lucas, REB (2002). 'The impact of financial crises on labor markets, household incomes, and poverty: A review of evidence', *World Bank Research Observer*, 17(1), 21–45. doi.org/10.1093/wbro/17.1.21.

International Monetary Fund (IMF) (2007). 'Globalization and inequality'. In *World Economic Outlook 2007* (pp 135–69). Washington DC: International Monetary Fund.

Jaumotte, F, Lall, S & Papageorgiou, C (2013). 'Rising income inequality: Technology, or trade and financial globalization', *IMF Economic Review*, 61(2), 271–309. doi.org/10.1057/imfer.2013.7.

Lloyd, PJ & MacLaren, D (2000). 'Openness and growth in East Asia after the Asian crisis', *Journal of Asian Economics*, 11(1), 89–105. doi.org/10.1016/S1049-0078(00)00042-7.

Milanovic, B (2005). 'Can we discern the effect of globalization on income distribution? Evidence from household surveys', *World Bank Economic Review*, 19, 21–44. doi.org/10.1093/wber/lhi003.

Taylor, L (2000). *External liberalisation, economic performance and distribution in Latin America and elsewhere*, UNU/WIDER Working Paper, No. 215. World Institute for Development Economics Research, United Nations University.

Topalova, P (2007). 'Trade liberalization, poverty, and inequality: Evidence from Indian districts'. In A Harrison (ed.), *Globalization and poverty* (pp 291–336). University of Chicago Press. doi.org/10.7208/chicago/9780226318004.003.0008.

Wade, RH (2004). 'Is globalization reducing poverty and inequality?', *World Development*, 32(4), 567–89. doi.org/10.1016/j.worlddev.2003.10.007.

6

AUTOMATION, THE FUTURE OF WORK AND INCOME INEQUALITY IN THE ASIA–PACIFIC REGION[1]

Yixiao Zhou

Introduction

> Last year, it was still quite humanlike when it played. But this year,
> it became like a god of Go.
>
> – Ke Jie

Ke Jie, the current world champion of the ancient Chinese board game Go, made the statement above after he was beaten by AlphaGo, an artificial intelligence (AI) software developed by DeepMind, the AI arm of Google's parent, Alphabet.[2] AlphaGo distilled thousands of years of human knowledge of Go into better moves of its own. The latest evolution of AlphaGo, AlphaGo Zero, has been hailed as a major advance because

---

1   I sincerely thank discussants Robert Scollay, Somkiat Tangkitvanich and participants at the 50th anniversary PAFTAD conference in Tokyo from 31 January to 2 February 2018 for insightful comments and suggestions that helped to improve the paper significantly. All errors are my own.
2   Refer to Paul Mozur, 'Google's AlphaGo defeats Chinese Go master in win for A.I.', *New York Times*, 23 May 2017, www.nytimes.com/2017/05/23/business/google-deepmind-alphago-go-champion-defeat.html.

it mastered the game from scratch, with no human help beyond being told the rules. In games against its 2015 version, which famously beat the South Korean Go grandmaster Lee Se-dol, AlphaGo Zero won 100 to 0.[3]

Such is the speed of the development of AI that its mastery of human intelligence is in prospect. Not only has AI developed rapidly in recent years, other major technological advances including big data analytics, advanced robotics, 3D printing and Industry 4.0, have also progressed at pace.

In this paper, the main question to be addressed is the impact of recent developments in AI and advanced robotics on employment and income distribution in the Asia–Pacific region. The paper explores, firstly, recent trends in technological progress, followed by potential drivers of development, the effect of new technologies on employment and income inequality and finally, the geography of innovation and future markets from a perspective focusing on countries' innovation capabilities.

Recent trends in technological progress and the development of automation technologies

Technological progress as reflected by total factor productivity (TFP) growth

In the early 2000s, prior to the global financial crisis (GFC), the growth of total factor productivity (TFP) experienced a turning point and slowed down in key Organisation for Economic Co-operation and Development (OECD) economies including the United States, the United Kingdom and Australia (Figure 6.1). Performance has been divergent amongst economies in the Asia–Pacific region: between 1970 and 2014, the Republic of Korea, China, Taiwan, India and Thailand achieved greater percentage growth in TFP than the OECD average, whereas Malaysia, Singapore, Indonesia and Japan scored less expansion in TFP than the OECD average. Similar to the situation in OECD economies, TFP growth in countries in the Asia–Pacific region slowed down post-GFC as well, with Indonesia being an exception (Figure 6.2).

---

3   Refer to 'AlphaGo Zero: learning from scratch', *Deepmind*, deepmind.com/blog/alphago-zero-learning-scratch/.

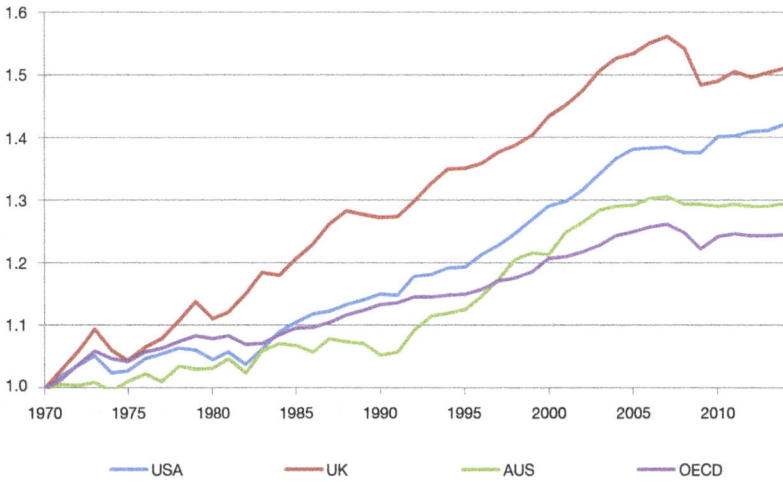

Figure 6.1. Total factor productivity, 1970–2014 (United States, United Kingdom, Australia and the OECD average)

Source. Penn World Tables (Feenstra et al. 2015), international comparisons of production, income and prices, version 9.0. TFP is the portion of output change not explained by the quantities of inputs used in production and is reported at constant national prices (2011=1). Data are normalised to set TFP in 1970 at unity

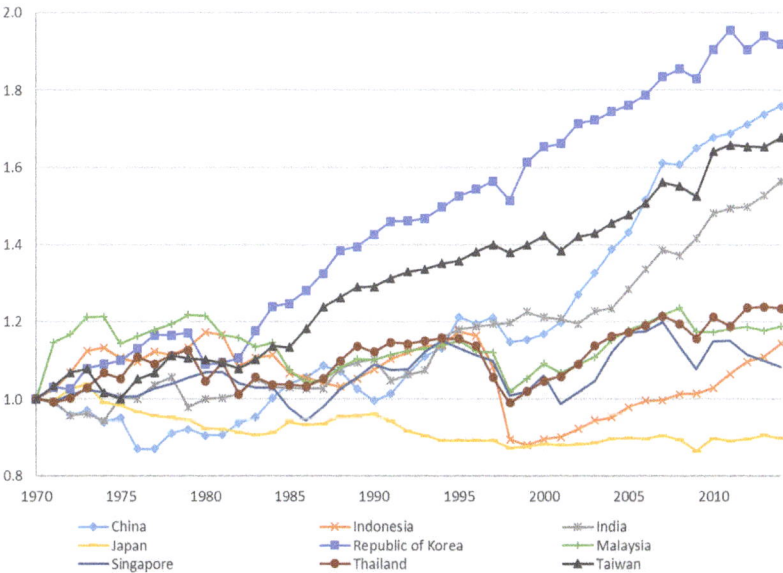

Figure 6.2. Total factor productivity, 1970–2014 (selected economies in the Asia–Pacific region)

Source. Penn World Tables (Feenstra et al. 2015)

What explains the slowdown in TFP growth despite the perceived rapid changes in technologies? Gordon (2014, 2015) argues that the major gains in capital-embodied productivity are in the past and that advances in information and communications technology (ICT) since the 1980s have contributed little thus far. He identifies massive gains accruing from the great discoveries of the nineteenth and twentieth centuries, which include the internal combustion engine, revolutions in materials science, transmitted electricity, sanitation, and health advances such as antibiotics. The more recent ICT advances, he claims, have not revolutionised quality of life and business practices in the way these major innovations did. In response to the claim that the gains from the most recent ICT developments are under-measured (the 'Solow paradox'[4]), Gordon asserts that this is typical of all periods of innovation and is also characteristic of the major gains delivered by older technologies. These views are shared by Clark (2016), Crafts (2016) and Friedman (2016).

In contrast with Gordon and others, the techno-optimists see immense potential for productivity and lifestyle improvements from further expansion of modern ICT, AI and advanced robotics. Mokyr (2013) and Mokyr et al. (2015) argue that, technology anxiety notwithstanding, we are on the cusp of a new era of progress in innovation that will provide an unprecedented boost to productivity. Mokyr et al. (2015) point out what is known as Amara's law, 'We tend to overestimate the effect of a technology in the short run and underestimate the effect in the long run'. Therefore, while TFP growth is often adopted to measure technological progress (Hulten 2001), relatively weak growth in TFP may not necessarily indicate the lack of technological progress, and may arise from implementation lags of new technologies. AI's most impressive capabilities, particularly those based on machine learning, may not have diffused widely. More importantly, like other general-purpose technologies, their full effects won't be realised until waves of complementary innovations are developed and implemented (Brynjolfsson et al. 2017).

Given the unsettled debate on whether weak growth in TFP implies slow technological progress, below I review key aspects of the development in automation and AI specifically in the context of Industry 4.0 that directly impact on firms' production and business models. By doing so, I aim to shed light on recent changes in technology and explore their potential impact on production and jobs in the future.

---

4   'You can see the computer age everywhere but in the productivity statistics' (Solow 1987).

A new wave of technological progress: Artificial intelligence, advanced robotics, big data analytics, and the rise of Industry 4.0

The new digital economy, such as deep learning and greater collection of data, disrupts all sectors. Data joins traditional production factors such as labour and capital as a new factor of production in various sectors. For example, data generated by sensors or agricultural drones at farms, out on the field or during transportation offer a wealth of information about soil, seeds, livestock, crops, costs, farm equipment, the use of water and fertiliser. Internet of Things (IoT) technologies and advanced analytics help farmers analyse real-time data like weather, temperature, moisture, prices or GPS signals and provide insights into how to optimise and increase yield, improve farm planning, make smarter decisions about the level of resources needed and when and where to distribute them in order to prevent waste (Irima 2016).

The manufacturing sector is also experiencing great changes due to the rise of new technologies. The term 'Industry 4.0' refers to a new developmental stage in the organisation and management of the manufacturing industry's value chain. Industry 4.0 utilises big data analytics to improve the efficiency of firms. According to the Australian Government's Department of Industry, Innovation and Science (2019), Industry 4.0 (the 'fourth industrial revolution') refers to the current trend of improved automation, machine-to-machine and human-to-machine communication, AI, continued technological improvements and digitalisation in manufacturing.

This trend is enabled by four key drivers:

1. rising data volumes, computational power and connectivity
2. the emergence of analytics and business-intelligence capabilities
3. new forms of human–machine interaction, such as touch interfaces and augmented-reality systems
4. improvements in transferring digital instructions to the physical world, such as robotics and 3D printing.

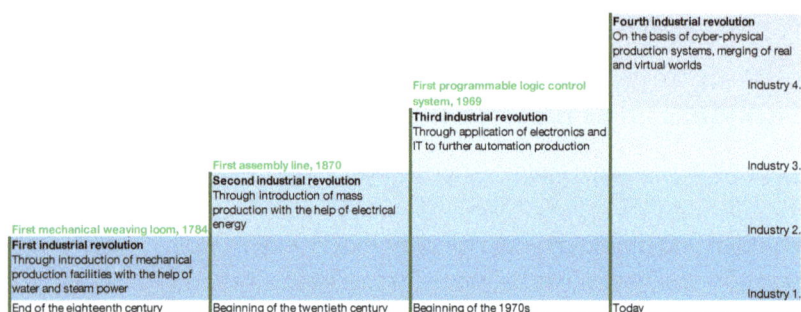

Figure 6.3. Industrial revolutions in history
Source. Deloitte (2014)

The evolution of the four rounds of industrial revolution is presented in Figure 6.3. Traditional manufacturing and production methods are in the throes of a digital transformation, going beyond the automation of production that was driven by developments in electronics and information technology (IT) since the early 1970s. Industry 4.0 features cyber-physical production systems, which are online networks of social machines that are organised in a similar way to social networks. In other words, IT is linked with mechanical and electronic components that communicate with each other via a network. Smart machines continually share real-time data and information about current stock levels, problems or faults, and changes in orders or demand levels, which is collected by sensors attached to robots. Data from one robot is compared to data from other robots in the same or different locations in cloud robotics. Thus, processes and deadlines are coordinated with the aim of boosting efficiency and optimising throughput times, capacity utilisation and quality in development, production, marketing and purchasing (Deloitte 2014). A number of production applications of Industry 4.0 are provided in Baur and Wee (2015), McKinsey Digital (2015), Geissbauer et al. (2016) and UNIDO (2017). The network of cloud robotics allows these connected robots to perform the same activities.

Industry 4.0 and its counterparts are pursued in several major economies including Germany, Japan, the United States, China and Malaysia. In 2015 the Chinese Government introduced its version of Industry 4.0 – 'Made in China 2025', which is an initiative to comprehensively upgrade Chinese industry. The initiative draws inspiration from Germany's Industry 4.0 plan, which was first discussed in 2011 and adopted in 2013. The heart of Industry 4.0 is intelligent manufacturing; i.e. applying the tools of information technology to production.

In the German context, this primarily means using IoT to more efficiently connect small and medium-sized companies in global production and innovation networks so that they not only more efficiently engage in mass production but, just as easily and efficiently, customise products. The Chinese effort is broader, as the efficiency and quality of Chinese producers is uneven, and multiple challenges need to be overcome in a short period of time if Chinese firms are to avoid being squeezed by emerging low-cost producers and more effectively cooperate and compete with advanced industrialised economies. The main objective of the strategy is to ensure that China's manufacturing is innovation-driven and green. It has 10 priority areas of development, including energy saving and new energy vehicles, power equipment, and modern railway equipment (Kennedy 2015; The State Council, The People's Republic of China 2017a, 2017b).

Other economies also regard Industry 4.0 as an opportunity to access the global value chain. Jeff Connolly, chair of Australia's Prime Minister's Industry 4.0 Taskforce, says 'Australia should see the fourth industrial revolution as an opportunity. If we establish a broad-based capability to use global engineering and manufacturing platforms based on advanced materials, the often spruiked access by our SMEs to global supply chains are more a reality now than they have been at any time in the past' (Department of Industry, Innovation and Science 2019).

Clearly, it will be a costly and disruptive process for society when firms transform to Industry 4.0. However, these costs are unlikely to prevent firms and governments from putting effort into developing and applying these new technologies and ways of production, as all participants realise that, unless they keep up with best-practice science and technology, they will fall hopelessly behind in the global competition (Mokyr et al. 2015). It is expected that competition between firms, nations, and major trading blocs will stimulate continued efforts for technological gains. For example, at the time of the introduction of mechanisation, including water and steam power, eighteenth-century British writers conceded that machinery might 'destroy the necessity of labour', but still recommended its introduction, because other nations would otherwise outcompete Britain (Mokyr 2013). An important driver of this development is that robot adoption is a response to faster business cycles in all manufacturing sectors, and the requirement to produce with greater flexibility tailored to customer demand. A new generation of industrial robots will pave the way for ever more flexible automation. 'Robots offer high levels of precision and their connectivity will play a key role in new digital manufacturing environments,' says Joe Gemma, president of the International Federation of Robotics (IFR): 'Increasing availability enables more and more manufacturers from companies of all sizes to automate' (IFR 2017).

Some robot manufacturers are also considering leasing models, particularly in order to accelerate adoption by small-to-medium-sized manufacturers. Simplification is a key trend for this market segment. The ongoing need for robots that are easier to program and use, and the increasing need for flexible automation, initiated the development of smarter solutions. This is especially useful for industries that do not employ in-house specialised production engineers. Robots that are simple to use will enable the deployment of industrial robots in many industries to sustain efficient and flexible manufacturing. The simplification of robots and the facilitation of deployment is exemplified by the sale of 3D printers to consumers who are essentially transformed into producers.

New technologies pose challenges and opportunities for firms in developing countries. On the one hand, firms in developed economies such as Germany, Japan and the United States host pools of technical talents that allow them to draw on significant technological knowhow. Their technological lead could be further strengthened in this new round of technological breakthrough, establishing them as superior to firms that lag in terms of productivity and product quality. On the other hand, firms in developing countries may be able to leapfrog to new technologies. Technology leaders may switch to new and more efficient technologies at a slower pace because their capital investment locks them in to vintage technology (Arther 1989; Brezis et al. 1993; Perkins 2003).

The Estonian Government's choice between a digital network and an analogue phone system is a case in point. The Finnish Government offered Estonia its analogue phone system for free following the collapse of the Soviet Union and as the Finns upgraded to a digital network. Estonia declined, choosing to bypass analogue telephony and move straight to a digital network of its own design. As it developed its own government, it skipped the typewriter-and-paper stage and began putting its services online from the outset. Every school in Estonia was online by 1998, just four years after the country was experiencing widespread fuel shortages and breadlines. Today, Estonia is one of the most connected countries in the world, having the world's fastest internet speeds and prosperous online services and businesses (Ross 2016).

Hallward-Driemeier and Nayyar (2017) recognise the possibility of technological leapfrog from a limited manufacturing base in developing economies. If countries can leapfrog into using new technologies, there may be no cost for not developing a manufacturing sector at this point. If, however, countries need to have a manufacturing sector using traditional (Industry 2.0) methods to build the capabilities required to support more sophisticated processes, the dynamic cost of not industrialising now could close off future manufacturing opportunities (Hallward-Driemeier & Nayyar 2017).

The market for robots and automation technologies

The market for robots is growing rapidly.[5] According to IFR, since 2010, the demand for industrial robots has accelerated considerably due to the ongoing trend toward automation, continued innovative technical improvements in industrial robots, and rapidly falling price of computing equipment (Figure 6.4).[6] Between 2011 and 2016, the average increase in industrial robot sales was 12 per cent per year and the average annual supply rose to about 212,000 units, which is an increase of about 84 per cent compared to the average annual supply between 2005 and 2008. This is a clear indication of the tremendous rise in worldwide demand for industrial robots. In terms of units, it is estimated that by 2020 the worldwide stock of operational industrial robots will increase from about 1,828,000 units at the end of 2016 to 3,053,000 units. This represents an average annual growth rate of 14 per cent between 2018 and 2020. Australasia is still the world's strongest growth market for industrial robots, followed by Europe and the Americas (Figure 6.5).

The operational stock of robots is estimated to increase by 16 per cent in 2017 in Australasia, by 9 per cent in the Americas and by 7 per cent in Europe. Since 2016, the largest number of industrial robots in operation are in China. In 2020, this will amount to about 950,300 units, considerably more than in Europe (611,700 units). The Japanese robot

---

5   Information and data on the international robotics market are from the website of the International Federation of Robotics (ifr.org/).

6   There are two general categories of robots: industrial and service robots. An industrial robot is designed to be used in goods manufacturing. A service robot operates semi- or fully autonomously to perform services useful to the wellbeing of humans and equipment, excluding manufacturing operations (Bekey et al. 2006).

stock will slightly increase in the period between 2018 and 2020. About 1.9 million robots will be in operation across Asia in 2020, which is almost equal to the global stock of robots in 2016.

There are five major markets representing 74 per cent of the total sales volume in 2016: China, the Republic of Korea, Japan, the United States, and Germany (Figure 6.5). China has significantly expanded its leading position as the largest market with a share of 30 per cent of the total supply in 2016. With sales of about 87,000 industrial robots, China came close to the total sales volume of Europe and the Americas combined (97,300 units). Chinese robot suppliers continued to expand their home market share to 31 per cent in 2016. Over the longer term, Chinese robot suppliers aim to grow into major suppliers of robots in the world market. Policymakers in China view robotics as a stepping stone to a broader strategic goal of succeeding in emerging markets for AI, driverless vehicles and digitally connected appliances and homes. The development of the robotics industry contributes to China's transition from a technology imitator to a technology innovator (Bloomberg News 2017).

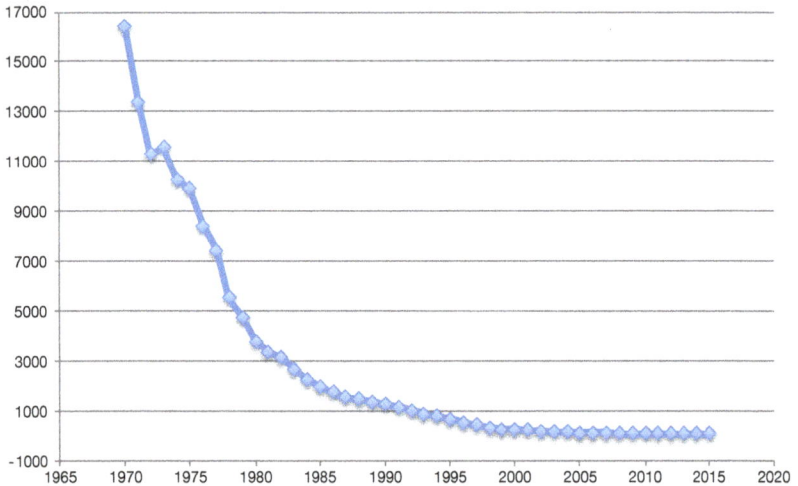

Figure 6.4. Price index of gross fixed capital formation in computing equipment (2010 = 100)

Source. EU KLEMS

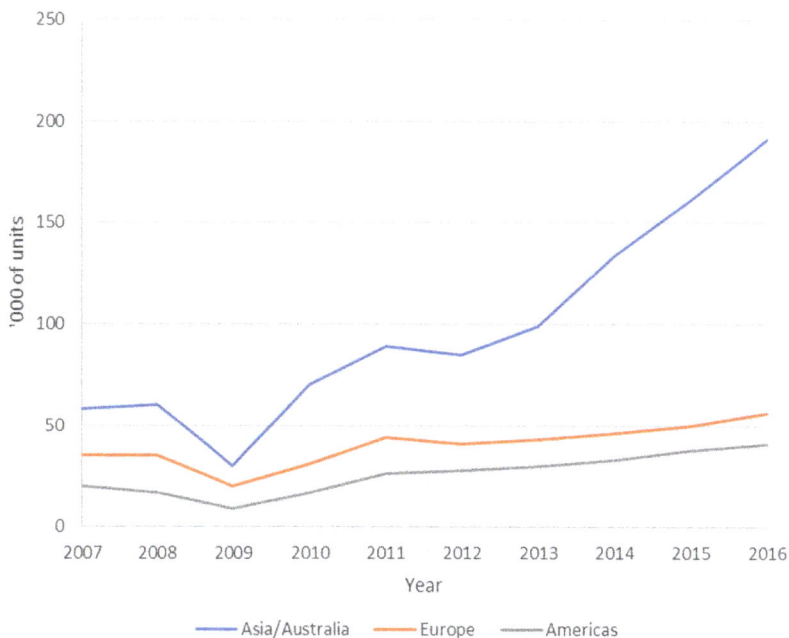

Figure 6.5. Estimated annual shipments of industrial robots by regions

Source. International Federation of Robotics (2017)

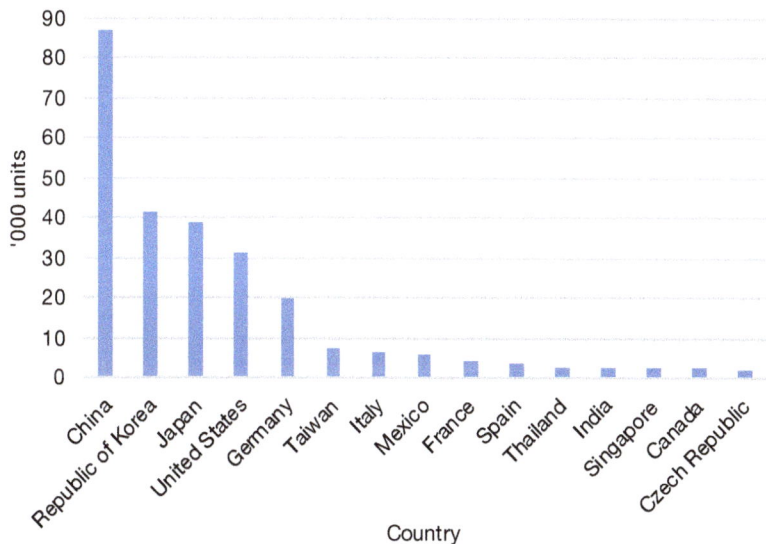

Figure 6.6. Annual supply of industrial robots in the 15 largest markets in 2016

Source. International Federation of Robotics (2017)

The Republic of Korea is the second-biggest market in the world. Due to major investments by the electrical and electronics industry in robots, annual sales have increased considerably. About 41,400 units were sold in 2016, which is a rise of 8 per cent compared to 2015. In Japan, robot sales increased by 10 per cent to about 38,600 units (2016), reaching the highest level since 2006 (37,400 units). Japan is the predominant robot-manufacturing country. Since 2010, the production capacity of Japanese robot suppliers has increased in order to meet the growing demand for industrial robots: production more than doubled from 73,900 units in 2010 to 152,600 units in 2016 (52 per cent of the global supply in 2016). In the United States, robot installations increased by 14 per cent to a peak of 31,400 units in 2016. This continued growth since 2010 is driven by the trend to automate production in order to strengthen the competitiveness of American industries in overseas markets. Germany is the fifth-largest robot market in the world and by far the largest in Europe. In Germany, the annual supply and operational stock of industrial robots in 2016 had a share of 36 per cent and 41 per cent respectively of total robot sales in Europe.

In terms of industry distribution, the automotive industry is the major customer for industrial robots with a share of 35 per cent of the total supply in 2016. The electrical/electronics industry has been catching up, reaching a share of 31 per cent of the total supply in 2016. If a country has a rapidly growing automotive and electrical/electronics industry, it tends to have higher robot density in the manufacturing sector; that is the number of industrial robots per 10,000 persons employed in manufacturing (this measure takes into account differences in the size of the manufacturing industry in various countries). The average global density of robots in the manufacturing industry in 2016 is approximately 74 industrial robots installed per 10,000 employees. The most automated countries in the world measured by this statistic in 2016 were the Republic of Korea (631 units of industrial robots per 10,000 employees), Singapore (488 units of industrial robots per 10,000 employees), Germany (309 units of industrial robots per 10,000 employees), and Japan (303 units of industrial robots per 10,000 employees).

The development of robot density in China was the most dynamic in the world due to the significant growth of robot installations in recent years. Particularly between 2013 and 2016, the rate of robot density accelerated in China, from 25 units to 68 units. Due to the dynamic development of robot installations since 2010, the robot density in China rose from 25 industrial robots per 10,000 employees in the manufacturing industry in 2013 to 68 units in 2016, and that in the United States increased significantly from 114 installed robots per 10,000 employees in the manufacturing industry in 2009 to 189 robots in 2016. In 2016, the average robot density was: 99 units in Europe, 84 in the Americas and only 63 in Asia. Overall, the potential for robot installations in countries with low robot density is high, and Asia will continue to be a leading growth centre of robotics.

Drivers of automation

What drives the significant growth in robotics investment in the Asia–Pacific region? Striving for lower cost production and higher quality output to stay competitive in international competition is an important motivation. An underlying driver of automation in the Asia–Pacific region could be an ageing population. In general, economies in this region are experiencing a demographic transition toward older populations. Figure 6.7 and Figure 6.8 show the old-age ratio – the ratio of those aged 65 or older to the working-age population (people aged 15–64); and the youth-dependency ratio – the ratio of those aged 0–14 to the working-age population.

The increasing number of elderly has been evident throughout the region and the cohort is projected to grow further in the next two decades. Conversely, the youth cohort has shrunk and will continue to decline in the coming years, except for Hong Kong (Figure 6.7 and Figure 6.8). Due to its rapid economic growth, developing Asia is compressing industrialisation and economic transformation into a much shorter time period than did the advanced economies, and the region is also replicating the demographic transition of the advanced economies within a much shorter time frame. In fact, the unprecedented speed and scale of the ageing of the region's population are largely driven by the region's exceptional economic growth (Park & Shin 2011).

Demographic change can have significant impacts on economic growth. The economic needs and contributions of individuals vary over the course of their economic lives. Firstly, working-age adults tend to work more than the young or elderly. As emphasised by Gordon (2016), demographic change is the first 'headwind' to slow down economic growth in the developed world, for an older population reduces labour-force participation and productivity. A larger labour force, therefore, contributes directly to economic growth. Secondly, working-age adults tend to save more than the young or elderly. A larger labour force indirectly contributes to growth through higher savings rates that boost the investment rate and the accumulation of capital, especially if newly added capital is embodied with new technologies. Thirdly, building on Hansen (1938), an increasingly popular thesis is that developed economies are afflicted by 'secular stagnation', partly because an ageing population creates an excess of savings relative to investments (Summers 2013; Teulings & Baldwin 2014). Fourthly, to the extent that physical capital can substitute for labour, an economy can accumulate more capital to compensate for the slowdown in the growth of the labour force. For example, older workers may need more capital than younger workers to compensate for their diminished physical strength and, therefore, there is more rapid adoption of automation technologies in countries with a larger ageing population (Acemoglu & Restrepo 2017b). Last but not least, demographic change has a sizable effect on a society's demand for goods and services and may induce structural changes in output and production. For example, in ageing economies, the need for care outstrips the number of available caregivers. Caregiver robots or 'carebots' have been developed to perform care-giving jobs that involve dull, dangerous, heavy and dirty work as well as tasks requiring a high level of knowledge and skill (Gallagher et al. 2016).

Another driver of automation is the rising cost of labour in the Asia–Pacific region. By following the East Asian model, a number of countries in the region achieved stellar performance in economic growth via the agency of moving into the global production chain and accessing the global goods and capital market (Perkins 2013). With the factor-price-equalisation theorem of Stolper and Samuelson (1941), free trade in finished goods leads to equal relative compensation across trading partners for productive input, albeit under a set of highly restrictive assumptions. Subsequent theorising has maintained the focus on the market-integrating impact of trade but without relying on the Stolper–Samuelson framework. For example, a recent contribution by Baldwin and Robert-Nicoud (2014) demonstrates the impact on wage convergence under outsourcing (trade-in-tasks) rather than trade-in-goods. Empirical evidence suggests a convergence across countries in the wage rates of workers of the same skill group within the same industry classification (Zhou & Bloch 2017).

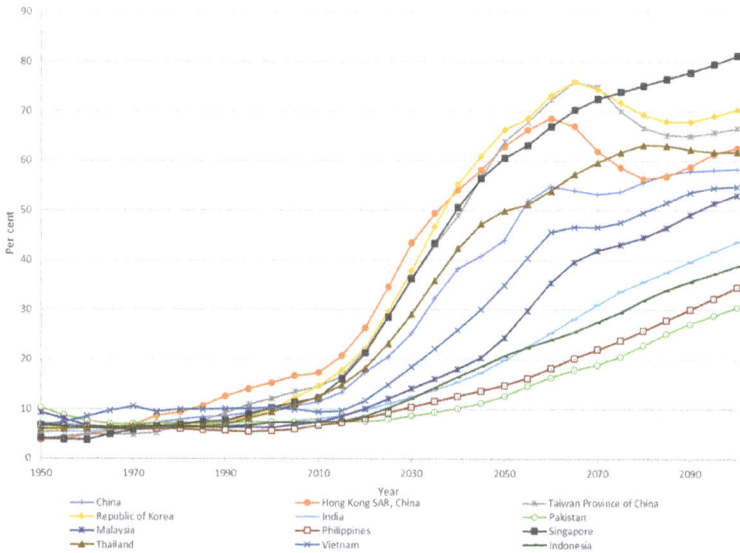

Figure 6.7. Dependency ratios in selected Asian economies, defined as population aged 65 and older as a share of population aged 15 to 64, 1950–2100

Source. United Nations (2017)

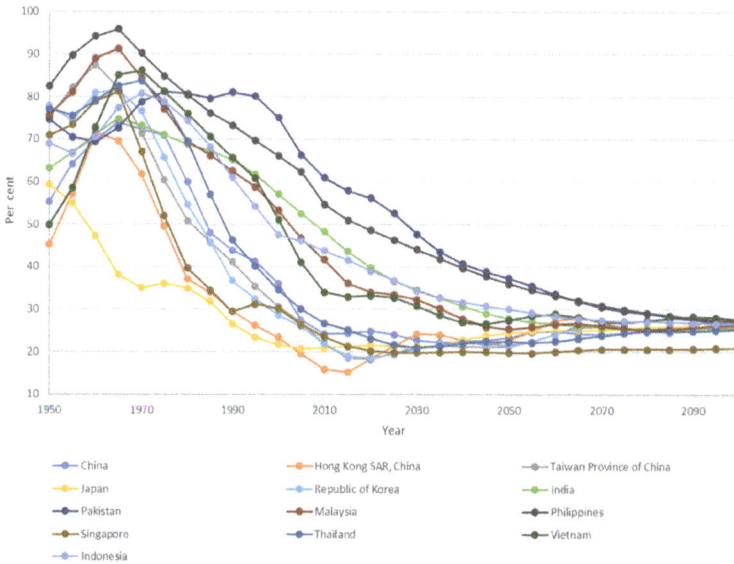

Figure 6.8. Dependency ratios in selected Asian economies, defined as population aged below 14 as a share of population aged 15 to 64, 1950–2100

Source. United Nations (2017)

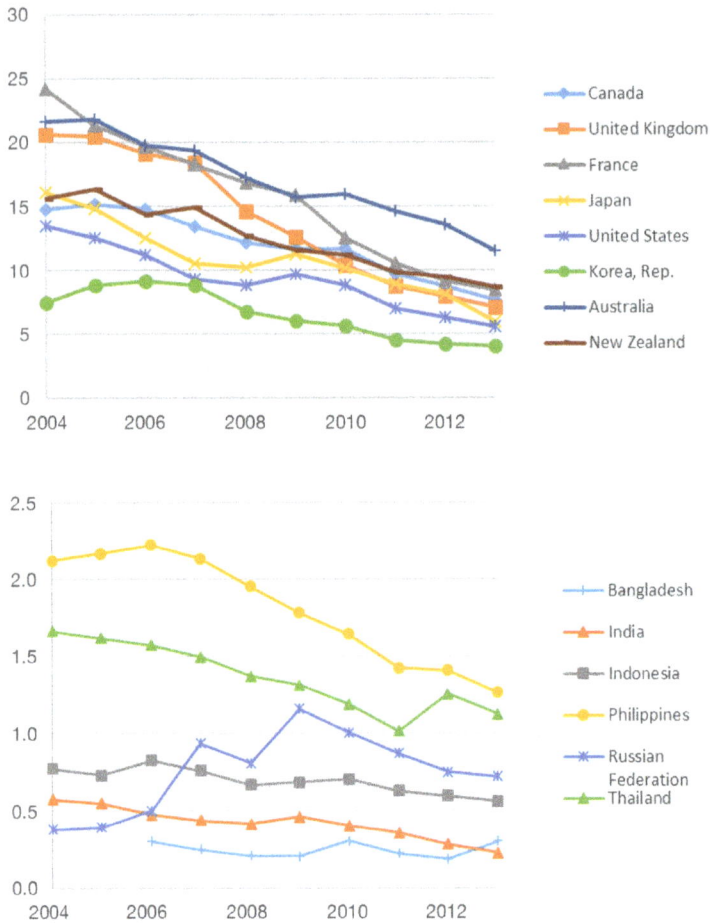

Figure 6.9. Minimum wages in selected countries divided by the minimum wage in China (2004–13)

Note. The calculation uses a harmonised series of statutory nominal gross monthly minimum wages in US dollar terms in various economies.

Source. Author's calculation based on data from the International Labour Organization (ILO) (2017)

Wage rates in developing Asia have converged towards those in advanced countries. Figure 6.9 presents minimum wages in selected countries divided by the minimum wage in China. The minimum wage can be a proxy for the cost of low-skill labour. The results show that the minimum wage in China has caught up rapidly with those in advanced economies but less strongly with minimum wages in other Asian economies. This cross-country pattern of minimum wages suggests that, overall, minimum wages in the emerging Asian countries as a group are catching up with those in advanced economies.[7]

Unit labour costs (ULC) are often viewed as a broad measure of international price competitiveness. They are defined as the average cost of labour per unit of output produced. They can be expressed as the ratio of labour cost per worker[8] to output per worker (labour productivity) (OECD 2017). To derive a country's international price competitiveness, it is necessary to calculate both labour cost per worker and labour productivity. Figure 6.10 presents ratios of labour productivity (output per worker) of selected countries over that of China. Overall, the extent of China's labour productivity catch-up towards the labour productivity of advanced economies is greater than the extent of the relative rise in China's minimum wage. This suggests that ULC in China have fallen against those in advanced economies and hence its international price competitiveness has risen. The change in China's international competitiveness compared with other developing economies in the sample is more attenuated and, therefore, the emerging Asian countries overall have achieved stronger international price competitiveness compared with advanced economies. The fall of ULC, however, is slowing down as developing Asia's labour productivity has gradually plateaued following the global financial crisis (GFC) of 2007–08, as seen in Figure 6.10. This trend of ULC threatens developing Asia's international price competitiveness in the long run. To maintain competitiveness in international markets, firms are investing in automation to enhance labour productivity and to save labour costs in production. Firms in advanced economies are also ramping up investment in automation and AI to maintain the lead in labour productivity and thus their competitiveness. This mechanism is potentially the key to driving the surge in investment in automation and AI in developing and advanced economies.

---

7   Because the International Labour Organization database (www.ilo.org/travail/areasofwork/wages-and-income/WCMS_142568/lang--en/index.htm) does not consistently provide wages by skill level for countries of interest, but does provide such data for the minimum wage across time, the minimum wage is adopted as a proxy for the wages of low-skilled workers.

8   In recent years, anecdotal evidence and empirical analysis suggests that the Chinese economy has reached the so-called 'Lewisian turning point' wherein the labour population starts to decline, while the movement of labourers from agricultural communities to the cities comes to an end (Lewis 1954; *The Economist* 2012; Cai & Du 2011; Cai & Wang 2010). And yet, precisely whether China has moved into an integrated national labour market without difference between rural and urban sectors is still debated. Athukorala and Wei (2017), for example, claim that labour shortages and wage increases in booming provinces reflect institutional constraints on labour mobility, rather than the rapid depletion of the economy-wide surplus labour pool. Despite the debate, wage growth is clearly strong.

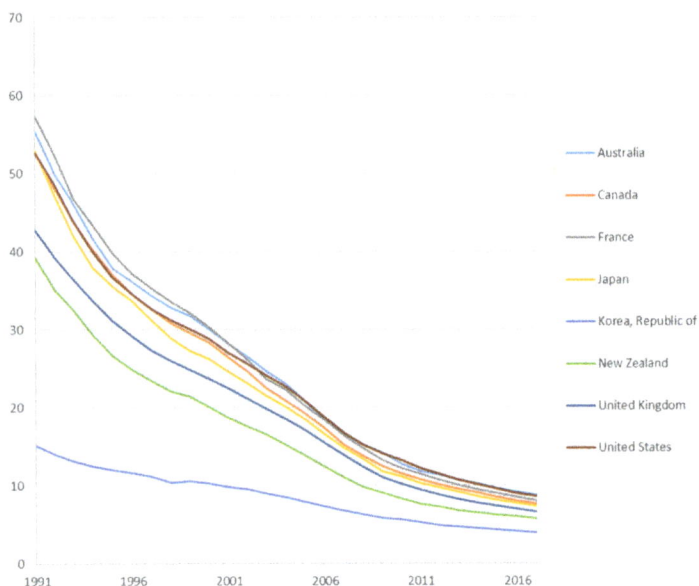

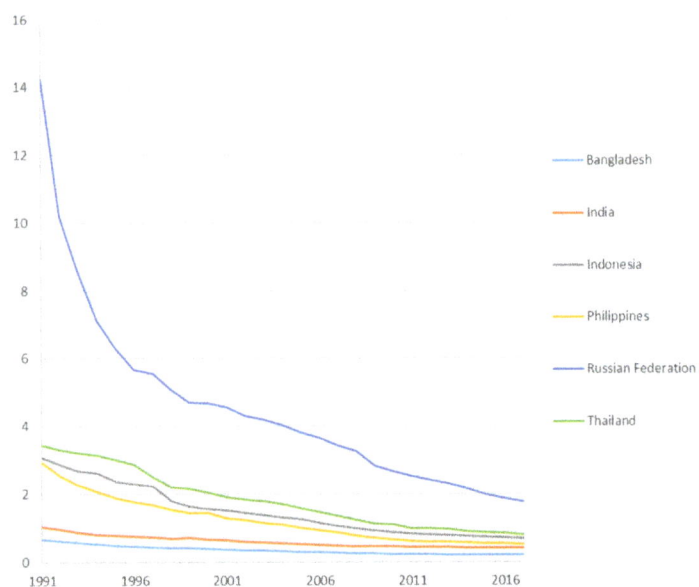

Figure 6.10. Ratios of labour productivity (real output per worker) in selected countries over labour productivity in China

Note: This measure of labour productivity is calculated using data on GDP in constant 2005 US dollars in PPP derived from the World Bank's World Development Indicators database. ILO estimates for total employment are used to compute labour productivity as GDP per worker.

Source. ILO (2017)

Robots and their impact on employment and income inequality

Angst over the rise of robots, job polarisation and income inequality

In the last several decades, substantial changes in wage inequality and job polarisation occurred in most advanced economies, though the United States is a representative case (Acemoglu & Autor 2011). Figure 6.11 shows changes in the US mean real income of males above 25 years old. For males with less than high school or high school and some college education, their mean real incomes fell below the levels in 1991 after the GFC and started to recover only recently. There is a significant divergence in real income earned by males with and without bachelor education and above.[9] In emerging economies such as China, real wages of high-skilled workers have been growing more quickly than those of medium- and low-skilled workers (Figure 6.12). As wage income is a major component in overall income, the distribution of income in these economies has become more unequal, as seen from the rising Gini coefficients. Figure 6.13 shows levels of income inequality, as measured by Gini coefficients, along with the restorative effects of fiscal policies on income distributions. The worsening of labour market conditions for low- and medium-skilled workers is also reflected by their falling share of payment in total value-added in key OECD economies and China (Tyers & Zhou 2017; Zhou & Tyers 2017).

Two main causes of job polarisation in advanced economies are automation and offshoring. Autor et al. (2003) link job polarisation to rapid improvements in the productivity – and declines in the real price – of information and communications technologies. The real cost of performing a standardised set of computational tasks – where cost is measured relative to the labour cost of performing the same calculations – fell by at least 1.7 trillion-fold between 1850 and 2006, with the bulk of this decline occurring in the last three decades (Nordhaus 2007). More recent work also reveals the dramatic fall in real ICT investment prices since 1959 (Byrne & Corrado 2016a, 2016b).

---

9 For information on wage differentials between skills, please refer to Katz and Autor (1999). This study reports that most industrialised economies experienced a compression of skill differentials and wage inequality during the 1970s, and a modest-to-large rise in differentials in the 1980s, with the greatest increase seen in the United States and United Kingdom.

121

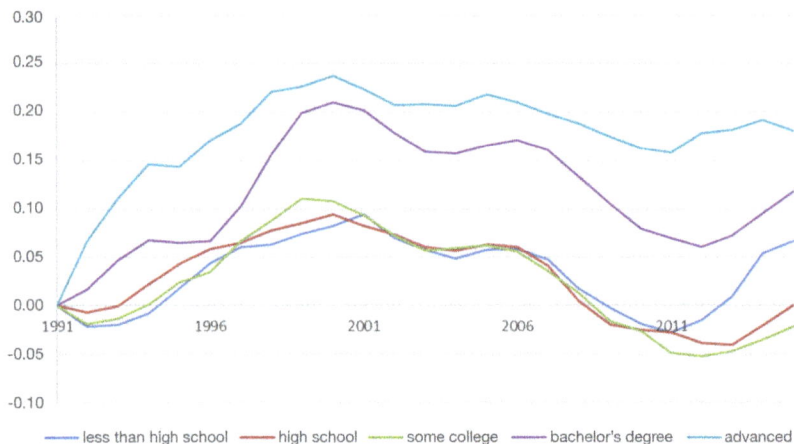

Figure 6.11. Percentage changes in US mean real income from the level in 1991, males above 25 years old (1991–2015)

Source. Reproduced from Figure 4 in Tyers and Zhou (2017)

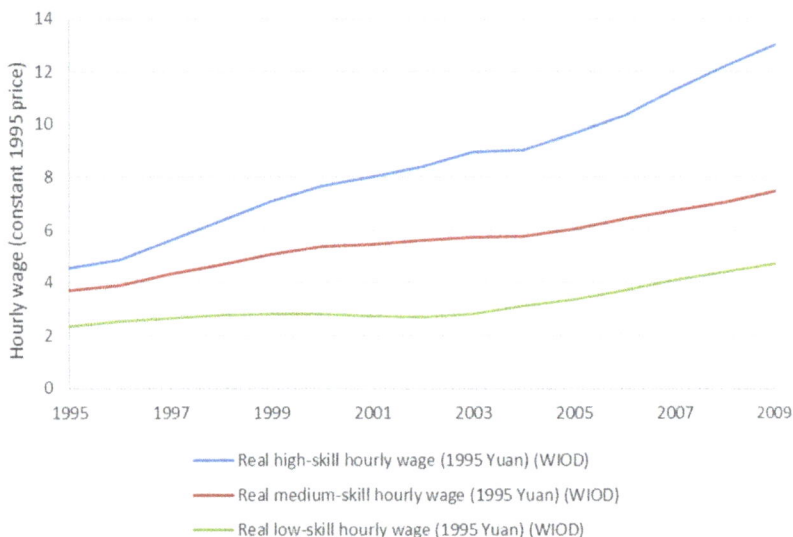

Figure 6.12. Changes in real hourly wages in China by skill level, constant 1995 yuan, 1995–2009

Source. Reproduced from Figure 5 in Zhou and Tyers (2017)

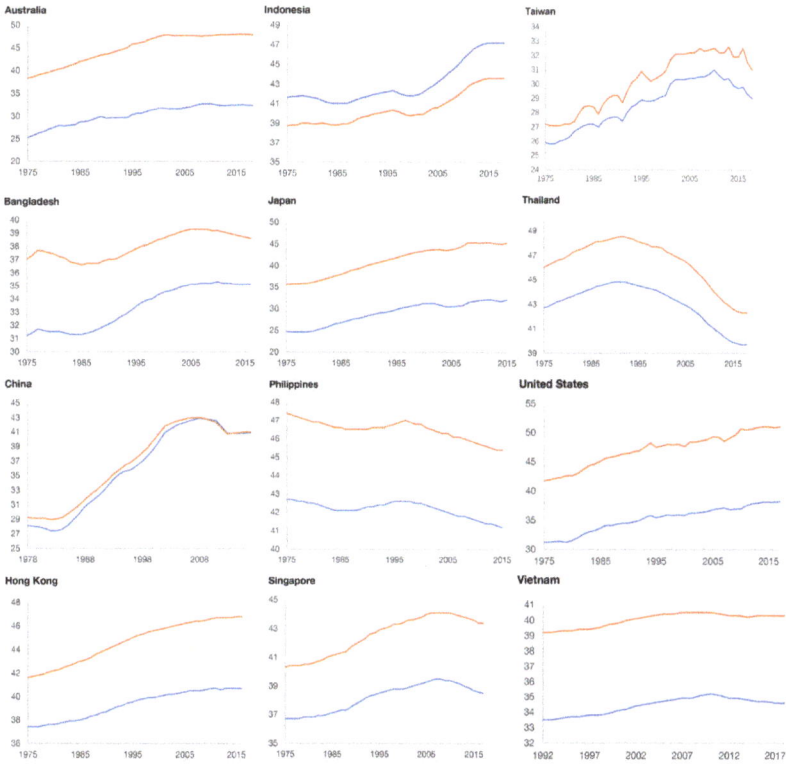

Figure 6.13. Gini coefficient pre-tax and pre-transfer and Gini coefficient post-tax and post-transfer in selected economies in the Asia–Pacific region

Note: The orange line is the Gini index of income inequality in equivalised household (pre-tax and pre-transfer) income. The blue line is the Gini index of inequality in equivalised household disposable (post-tax and post-transfer) income.

Source. The Standardized World Income Inequality Database, Version 8

The rapid, secular price decline in the real cost of symbolic processing creates enormous economic incentives for employers to substitute information technology for expensive labour in performing workplace tasks. Simultaneously, it creates significant advantages for workers whose skills become increasingly productive as the price of computing falls. Computers are increasingly good at replacing human labour in performing routine tasks that are procedural, rule-based, sufficiently well understood and fully specified as a series of instructions to be executed by a machine. Furthermore, these technological advances have dramatically lowered the cost of offshoring. This process of automation and offshoring of routine tasks, in turn, raises relative demand for workers who can perform complementary non-routine tasks: abstract tasks that require problem-solving, intuition, persuasion; and creative and manual tasks that require situational adaptability, visual and language recognition, and in-person interactions. Since these jobs are found at opposite ends of the occupational skill spectrum – in professional, managerial and technical occupations on the one hand, and in service and labourer occupations on the other – the consequence may be a partial 'hollowing out' or polarisation of employment opportunities (Acemoglu & Autor 2011).

Advanced robotics, artificial intelligence and future work

With the maturing of a new raft of technologies, including Industry 4.0, 3D printing, IoT, AI, automation, augmented reality and virtual reality, the fear of an imminent wave of technological unemployment is again one of the dominant economic themes of our time. Will smart machines replace humans, just as the internal combustion engine replaced horses? The popular narrative often goes as follows: as software and AI advance, production processes become increasingly automated. Workers can be replaced by new and smarter machines – industrial robots, in particular – that are capable of faster and more efficiently performing the tasks formerly carried out by humans. The robots will therefore make millions of workers redundant, especially those with low and medium qualifications, and reshape society in a fundamental way.

There have been dramatic estimates of how many occupations are at risk of being automated, given the type of work they usually conduct (Frey & Osborne 2017). Building on the literature on task content of employment, Frey and Osborne (2017) asked the question: how susceptible are current jobs to these technological developments? To assess this, they implemented a novel methodology to estimate the probability of computerisation for 702 detailed occupations. The data was collected from a survey provided to each worker who answered a set of specific questions relating to activities of their occupation. Frey and Osborne created an algorithm that assigned probabilities of automation to the nine O*NET[10] variables: finger dexterity, manual dexterity, cramped workspace, originality, fine arts,

---

10   O*NET data is an online service developed for the US Department of Labor. It provides detailed descriptions of the world of work for use by job seekers, workforce development and HR professionals, students and researchers. O*NET data is available at www.onetonline.org/.

social perceptiveness, negotiations, persuasion, assisting and caring for others and, ultimately, the probability of automation of each occupation. According to their estimates, about 47 per cent of total US employment is at risk.

One counterargument to Frey and Osborne (2017) is that, while existing occupations are prone to replacement by robots, there will be new products and industries and hence jobs or tasks created to demand labour. Acemoglu and Restrepo (2015) demonstrate that, although automation tends to reduce employment and the share of labour in national income, the creation of more complex tasks has the opposite effect and, under reasonable conditions, there exists a stable balanced growth path in which the two types of innovations go hand-in-hand. This issue is examined in a task-based framework wherein tasks previously performed by labour are automated, more complex versions of existing tasks can be created and, in performing these new tasks, labour tends to have a comparative advantage. An increase in automation reduces the wage-to-rental-rate ratio, which discourages further automation and encourages greater creation of more labour-intensive tasks, restoring the share of labour in national income and the employment-to-population ratio back towards their initial values.

Until very recently, systematic empirical analyses of the general equilibrium impact of robots and other new technologies on employment were scarce. Acemoglu and Restrepo (2017a) analyse the effect of the increase in industrial robot usage on local US labour markets from 1993 to 2014. Using a model in which robots compete against human labour in the completion of different tasks, it is shown that industrial robots may reduce employment and wages, and that the local labour market effects of industrial robots can be estimated by regressing the change in employment and wages on the exposure to robots in each local labour market – defined from the national penetration of robots into each industry and the local distribution of employment across industries. Using this approach, Acemoglu and Restrepo (2017a) identify large and robust negative effects of industrial robots on employment and wages across commuting zones. The commuting zones most exposed to robots in the post-1990 era do not exhibit any differential trends before 1990. The impact of industrial robots is distinct from the impact of imports from China and Mexico, the decline of routine jobs, offshoring, other types of IT capital, and the total capital stock. According to the estimates, one more industrial robot per thousand workers reduces the employment-to-population ratio by about 0.18–0.34 percentage points and wages by 0.25–0.5 per cent. The empirical picture that emerges confirms some of the US labour market's darkest concerns about robots.

Whilst the above research shows that industrial robots have caused job and earnings losses in the United States, Dauth et al. (2017) explore the impact of robots on the German labour market. Germany's robot density is higher than the United States, as seen in the discussion above on the market for robots and automation. Despite there being many more robots in operation, Germany is still among the world's major manufacturing powerhouses with an exceptionally large employment share. It ranges from 25 per cent in 2014 (compared to less than 9 per cent in the United States), and has declined less dramatically over the last 25 years. Moreover, Germany is not only a heavy user but also an important producer of industrial robots. The analysis for Germany thus elicits the causal labour market effects of robots in a context with many more manufacturing jobs per capita than could potentially be replaced, but also with many more robots installed in production and robotic producers located close by. Dauth et al. (2017) find that robots have had no *aggregate* effect on German employment. Although robots do not affect total employment, they do have strongly negative impacts on manufacturing employment in Germany. One additional robot replaces two manufacturing jobs on average. This implies that robots performed roughly 275,000 full-time manufacturing jobs in the period 1994–2014. But, those sizable losses are fully offset by additional jobs in the service sector. In other words, robots have strongly changed the composition of employment by driving the decline of manufacturing jobs. Importantly, robot exposure is found to increase the chances of workers staying with their original employer. That is, robot exposure increased job stability for these workers, although some of them went on to perform different tasks to those they were engaged in before robot exposure. This effect seems to be largely down to the efforts of work councils and labour unions, but is also the result of fewer young workers entering manufacturing careers.

The negative equilibrium effect of robots on aggregate manufacturing employment is not, therefore, brought about by direct displacements of incumbent workers and is instead driven by smaller flows of labour market entrants into more robot-exposed industries. In other words, robots do not destroy existing manufacturing jobs, but they do induce firms to create fewer new jobs for young people. Robot exposure causes notable on-the-job gains in earnings for high-skilled workers, especially in scientific and management positions. Those workers may gain from robots, because they possess complementary skills to this technology and perform tasks that are not easily replaceable. But for low-skilled and especially for medium-skilled manufacturing workers, sizable negative impacts are found. The introduction of robots results in medium-skilled workers, such as machine operators, receiving lower wages and cumulative earnings losses, but even for them no increased displacement risk is found, rather positive employment effects are identified.

These empirical findings reflect a key feature of industrial relations in the German labour market – the manufacturing sector is still highly unionised, and blue-collar wages are typically determined collectively with strong involvement of work councils. It has been frequently argued that German unions prefer maintaining high employment levels, and are willing to accept flexible wage setting arrangements, such as opening clauses, in the presence of negative shocks in order to keep jobs. This flexibility of unions and the resulting wage restraints are seen as one of the leading hypotheses for the strong overall performance of the German labour market (the 'employment miracle') since the mid-2000s.

Another mechanism through which robotics may negatively affect employment and growth is discussed in Benzell et al. (2015). They find that, under the right conditions, more supply produces, over time, less demand as the smart machines undermine their customer base. Highly tailored skill- and generation-specific redistribution policies can keep smart machines from immiserating humanity. But blunt policies, such as mandating open-source technology, can make matters worse.

The above discussion is mainly focused on the impact of automation within an economy. It is also important to examine how trade activities between countries are affected by automation technologies and how these changes influence employment and income inequality across countries. As discussed above, medium- and low-skilled workers in advanced economies experienced decline in employment opportunities over the past several decades. Automation and offshoring are the two causes identified, with the two interrelated. While politicians tend to draw attention to offshoring and the 'hollowing out' of manufacturing activities as the main driver of slack in the low- and medium-skilled labour market, academic research shows that automation exerts greater impact (Acemoglu & Restrepo 2017b; Rotman 2017).

The potential effects of automation on trade activities and employment can be considered in light of the fact that the labour cost differential is a main reason for offshoring (Dachs et al. 2012). A smaller labour cost differential leads, therefore, to more re-shoring. Although the shrinkage of the labour cost differential is favourable for re-shoring, counterforces exist. Firstly, the advantages of production taking place in close proximity to the customer do not favour re-shoring if the customer is not located in the company's home country or region. Offshoring is not only motivated by seeking lower costs, but also as a step towards entering new markets by locating production closer to the customers in foreign countries. So for some firms, closeness to customers works in favour of staying offshore, and was already an essential motive for their previous offshoring decision. According to Sebastien Duchamp, a spokesman for the multinational GE, 'The global environment for manufacturing is changing in a way where we must innovate differently … innovation has to be in the markets you play in, close to your customers; and close to access the best talent wherever it exists in the world' (Khan 2013). GE, like other companies, is responding to the trend of what is called 'mass customisation', or making products to a customer's preferences. As a result, companies are finding it more suitable to have plants closer to their markets and to their research and development units (Khan 2013). Industry 4.0 enhances production for customised products, thereby better serving local customers and preventing offshoring.

Secondly, production in certain industries is difficult to automate as yet. For example, in the sportswear industry, the chief executive of Adidas said 'Asian plants will become more automated, but there were some processes of the roughly 120 steps in creating an Adidas shoe that remain stubbornly resistant to automation … The biggest challenge the shoe industry has is how do you create a robot that puts the lace into the shoe … I'm not kidding. That's a complete manual process today. There is no technology for that' (Hancock 2017). Bottlenecks in automation technologies will slow down re-shoring activities.

Thirdly, being a supplier reduces the likelihood of re-shoring in all specifications of the regression. This can be explained by the fact that many suppliers have offshored production to follow their clients. These customer relations provide an effective 'glue' to keep manufacturing activities at foreign locations, even if external factors like wages or costs of material change (Dachs et al. 2017). If Industry 4.0 strengthens supply linkages between firms, it could act as a force preventing re-shoring.

For systematic reviews of manufacturing re-shoring, refer to Brennan et al. (2015), Stentolft et al. (2016), Dachs et al. (2017) and Delis et al. (2017). How new technologies will affect re-shoring is still under debate.

For advanced economies, the risk to employment is likely to prevail even if re-shoring does occur. This is because new manufacturing plants in advanced economies may translate into more jobs for robots than humans. Lower cost of automation technologies could mean that firms are simply completing the transition that would have taken place earlier without offshoring. Therefore re-shoring may not necessarily boost employment. Chances are that, if there were any positive effect on employment, automated factories would require highly skilled workers, often with training in technology and computers. For developing economies, the concern is firstly that the increased use of robots in developed countries risks eroding the traditional labour-cost advantage of developing countries; secondly, that robot use is working to the advantage of countries with established industrial capacity; and, thirdly, that the share of occupations that could experience significant automation is higher in developing countries than in more advanced ones, where many of these jobs have already disappeared. This could further damage growth prospects in developing countries where manufacturing has stalled or that are already experiencing 'premature deindustrialisation' (UNCTAD 2017). Furthermore, if future international competition hinges on the intensification of the use of robots, the observed effects of automation on employment and wages in advanced economies may also take place in developing economies as these robots are increasingly adopted.

Overall, robots may replace labour in both advanced and developing economies, at least in the short run. Some existing skills will become obsolete and new skills will be in demand. It will be critical to ensure that replaced workers can be retrained to gain skills for new and more complex tasks, and also that all workers develop the mindset of continuous learning to face more rapid technical change and job churning. Clearly public policies, including educational reform and infrastructure investment, will have important roles to play.[11] In the next section, I consider income inequality and the consequences of education and upskilling being insufficient for the smooth transition to new technologies.

---

11 Another important headwind of the transition is macro-economic in nature and is not discussed in detail here. The anxiety surrounding robots does not lie in their wider scope, faster speed or greater intrusiveness alone, but in their arrival at a time of subdued global macro-economic dynamism. This has held back the investment needed to create new sectors, where workers displaced by robots could find better jobs (UNCTAD 2017).

Automation and income inequality and the policy response

Alongside the fear that automation will lead to the replacement of labour is concern about the impact of automation on income inequality and the fiscal capacity of nations to redistribute income. Automation may exert upward pressure on income inequality, at least in the short run. Acemoglu and Restrepo (2015) introduce a distinction between low-skilled and high-skilled labour, where the latter has a comparative advantage in producing with newer technologies. This structure implies that both automation, which squeezes out tasks previously performed by low-skilled labour, and the creation of new tasks, which directly benefits high-skilled labour, will increase inequality between the two labour types during the short-run transitions. Nevertheless, the medium-term implications of creation of new tasks could be very different, because these tasks are later standardised and undertaken by low-skilled labour. As a result, there exists a uniquely balanced growth path on which not only the factor distribution of income (between capital and labour) but also inequality between the two skill types is constant.

Technological changes can affect the distribution of income among different factors of production. The introduction of new technology, which usually accelerates growth, may benefit relatively richer segments of the population, and worsen income inequality. If the technological change benefits skilled labour more than unskilled labour, skill premium will go up, which might increase inequality. If the technology is capital-biased, it also could increase income inequality because capital incomes usually accrue to the rich more than to the poor (Yang & Greaney 2017). Based on an elemental three-household general equilibrium model, Zhou and Tyers (2017) quantify the links in China between real income inequality on the one hand and, on the other, changes in factor abundance, total factor productivity, factor bias, the relative cost of capital goods, labour-force participation rates, the fiscal deficit and the unemployment rate. Relative expansion in the stocks of skill and physical capital have, by themselves, mitigated inequality. Yet their effects have been dominated by the combination of structural change and biased technical change, with the latter having the dominant effect. Looking into the future, which is expected to bring a continuation in structural change and a further technical twist away from low-skill labour, this time toward physical capital due to automation, Zhou and Tyers (2017) find that if the new technology delivers only a shift in technical bias then aggregate performance is impaired by worker displacement that could cause the unemployment rate to rise to anywhere between 20 and 55 per cent so that low-skilled wages are downwardly rigid. If the government protects the welfare of low-skilled households via tax-funded transfers, the transfer burden, either to maintain the welfare of low-skilled households or to constrain income equality, makes capital-owners significant losers. Worker displacement and the capital income tax rate required to contain the rise of income inequality are lessened the more the new technology also delivers increments to total TFP. But the required rates of TFP growth are high relative to what has been achieved by China in recent decades and the potential for continuing this pattern, constrained as it is by the shrinkage of opportunities for 'catch-up' productivity advances, will rely on the productivity effects of AI and robotic advances.

Tyers and Zhou (2017) examine the issue of robotics and income inequality in the US economy using a similar elemental three-household general equilibrium model as in Zhou and Tyers (2017). Applied to the United States, changes in factor bias are shown to have been the primary cause of the observed increase in inequality between 1990 and 2016. The widely anticipated future twist away from low-skilled labour toward capital is examined in combination with expected changes in population and its skill composition. With downward rigidity of low-skilled wages the potential is identified for unemployment to rise to extraordinarily high levels, with possible exacerbation from intensive low-skilled population growth and productivity growth that is no greater than that achieved since 1990. Indeed, the results suggest that productivity growth at twice the pace since 1990 would be needed to constrain unemployment, though even this would not slow the concentration of income. The superior policy response is shown to be a generalisation of the US 'earned income tax credit' system, with financing from taxes on consumption, rather than capital income.

Besides affecting within-county income inequality, the rise of automation may also affect cross-country income inequality. Research has found that after 1985, the growth in absolute global inequality was driven primarily by the accelerated growth of within-country income differences and that, currently, within-country inequality explains 70 per cent of absolute global market inequality (Goda & García 2017). The concern that cross-country income inequality may rise in the future arises from the potential for massive inequality stemming from automation and the 'winner-takes-all' global economic scenario that pushes low-skilled workers and low-income nations out of competitive positions, thus pushing up inequality levels further. Developed nations may bring back manufacturing and industrial jobs from overseas due to their technological advances in automation, reducing the need for low-skilled labour. Thus, as the World Bank argues, these changes will challenge traditional economic growth models, concluding that the risk of rising inequality in the coming decades is high.

With the rise of automation and AI, how can individuals adapt to these rapid technological changes? On the one hand, automation and AI may demand more workers who have skills in programming and mathematics. On the other hand, the new technologies may reach a stage of maturity that people no longer need advanced maths or programming skills to utilise the technology, that is 'singularity' in which machines surpass humans and produce more machines (Korinek & Stiglitz 2017). At that stage, skills in liberal arts will become more important and the most important skills are likely to be emotional and communication skills. Before singularity is reached, however, problem-solving and analytical skills and mathematics and programming skills are likely to be increasingly in demand in the future.

It is clear that as automation replaces low-skilled labour and increases demand for workers of higher skill levels, access to high-quality education becomes more important. Relatively well-off households will be able to provide their children with an education to give them the skills and capacity to compete in the labour market in the future. If there is strong inequality of opportunity, income inequality could deteriorate over generations (Golley et al. 2019; UN ESCAP 2017). Policies that aim at reducing inequality of opportunity will help alleviate income inequality and its negative impact when societies are increasingly faced with the rise of robotics and AI. Whether policies such as universal basic income or earned income credit could be adopted to help support the welfare of individuals experiencing job loss due to technical change and to help constrain income inequality is the subject of heated debate (Jessen et al. 2017; Stiglitz 2017).

The geography of innovation and future markets: A capability perspective

The development of automation and AI will have significant impact on the geography of innovation and future markets. Comparative advantages of countries are likely to be reshaped, which will affect export performance. Furthermore, the geography of future innovation is uncertain. It is not yet known whether several leading technology companies will dominate automation and AI and, hence, innovation will be clustered around places such as California's Silicon Valley, or these new technologies will be utilised by local markets and be developed into specialised frontier technologies in locations that suit markets and conditions in local economies. This will have significant impact on future income inequality between nations, as a geographically clustered model of innovation is likely to lead to higher income inequality between nations and a geographically distributed model of innovation will stimulate growth in lagging countries and thus reduce income inequality between nations. It is possible that lagging countries will leapfrog existing technologies and move straight into more advanced ones, thus gaining momentum in technological progress and growth. Firms in developing countries in the Asia–Pacific region could potentially develop niche technologies for domestic markets by leveraging and integrating into the existing platforms of Industry 4.0 of leading countries including China, Japan, Germany and the Republic of Korea (ILO 2016). Whether to stave off the loss of competitiveness relative to advanced economies or to leapfrog to new technologies, a country's key capabilities for technology absorption and innovation will be critical for the success of these efforts.

Future global comparative advantage will be reshaped, as inputs used in production will include not only labour, capital and land but also, and more importantly, information. For example, analytics based on big data require information as key input. Therefore, it is important that an economy maintains strong openness to ideas, international trade, international flow of capital and international migration to stay connected and competitive. To stay connected for information flows requires infrastructure such as broadband and mobile networks. Figure 6.14 and Figure 6.15 present the fixed broadband subscriptions per 100 people, and mobile cellular subscriptions per 100 people in selected economies as indicators of the development of ICT infrastructures. While mobile use shows convergence across these countries, the gap in the use of fixed broadband is significant.

Figure 6.16 shows the 2017 Global Connectivity Index and, again, there is significant opportunity for several economies in the Asia–Pacific region to catch up. Figure 6.17 presents the Networked Readiness Index, which assesses the factors, policies and institutions that enable a country to fully leverage ICT for increased competitiveness and well-being (Baller et al. 2016), and shows similar ranking as that in Figure 6.16.

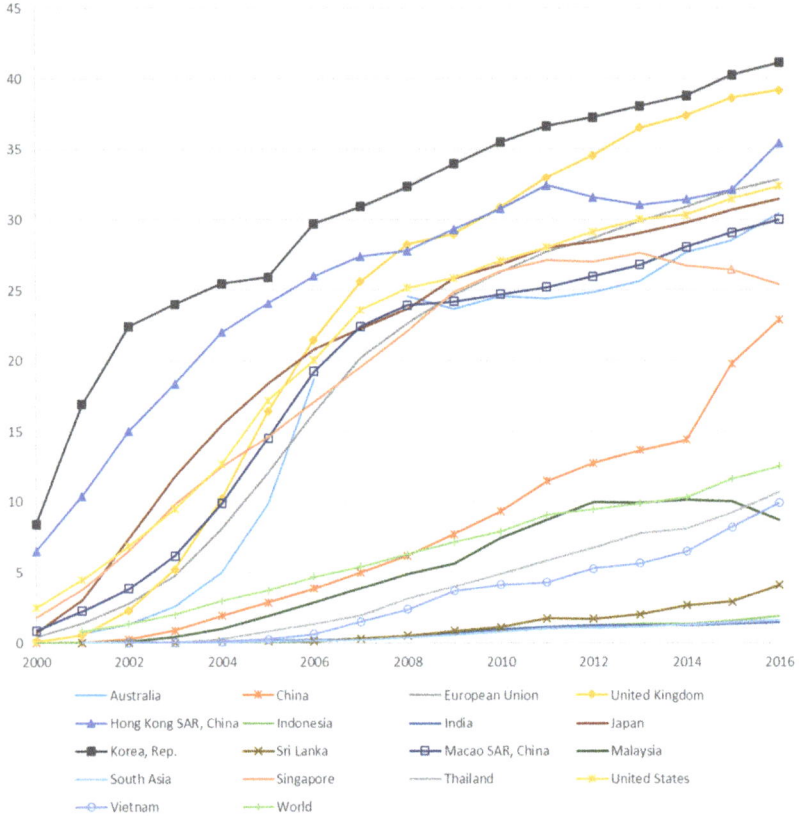

Figure 6.14. Fixed broadband subscriptions (per 100 people)
Source. World Development Indicators

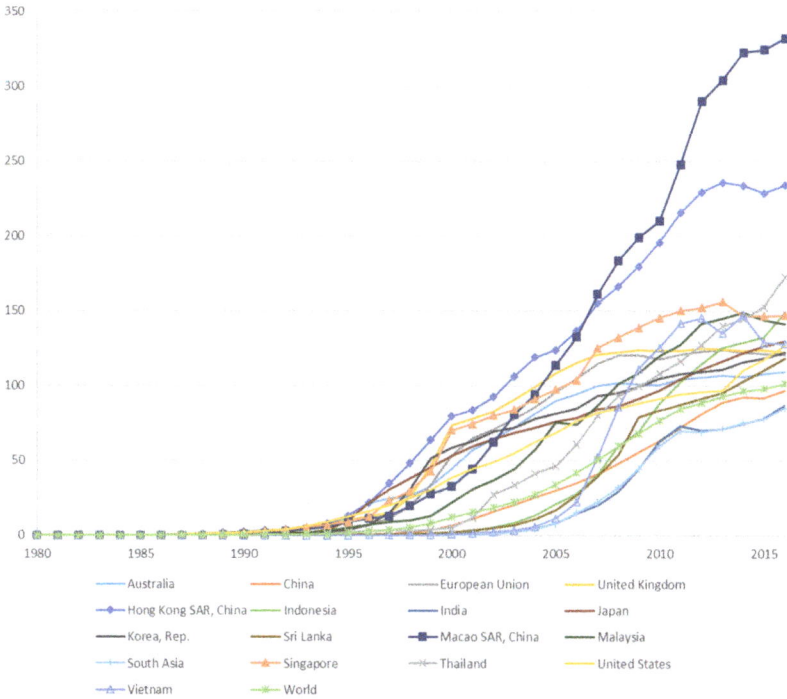

Figure 6.15. Mobile cellular subscriptions (per 100 people)

Source. World Development Indicators

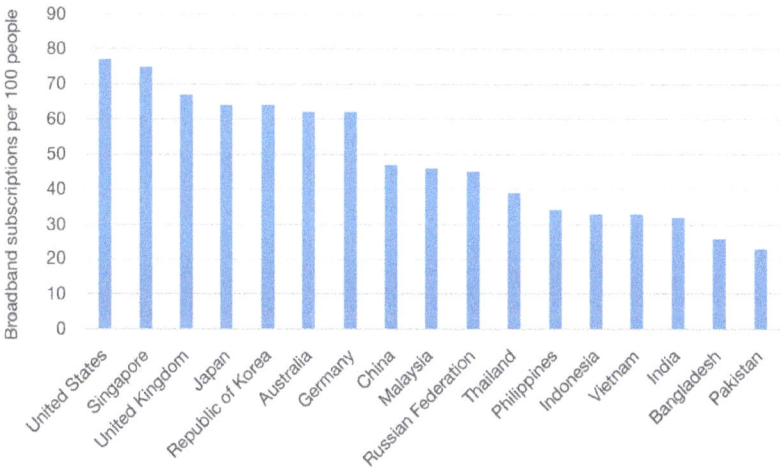

Figure 6.16. 2017 Global Connectivity Index

Source. Global Connectivity Index (2017)

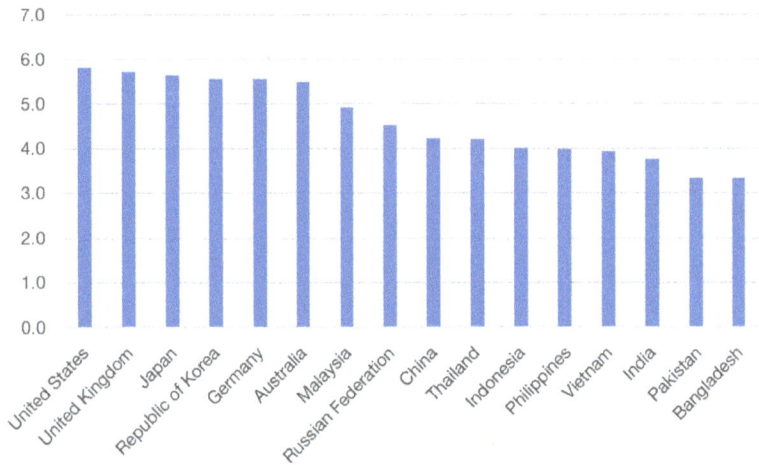

Figure 6.17. Networked Readiness Index
Source. Baller et al. (2016)

Human capital and institutional quality are another two factors that could shape the competitiveness of countries in riding this new wave of technological progress. As human capital and institutional quality complement each other in enabling an economy's technological progress and industrial upgrading, countries with better-educated workforces and better-developed institutions are more likely to lead the round of technological change (Zhou 2016). Table 6.1 shows the share of tertiary-educated people aged 25 and over in selected countries. The variation is wide, ranging from 2.3 per cent in Nepal to 34.8 per cent in the Republic of Korea. As demand for high-skilled workers to invent, improve and implement automation technologies continues in the future, countries with an abundant, well-educated labour force are likely to enjoy higher competitiveness. Firms that aim to be integrated in the Industry 4.0 platform will increasingly demand high-skilled labour, whether in programming and analytics or in liberal arts and creative thinking. A highly educated and well-trained labour force will allow the economy to specialise in niche and advanced technologies, and to better adapt to the servicification of manufacturing under Industry 4.0; that is the development whereby manufacturing firms not only buy and produce more services than before but also sell and export more services as integrated activities (World Bank 2017). Table 6.2 presents measures of ease of doing business and export, logistics performance, and legal protection in selected countries in the Asia–Pacific region. It is evident that, in this region, existing human capital and institutional quality varies significantly, which will potentially affect a nation's technological capability in the era of robotics and AI.

The competitiveness of firms to embrace new technologies and new ways of production also depends on investment in intangible capital and research and development (R&D). Figure 6.18 presents the share of ICT capital of the total capital of selected economies. An economy's total capital consists of structures, transport equipment, machinery, and ICT capital – which includes computers, communication equipment, and software. The share of ICT capital in total capital reflects the importance of information technologies in an economy. Countries in the Asia–Pacific region vary significantly in their share of ICT capital. In 2015, the share is around 25 per cent in the United States; 20 per cent in the Republic of Korea, Taiwan and Germany; 15 per cent in Singapore; 10 per cent in Japan and Australia; 5 per cent in Hong Kong and India; and 1.8 per cent in China. Countries with high ICT share are equipped with strong capability in ICT technologies and are better positioned for competition in automation and AI. There is great potential for countries with low ICT share to catch up in ICT investment in the future. Figure 6.19 shows the share of research and development expenditure in gross domestic product (GDP) in selected countries in the Asia–Pacific region from 1996 to 2015. The Republic of Korea takes the lead in 2015 with R&D intensity of 4.1 per cent, far surpassing East Asia's average of 2.5 per cent. China's R&D intensity is catching up the most rapidly, reaching 2 per cent in 2015 and outpacing Malaysia, Hong Kong, Thailand and Macao SAR.

Establishing a business environment that is friendly to entrepreneurship will stimulate the growth of new firms based on cutting-edge technologies and generate employment opportunities. Unlike traditional routes to industrialisation, when factories employ mass workers and combine workers with machines to produce output under relatively stable technologies, the new model of industrialisation is likely to see more frequent disruptive technological changes and continuous creative destruction aka Schumpeterian growth. Hence, for firms in developing Asia to stay competitive under such a technological paradigm, entrepreneurship plays an important role as the competitive behaviour that drives the market process, alternatively phrased as the introduction of new economic activity that leads to change in the marketplace (Davidsson 2016). Demographics may also have a role to play. Countries with relatively young populations having the opportunity to move into senior management positions will nurture more entrepreneurs and innovation and higher TFP and economic growth (Liang et al. 2014). This mechanism is important when firms adopt and develop a new wave of technologies.

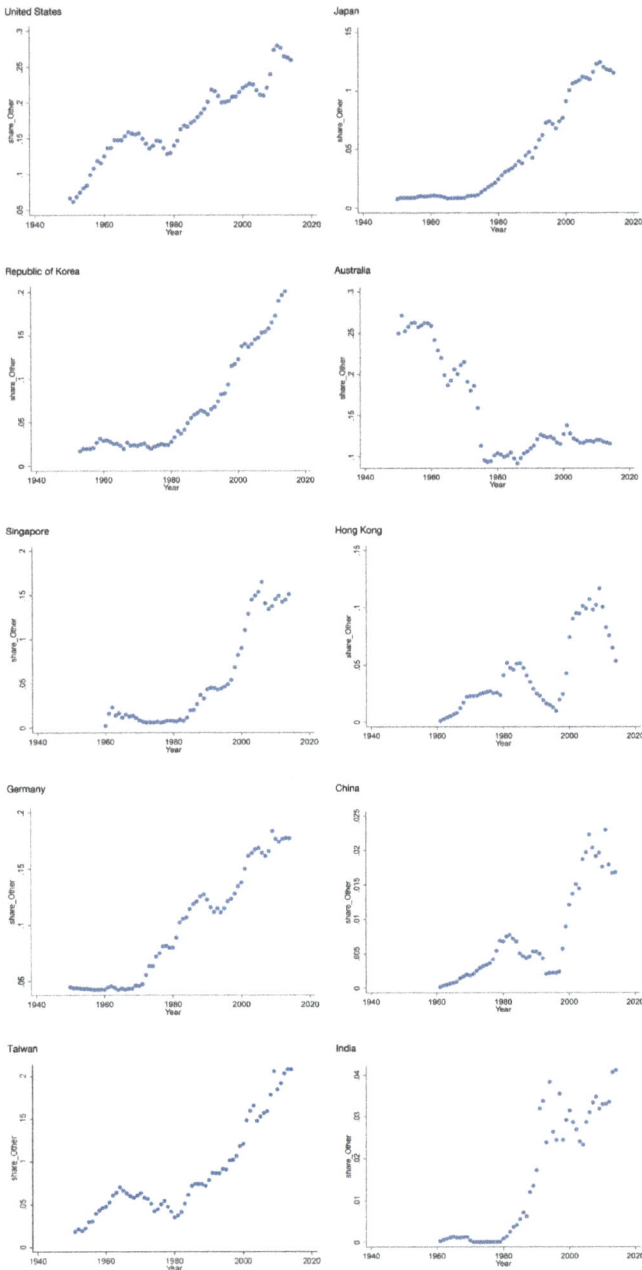

Figure 6.18. Share of real investment in ICT capital in the total capital in selected economies

Note: 'share_other' is the share of real investment in ICT capital in the total capital.

Source. Author's calculation based on capital data in Penn World Table 9.0

Another important determinant of an economy's capability to nurture new technologies is whether government policymakers and regulators are prepared and able to effectively and quickly regulate these new technologies. One policy approach in response to the opportunity and risk associated with emerging new technologies is the regulatory sandbox. A regulatory sandbox creates a 'safe space' in which businesses can test innovative products, services, business models and delivery mechanisms in the context of regulation, with regulators. The sandbox framework enables firms to manage regulatory risks during the testing stage (Zilgalvis 2018). Countries like China, Japan, Singapore, the United Kingdom and Thailand have 'regulatory sandboxes' in which to experiment with regulations for new digital technologies; for example, areas that permit self-driving cars and financial technology.[12] Different countries have different regulatory approaches, which will in turn impact on the uptake and development of new technologies in these countries.

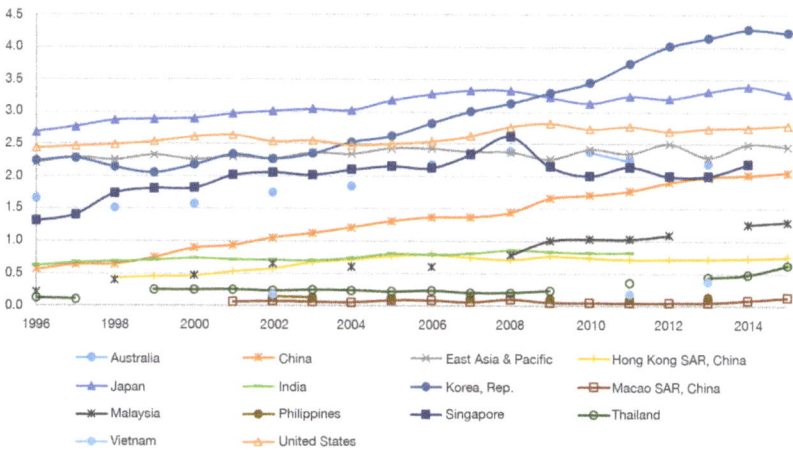

Figure 6.19. Research and development expenditure (% of GDP) in selected countries from 1996 to 2015

Source. World Development Indicators (2017)

---

12   Overview of regulatory sandbox, Monetary Authority of Singapore, www.mas.gov.sg/Singapore-Financial-Centre/Smart-Financial-Centre/FinTech-Regulatory-Sandbox.aspx; Regulatory sandbox, Financial Conduct Authority, www.fca.org.uk/firms/regulatory-sandbox; *The Westside Story*, From autonomous vehicles to blockchain: regulatory sandboxes are taking off (2018). 5 March, thewestside story.net/autonomous-vehicles-blockchain-regulatory-sandboxes-taking-off/

Table 6.1. People with completed tertiary education as percentage of population aged 25 and over

Country	Completed tertiary education, % of population aged 25 and over
Republic of Korea	34.8
USA	30.9
Singapore	30.6
Australia	25.2
Mongolia	22.5
Japan	19.9
United Kingdom	18.8
Germany	16.1
Hong Kong SAR China	14.8
Macao SAR China	12.3
Thailand	10.0
Sri Lanka	9.5
Taiwan	8.6
Philippines	7.2
India	6.1
Malaysia	5.9
Pakistan	5.5
Myanmar	4.9
Vietnam	4.6
Bangladesh	3.1
China	2.4
Nepal	2.3

Source. Barro and Lee (2013)

Table 6.2. Ease of doing business, infrastructure, legal protection and ease of exporting in selected countries in the Asia–Pacific region

Country	2016 logistics performance index: Overall (1 = low to 5 = high)	2016 strength of legal rights index (0 = weak to 12 = strong)	2014 time to export (days)	2017 ease of doing business index (1 = most business-friendly regulations)
Singapore	4.1	8	6	2
Korea, Rep.	3.7	5	8	4
Hong Kong SAR, China	4.1	8	6	5
United States	4.0	11	6	6

Country	2016 logistics performance index: Overall (1 = low to 5 = high)	2016 strength of legal rights index (0 = weak to 12 = strong)	2014 time to export (days)	2017 ease of doing business index (1 = most business-friendly regulations)
Australia	3.8	11	9	14
Malaysia	3.4	7	11	24
Thailand	3.3	3	14	26
Japan	4.0	5	11	34
Vietnam	3.0	7	21	68
Indonesia	3.0	6	17	72
China	3.7	4	21	78
India	3.4	6	17.1	100
Nepal	2.4	6	40	105
Sri Lanka	N.A.	2	16	111
Philippines	2.9	1	15	113
Bangladesh	2.7	5	28.3	177

Source. World Development Indicators

Conclusion

Despite sluggishness in the growth of total factor productivity in major economies since the GFC, a new round of technological revolution characterised by automation, robotics, AI, big data analytics and Industry 4.0 is rapidly approaching and the full impact of these new technologies is yet to be realised. Industrial robots have been growing quickly in Asia, surpassing the speed of development in Europe and the Americas. This growth in robotics is driven by firms' need to maintain competitiveness in international markets given the ageing population and rising labour costs in the Asia–Pacific region.

The dark side of the rise of robotics is to potentially cause unemployment and aggravate income inequality as future technological progress is skill-biased. Two mechanisms with opposite effects on employment are identified: the labour-replacing effect and the productivity-enhancing effect, with the former reducing employment and the latter creating new jobs and tasks. Income inequality is likely to rise in the short run if the labour-replacing effect dominates before new industries, tasks and jobs are generated.

The rise of automation in major economies including China, the Republic of Korea, Japan, Germany and the United States will have significant impact on the growth trajectory of emerging economies in Asia. If capital deepening continues in China on a large scale, there is less hope that emerging economies can continue to follow the East Asian growth model to prosperity. Instead, firms in these countries could develop technological capability to integrate into the Industry 4.0 platforms of major economies and leverage these new technologies to leapfrog and be successful in niche markets. Staying open and connected, investing in human capital, improving the business environment and stimulating entrepreneurship are strategies that will help firms in the Asia–Pacific region to prosper in the new wave of technological progress.

References

Acemoglu, D & Autor, D (2011). 'Skills, tasks and technologies: Implications for employment and earnings', *Handbook of Labor Economics*, 4, 1043–171. doi.org/10.1016/S0169-7218(11)02410-5.

Acemoglu, D & Restrepo, P (2015). *The race between man and machine: Implications of technology for growth, factor shares and employment*, NBER Working Paper, No. 22252.

—— (2017a). *Robots and jobs: Evidence from US labour markets*, NBER Working Paper, No. 23285.

—— (2017b). *Secular stagnation? The effect of aging on economic growth in the age of automation*, NBER Working Paper, No. 23077, www.nber.org/papers/w23077.

Arther, WB (1989). 'Competing technologies, increasing returns, and lock-in by historical events', *The Economic Journal*, 99, 116–31. doi.org/10.2307/2234208.

Athukorala, P & Wei, Z (2017). 'Economic transition and labour markets in China: An interpretive survey of the "turning point" debate', *Journal of Economic Surveys*. doi.org/10.1111/joes.12206.

Autor, DH, Dorn, D & Hanson, GH (2013). *Untangling trade and technology: Evidence from local labour markets*, NBER Working Paper, No. 18938. doi.org/10.3386/w18938.

—— (2016). 'The China shock: Learning from labor-market adjustment to large changes in trade', *Annual Review of Economics*, 8, 205–40. doi.org/10.1146/annurev-economics-080315-015041.

Autor, DH, Levy, F & Murnane, RJ (2003). 'The skill content of recent technological change: An empirical exploration', *Quarterly Journal of Economics*, 116(4), 1279–333. doi.org/10.1162/003355303322552801.

Baldwin, R & Robert-Nicoud, F (2014). 'Trade-in-goods and trade-in-tasks: An integrating framework', *Journal of International Economics*, 92(1), 51–62. doi.org/10.1016/j.jinteco.2013.10.002.

Baller, S, Dutta, S & Lanvin, B (2016). *Global information technology report 2016: Innovating in the digital economy*. World Economic Forum and INSEAD.

Barro, R & Lee, JW (2013). 'A new data set of educational attainment in the world, 1950–2010', *Journal of Development Economics*, 104, 184–98. doi.org/10.1016/j.jdeveco.2012.10.001.

Baur, C & Wee, D (2015). 'Manufacturing's next act', *McKinsey & Company*, www.mckinsey.com/business-functions/operations/our-insights/manufacturings-next-act.

Bekey, G, Ambrose, R, Kumar, V, Sanderson, V, Wilcox, B & Zheng, Y (2006). *International assessment of research and development in robotics*, WTEC Panel Report, wtec.org/robotics/report/screen-robotics-final-report.pdf.

Benzell, SG, Kotlikoff, LJ, LaGarda, G & Sachs, JD (2015). *Robots are us: Some economics of human replacement*, NBER Working Paper, No. 20941. doi.org/10.3386/w20941.

Bloomberg News (2017). 'Inside China's plans for world robot domination'. 25 April, www.bloomberg.com/news/articles/2017-04-24/resistance-is-futile-china-s-conquest-plan-for-robot-industry.

Brennan, L, Ferdows, K, Godsell, J, Golini, R, Keegan, R, Kinkel, S, Srai, JS & Taylor, M (2015). 'Manufacturing in the world: Where next?', *International Journal of Operations & Production Management*, 36(9), 1253–74. doi.org/10.1108/IJOPM-03-2015-0135.

Brezis, ES, Krugman, P & Tsiddon, D (1993). 'Leapfrogging in international competition: A theory of cycles in national technological leadership', *The American Economic Review*, 83(5), 1211–19.

Brynjolfsson, E, Rock, D & Syverson, C (2017). *Artificial intelligence and the modern productivity paradox: A clash of expectations and statistics*, NBER Working Paper, No. 24001. doi.org/10.3386/w24001.

Byrne, D & Corrado, C (2016a). *ICT prices and ICT services: What do they tell us about productivity and technology?*, Economics Program Working Paper Series, #16-05. The Conference Board.

—— (2016b). *ICT asset prices: Marshaling evidence into new measures*, Economics Program Working Paper Series, #16-06. The Conference Board.

Cai, F & Du, Y (2011). 'Wage increases, wage convergence and the Lewis turning point in China', *China Economic Review*, 22(4), 601–10. doi.org/10.1016/j.chieco.2011.07.004.

Cai, F & Wang, M (2010). 'Growth and structural changes in employment in transition China', *Journal of Comparative Economics*, 38(1), 71–81. doi.org/10.1016/j.jce.2009.10.006.

Clark, G (2016). 'Winter is coming: Robert Gordon and the future of economic growth', *American Economic Review*, 106(5), 68–71. doi.org/10.1257/aer.p20161072.

Crafts, N (2016). 'The rise and fall of American growth: exploring the numbers', *American Economic Review*, 106(5), 57–60. doi.org/10.1257/aer.p20161070.

Dachs, B, Borowiecki, M, Kinkel, S & Schmall, TC (2012). *The offshoring of production activities in European manufacturing*, MPRA Working Paper.

Dachs, B, Kinkel, S & Jager, A (2017). *Bringing it all back home? Backshoring of manufacturing activities and the adoption of Industry 4.0 technologies*, MPRA Working Paper.

Dauth, W, Findeisen, S & Suedekum, J (2017). *German robots – The impact of industrial robots on workers*, CEPR Discussion Paper, No. 12306.

Davidsson, P (2016). 'What is entrepreneurship?' In *Researching entrepreneurship: conceptualisation and design* (pp 1–19). Switzerland: Springer. doi.org/10.1007/978-3-319-26692-3.

Delis, A, Driffield, N & Temouri, Y (2017). 'The global recession and the shift to re-shoring: Myth or reality?', *Journal of Business Research*, 1–12. doi.org/10.1016/j.jbusres.2017.09.054.

Deloitte (2014). *Industry 4.0: Challenges and solutions for the digital transformation and use of exponential technologies*, www2.deloitte.com/content/dam/Deloitte/ch/Documents/manufacturing/ch-en-manufacturing-industry-4-0-24102014.pdf.

Department of Industry, Innovation and Science (2019). 'Industry 4.0', www.industry.gov.au/funding-and-incentives/industry-40.

EU KLEMS Growth and Productivity Accounts: Statistical Module (EU KLEMS), www.euklems.net/.

Feenstra, RC, Inklaar, R & Timmer, MP (2015). 'The next generation of the Penn World Table', *American Economic Review*, 105(10), 3150–82, www.ggdc.net/pwt.

Frey, CB & Osborne, MA (2017). 'The future of employment: How susceptible are jobs to computerisation?', *Technological Forecasting and Social Change*, 114, 254–80. doi.org/10.1016/j.techfore.2016.08.019.

Friedman, B (2016). 'A century of growth and improvement', *American Economic Review*, 106(5), 52–56. doi.org/10.1257/aer.p20161069.

Gallagher, A, Naden, D & Karterud, D (2016). 'Robots in elder care: Some ethical questions', *Nursing Ethics*, 23(4), 369–71. doi.org/10.1177/0969733016647297.

Geissbauer, R, Vedso, J & Schrauf, S (2016). *Industry 4.0: Building the digital enterprise*, PwC, www.pwc.com/gx/en/industries/industries-4.0/landing-page/industry-4.0-building-your-digital-enterprise-april-2016.pdf.

Global Connectivity Index. Huawei, www.huawei.com/minisite/gci/en/.

Goda, T & García, AT (2017). 'The rising tide of absolute global income inequality during 1850–2010: Is it driven by inequality within or between countries?', *Social Indicators Research*, 130, 1051–72. doi.org/10.1007/s11205-015-1222-0.

Golley, J, Zhou, Y & Wang, M (2019). 'Inequality of opportunity in China's labor earnings: the gender dimension'. *China & World Economy*, 27(1), 28–50. doi.org/10.1111/cwe.12266.

Gordon, RJ (2014). 'The turtle's progress: Secular stagnation meets the headwinds'. In C Teulings & R Baldwin (2014). *Secular stagnation: Facts, causes and cures* (pp 131–42) voxeu.org/content/secular-stagnation-facts-causes-and-cures. London: Centre for Economic Policy Research (CEPR), scholar.harvard.edu/files/farhi/files/book_chapter_secular_stagnation_nov_2014_0.pdf.

—— (2015). *The rise and fall of American growth: The US standard of living since the Civil War*. Princeton University Press.

—— (2016). *The rise and fall of American growth*. Princeton University Press.

Hallward-Driemeier, M & Nayyar, G (2017). *Trouble in the making? The future of manufacturing-led development*. Washington, DC: World Bank. doi.org/10.1596/978-1-4648-1174-6.

Hancock, T (2017). 'Adidas boss says large-scale reshoring is "an illusion"', *Financial Times*, 24 April.

Hansen, A (1938). 'Economic progress and the declining population growth', *American Economic Review*, 29(1), 1–15.

Hulten, CR (2001). *Total factor productivity: a short biography*, NBER Working Paper, No. 7471.

International Federation of Robotics (2017). ifr.org/.

International Labour Organization (ILO) (2016). *Regional Reports: ASEAN in transformation*, www.ilo.org/actemp/publications/WCMS_579558/lang--en/index.htm.

Irima, M (2016). 'Five ways agriculture could benefit from artificial intelligence', *AI for the Enterprise*. IBM, www.ibm.com/blogs/watson/2016/12/five-ways-agriculture-benefit-artificial-intelligence/.

Jessen, R, Rostam-Afschar, D & Viktor, S (2017). 'Getting the poor to work: Three welfare-increasing reforms for a busy Germany', *Public Finance Analysis*, 73(1), 1–41. doi.org/10.1628/001522117X14864674910065.

Katz L & Autor, DH (1999). 'Changes in the wage structure and earnings inequality'. In O Ashenfelter & D Card (eds), *Handbook of Labor Economics*, 3A, pp 1463–555.

Katz, L & Murphy, K (1992). 'Changes in relative wages: Supply and demand factors', *Quarterly Journal of Economics*, 107, 35–78. doi.org/10.2307/2118323.

Kennedy, S (2015). 'Made in China 2025', *Center for Strategic and International Studies* (CSIS), www.csis.org/analysis/made-china-2025.

Khan, MS (2013). 'US manufacturing and the troubled promise of reshoring', *Guardian*, 25 July, www.theguardian.com/business/2013/jul/24/us-manufacturing-troubled-promise-reshoring.

Korinek, A & Stiglitz, JE (2017). *Artificial intelligence, worker-replacing technological progress and income distribution*, NBER Working Paper, No. 24174.

Lewis, WA (1954). 'Economic development with unlimited supplies of labour', *The Manchester School*, 22(2), 139–91. doi.org/10.1111/j.1467-9957.1954.tb00021.x.

Liang, J, Wang, H & Lazear, EP (2014). *Demographics and entrepreneurship*, NBER Working Paper, No. 20506. doi.org/10.3386/w20506.

McKinsey Digital (2015). *Industry 4.0: How to navigate digitization of the manufacturing sector*. McKinsey & Company, www.mckinsey.com/business-functions/operations/our-insights/industry-four-point-o-how-to-navigae-the-digitization-of-the-manufacturing-sector.

Mokyr, J (2013). *Is technological progress a thing of the past?*, 8 September. London: Centre for Economic Policy Research (CEPR), voxeu.org/article/technological-progress-thing-past.

Mokyr, J, Vickers, C & Ziebarth, NL (2015). 'The history of technological anxiety and the future of economic growth: Is this time different?', *Journal of Economic Perspectives*, 29(3), 31–50. doi.org/10.1257/jep.29.3.31.

Nordhaus, WD (2007). 'Two centuries of productivity growth in computing', *Journal of Economic History*, 67(1), 128–59. doi.org/10.1017/S0022050707000058.

Observatory of Economic Complexity. (2017). 'Economic complexity index (ECI)', atlas.media.mit.edu/en/rankings/country/eci/?year_range=2011-2016.

Organisation for Economic Co-operation and Development (OECD) (2017). 'Unit labour costs', *Data*, data.oecd.org/lprdty/unit-labour-costs.htm.

Park, D & Shin, K (2011). *Impact of population aging on Asia's future growth*, ADB Economics Working Paper Series, No. 281. doi.org/10.2139/ssrn.1956869.

Perkins, D (2013). *East Asian development: Foundations and strategies*. Cambridge, MA: Harvard University Press. doi.org/10.4159/harvard.9780674726130.

Perkins, R (2003). 'Technological "lock-in". In E Neumayer (ed.), *Internet encyclopaedia of ecological economics*. The International Society for Ecological Economics, isecoeco.org/pdf/techlkin.pdf.

Ross, A (2016). *The industries of the future*. Simon and Schuster.

Rotman, D (2017). 'Artificial intelligence could dramatically improve the economy and aspects of everyday life, but we need to invent ways to make sure everyone benefits', *MIT Technology Review*, www.technologyreview.com/s/603465/the-relentless-pace-of-automation/.

Solow, R (1987). 'We'd better watch out', *New York Times Book Review*, 12 July, p 36.

Stentolft, J, Olharger, J, Heikkila, J & Thomas, L (2016). 'Manufacturing backshoring: A systematic literature review', *Operations Management Research*, 9(3–4), 53–61. doi.org/10.1007/s12063-016-0111-2.

Stiglitz, JE (2017). *The welfare state in the twenty-first century.* Roosevelt Institute, policydialogue.org/files/publications/The_Welfare_State_in_the_Twenty-First_Century.pdf.

Stolper, W & Samuelson, PA (1941). 'Protection and real wages', *Review of Economic Studies*, 9(1), 58–73. doi.org/10.2307/2967638.

Summers, L (2013). 'Why stagnation might prove to be the new normal', *Financial Times*, 16 December, www.ft.com/content/87cb15ea-5d1a-11e3-a558-00144feabdc0.

Teulings, C & Baldwin, R (2014). *Secular stagnation: Facts, causes and cures.* London: Centre for Economic Policy Research (CEPR), scholar.harvard.edu/files/farhi/files/book_chapter_secular_stagnation_nov_2014_0.pdf.

The Economist (2012). 'China's Achilles heel', 21 April, www.economist.com/node/21553056.

The Standardized World Income Inequality Database (SWIID), fsolt.org/swiid/.

The State Council, The People's Republic of China (2017a). english.gov.cn/2016special/madeinchina2025/.

—— (2017b). www.gov.cn/xinwen/2015-05/20/content_2865061.htm.

Tyers, R & Zhou, Y (2017). *Automation and inequality in China*, CAMA Working Paper, 59, papers.ssrn.com/sol3/papers.cfm?abstract_id=3036735.

United Nations (UN) (2017). World population prospects 2017, esa.un.org/unpd/wpp/Download/Standard/Population/.

United Nations Conference on Trade and Development (UNCTAD) (2017). *Trade and development report 2017 – Beyond austerity: Towards a new global deal*, unctad.org/en/PublicationsLibrary/tdr2017_en.pdf.

United Nations Economic and Social Commission for Asia and the Pacific (UN ESCAP) (2017). *Inequality of opportunity in Asia and the Pacific: Education*, www.unescap.org/resources/inequality-opportunity-asia-and-pacific-education.

United Nations Industrial Development Organization (UNIDO) (2017). *Industry 4.0: Opportunities behind the challenge*, Background Paper, www.unido.org/sites/default/files/files/2017-11/UNIDO%20Background%20Paper%20on%20Industry%204.0_27112017.pdf.

Yang, Y & Greaney, TM (2017). 'Economic growth and income inequality in the Asia-Pacific region: A comparative study of China, Japan, South Korea, and the United States', *Journal of Asia Economics*, 48, 6–22.

Zhou, Y (2016). 'Human capital, institutional quality and industrial upgrading: global insights from industrial data', *Economic Change and Restructuring*, 51(1), 1–27. doi.org/10.1007/s10644-016-9194-x.

Zhou, Y & Bloch, H (2017). 'Wage convergence and trade', working paper.

Zhou, Y & Tyers, R (2017). *Automation and inequality with taxes and transfers*, CAMA Working Paper, 70, cama.crawford.anu.edu.au/sites/default/files/publication/cama_crawford_anu_edu_au/2017-11/70_2017_tyers_zhou_0.pdf.

Zilgalvis, P (2018). 'Regulatory sandboxes: An innovation in policymaking', *Startup Nations Summit Surabaya 2018*, www.genglobal.org/startup-nations-estonia-gen-europe/regulatory-sandboxes-innovation-policymaking.

7

HISTORY RETURNS: INTERGENERATIONAL MOBILITY OF EDUCATION IN CHINA IN 1930–2010

Yang Yao and Zhi-An Hu

Introduction

During the twentieth century, China witnessed a dramatic episode of societal change when a series of revolutions toppled the social order that sustained the imperial rule for more than a thousand years. One of the most significant changes was the cessation of *keju* – the royal examination system that provided the only channel for upward social mobility – which permanently changed the nature of Chinese education. Education was no longer a bridge to enter officialdom, but a means to enhance one's productivity and life satisfaction. The spread of education, however, was slow until the communist revolution of 1949. The Chinese Communist Party (CCP) began massive campaigns to elevate the Chinese population's level of education. As a result, the number of illiterate or semi-illiterate people declined from 70 per cent among people born in the 1930s to about 10 per cent among those born around 1980.[1] The period of the Cultural Revolution (1966–76) saw the fastest growth in elementary and high school education, from which young

---

1   Unless otherwise stated, figures reported in this section are from the authors' calculations based on data from China Family Panel Studies (CFPS) 2010.

rural people most benefited. As a result, intergenerational mobility of education was greatly accelerated. Following the period of economic reform and opening (1978 onwards), however, the trend of improvement has reversed. Despite the government's efforts to enforce nine-year compulsory education for all children, the average schooling for rural youth between 20 and 29 years of age in 2010 was barely above eight years. In contrast, the average educational achievement of the same cohort in urban centres was close to 11 years. The figures for higher education are even worse. In their influential work (Liang et al. 2012), James Lee and his co-authors show that Peking University and Suzhou University, two of China's elite universities, had a 'silent revolution' that extended admission to lower class young people in the period 1949–2002. This experience may not, however, represent the whole country. While China entered a period of expansion of higher education at the turn of the century, it is unclear whether young rural people, who are disadvantaged by the increasing costs of higher education and their families' need for them to enter the labour market, have benefited from this expansion. The resulting urban–rural divide is the single-most important factor responsible for the stagnation in China's transmission of intergenerational education. The 70-year history of the People's Republic was an experiment in social transformation. In its first 30 years, equality was enhanced by the CCP's efforts of social and political transformation; the following 40 years have witnessed a return to inequality due to a weakening in the CCP's commitment to a socially and politically equal society.

This paper, using data provided by the China Family Panel Studies (CFPS), documents the trends of improvements and intergenerational mobility in education for people born between 1930 and 1985. While a full consideration of these trends needs a comprehensive study, this paper provides some tentative – in many cases conjectural – explanations and prescribes policy remedies to improve intergenerational mobility in China.

The general trends

The CFPS has had four waves of survey since 2010, but data from the latest wave (2016) were not released in time for this paper's preparation. This study refers to data from the 2010 survey and, because the paper is not concerned with long-term trends, the 2012 or 2014 surveys are not relevant here.

Improvement of education

The following analysis applies the five CFPS categories of education: 1 = not finishing elementary school, 2 = elementary school, 3 = middle school, 4 = high school, 5 = college or above. To ensure sufficient observations to make reasonable inferences, the sample is restricted to individuals who were 80 or younger in 2010 (i.e. those born in 1930 or later). In addition, to ensure the study considers only people who had completed their education, individuals younger than 25 in 2010 (i.e. those born later than 1985) are excluded. The resulting sample size is 62,219 people who were born between 1930 and 1985.

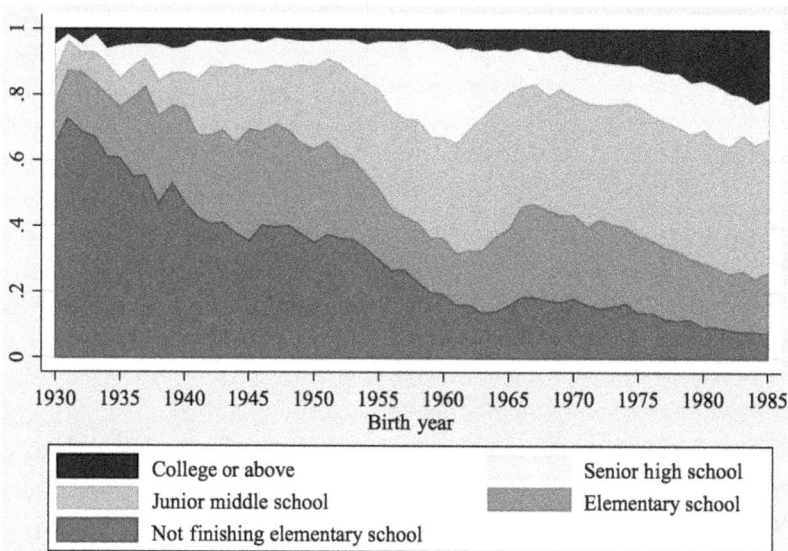

Figure 7.1. Education trend: Full sample
Source. CFPS 2010

Figure 7.1 presents the composition of educational achievements by birth year. A clear trend of improved education is evident in the 55 years covered by the figure. Among people born in 1930, close to 70 per cent did not finish elementary school; in contrast, this percentage dropped to 7.3 per cent for people born in 1985. The establishment of the New China in 1949 did not accelerate the progress and, on the other hand, a mild setback happened in the later stage of the Cultural Revolution. People born around 1965 should have received elementary education in the early 1970s, but fewer people among them finished elementary school than those who were born in the early 1960s. The New China did, however, accelerate the spread of middle school education; people born after 1940, who were supposed to obtain middle school education after 1949, were more likely to finish middle school than the earlier cohorts. The acceleration of high school education, though, had to wait until the 1960s. As the figure shows, the chance that people born after 1950 would finish high school increased at that time. This improvement culminated with the cohorts born in the early 1960s who received high school education in the early 1970s. This was consistent with the observation that high school education was greatly expanded during the Cultural Revolution. The quality of high school education at that time, however, was limited because teachers were required to impart to students practical skills instead of general knowledge. This is confirmed by CFPS 2010 data applied to the rate of return to education. People around 45 years old in 2010 (born around 1965) had the lowest rates of return to education among all the income earners in the sample (Yao & Cui 2015). After the death of Chairman Mao Zedong in 1976, the zeal of the Cultural Revolution receded quickly. The share of high school graduates has since stabilised at around 13 per cent.

In the early times of New China (the 1950s and early 1960s), there was a modest expansion of higher education. Among people born between 1935 and 1942 (who reached college age in the 1950s and early 1960s), 4.9 per cent had a college degree, compared with 4 per cent of people born before them. The expansion ceased, however, for the following 20 years when the chance that people born between 1945 and 1960 would attend college dropped to 3.8 per cent. The Cultural Revolution was clearly the cause for this setback because, during its first years, university admission was effectively stopped and, in its later years, only a small number of students were admitted (Liang et al. 2012). The expansion of higher education began again in 1978 when the birth cohorts of the early 1960s reached college age. The share of college graduates reached 21.2 per cent for the 1985 cohort.

Male

Female

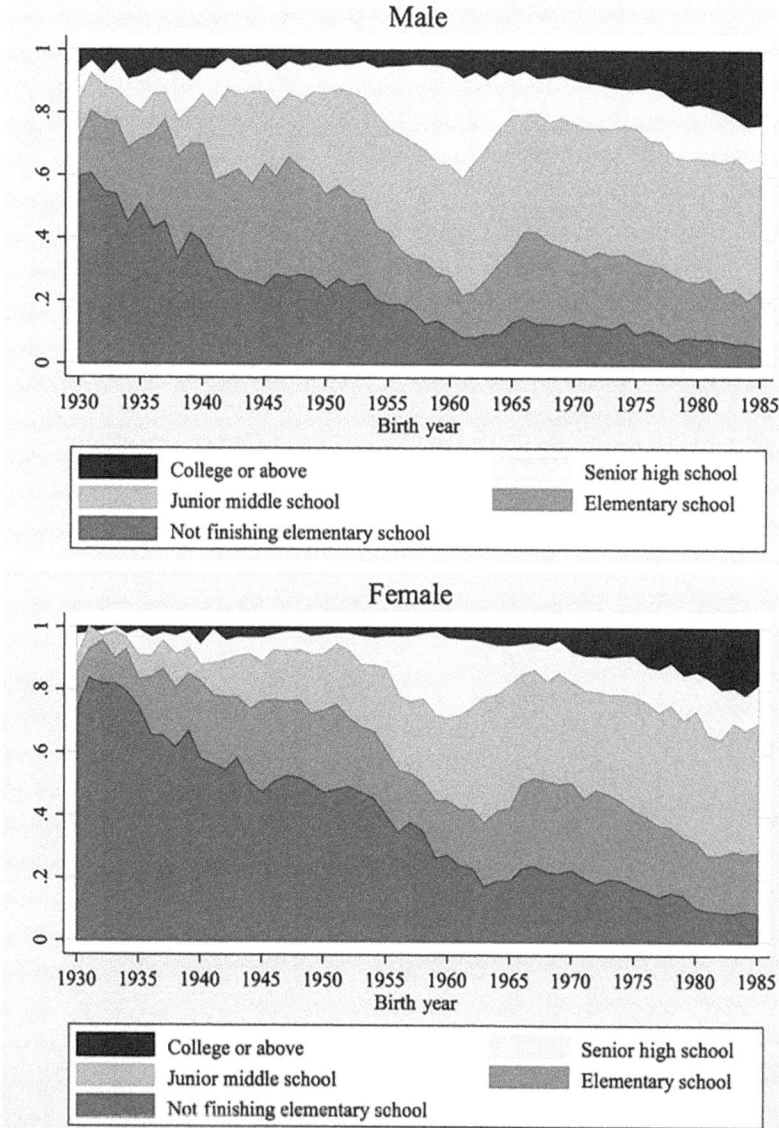

Figure 7.2. Education trend by gender
Source. CFPS 2010

The trends presented in Figure 7.2 are broadly similar, although differences are evident for different cohorts. A significantly higher ratio of women born before the early 1960s did not finish elementary school, compared to their male counterparts. The expansion of higher education before the Cultural Revolution benefited more men than women. So did the expansion of high school education during the Cultural Revolution. In general, however, gender gaps declined over the period and this was driven by female political participation. Using data provided by county chronicles and the 1990 Census, Yao and You (2018) found that, in counties with a faster expansion of female membership in the CCP, the female–male ratio of educational achievement increased more rapidly. Using data from CFPS 2010, they also found that living as an adolescent in a county with larger female party membership induced a person to invest more in his/her daughters.

The rapid decline in gender gaps in the 1980s was compounded by many factors, such as higher returns to education, smaller families, higher family income and continually changing social norms. By the 1985 cohort, the only significant remaining gender gap was at the level of college education. While 23.9 per cent of men born in 1985 had a college degree, the percentage for women born in the same year was 18.6 per cent.

Intergenerational transmission of education

The most commonly used indicator for intergenerational transmission of education is the coefficient of correlation between the educational achievements of two consecutive generations. We use this indicator in our paper. Subsequently, we will call it the 'transmission coefficient'. It is obtained by regressing the child's education on the higher achievement of his/her parents' educational achievements. A higher coefficient implies more stagnant intergenerational mobility and thus slower improvement of educational equality.

Figure 7.3 presents the transmission coefficients through a five-year moving cohort. The horizontal axis indicates the starting year of each five-year birth cohort. The figure conveys the main message of this paper: history is repeating itself. The transmission coefficients form a U curve with the lowest points situated at the birth cohorts of the mid-1950s. Intergenerational mobility was less dynamic for people born in the early 1930s and their transmission coefficients were around 0.55. The coefficient dropped rapidly, however, until the cohorts born around 1940, which shows that, even before the communist revolution, social mobility was accelerating. After a short set back, the decline continued until the birth cohorts of the mid-1950s when the transmission coefficient reached its lowest level of 0.32. Most of these people received their middle school and high school education during the Cultural Revolution. The political and social mobilisation during this period had a decisive impact on accelerating social mobility within the Chinese population. Soon after, China waved goodbye to Mao's radicalism when he died in 1976, however, history has quickly begun to repeat. The transmission coefficient has increased steadily across birth cohorts and, by the time of the cohorts of the mid-1970s (who would finish their education by the end of the 1990s), it went back to the levels of the cohorts of the mid-1930s. Despite dropping for a brief period, the coefficient turned upward again among more recent cohorts.

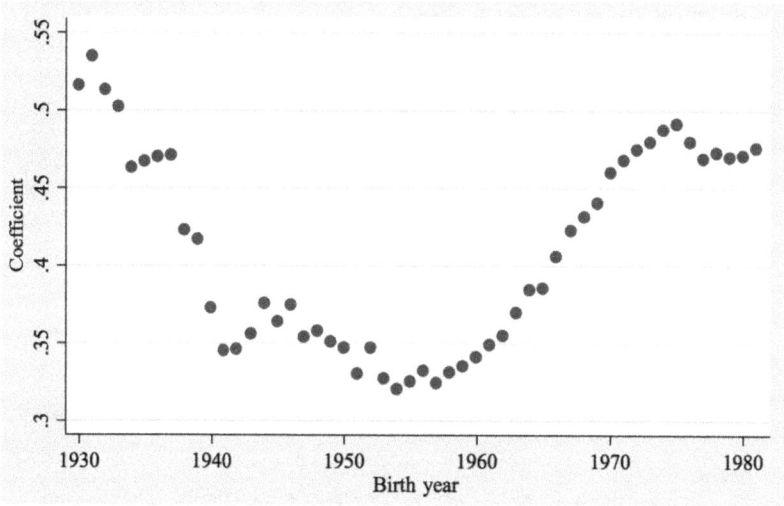

Figure 7.3. Transmission coefficient: Full sample

Note. 1. Education is measured in units of five

2. Each point is estimated using a five-year moving sample

3. X-axis indicates the starting year of each sample window

Source. CFPS 2010

Figure 7.4 presents an historical pattern of education transition from parents to children. The child sample is divided into three groups by birth cohort: 1930–44, 1945–64, and 1965–85. Most people in the first cohort, if they received any education at all, began their education before 1949. In the second cohort, most finished their elementary education before 1976, the last year of the Cultural Revolution. Most of the last cohort began their education after 1976. Several findings are evident in the figure. First, given parents' educational level, more recent cohorts had higher levels of education. This fits into the general trend of improved education shown by Figure 7.1; a rising tide lifts all boats. Second, the 1945–64 cohort had the smallest slope of transition (transmission coefficient), while the other two cohorts had almost the same and larger slopes. That is, after a period of more equitable improvement, intergenerational transmission of education again lost dynamism in more recent generations. Third, the reduced level of transmission for the 1945–64 cohort was achieved by raising the level of education of those born to parents of lower levels of education more than the level of people born to parents of higher levels of education. Lastly, the transmission coefficient of the 1965–85 cohort increased because people born to parents with lower levels of education did not improve much, while people born to parents with higher levels of education had large improvements.

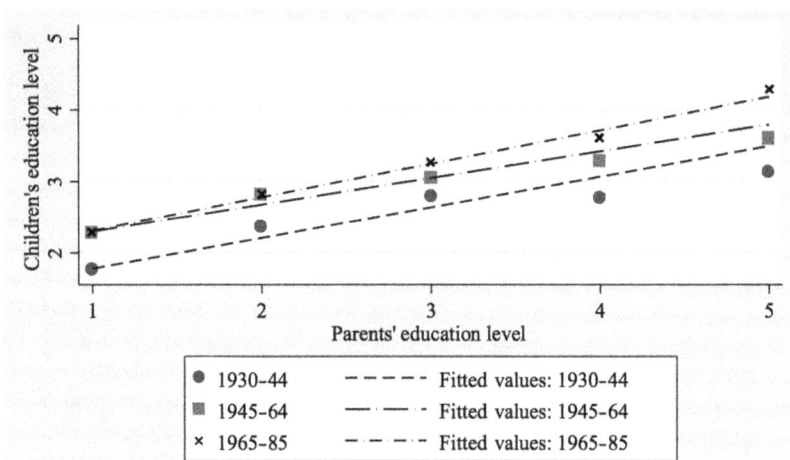

Figure 7.4. Transmission by cohorts

Note. 1 = Not finishing elementary school

2 = Elementary school

3 = Junior middle school

4 = Senior high school

5 = College or above

Source. CFPS 2010

The last finding is alarming because it indicates that inequality of intergenerational transmission has accelerated among more recent generations: children born to less-educated parents have been locked in by stagnant transmission while children born to more educated parents have been able to obtain much better education than their already highly educated parents. If they went to college at all, the members of the 1965–85 cohort started their college education before 2003. The increasing inequality among this cohort is inconsistent with the findings of James

Lee's team, which may be because they only studied two elite universities, Peking University and Suzhou University, and thus missed the larger picture of the whole country.

As expected, women's education was more dependent on their parents' education than men. Figure 7.5 shows that women had larger transmission coefficients than men, except for people born in the early 1930s. One possible explanation is that women born in that period of time had uniformly low education regardless of their family backgrounds.

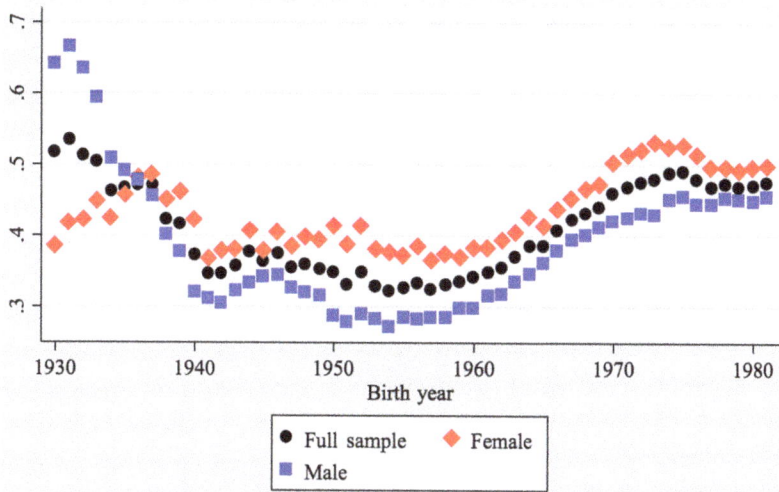

Figure 7.5. Transmission coefficient by gender

Note. 1. Education is measured in units of five

2. Each point is estimated using a five-year moving sample

3. X-axis indicates the starting year of each sample window

Source. CFPS 2010

How does China's experience compare with other countries? Hertz et al. (2008) find that the global average correlation between parents' and children's schooling held steady at about 0.4 for the 50 years before the global financial crisis (GFC) of 2007–08. Latin America had the highest transmission coefficient of 0.83, followed by Asia (0.69), sub-Saharan Africa (0.66), and Western Europe and the United States (0.52). The Eastern Bloc fared the best, having a transmission coefficient of 0.38. Large variations are evident within regions; for example, Azomahou and Yitbarek (2016) find that, among several sub-Saharan countries, Nigeria had the highest level of education inheritance, with its transmission coefficient reaching above 1.2 for people born around 1950, whereas

Ghana fared much better, with its transmission coefficient declining from 0.77 of the birth cohort of 1944–48 to 0.39 of the birth cohort of 1989–93. These findings, compared with this paper's findings about China, reveal that China did not fare badly even before 1949. The only region that outperformed China was the Eastern Bloc, which experienced communist revolutions. Similar to the Eastern Bloc, China's communist revolution also had a significant levelling effect, so that, by the time of the Cultural Revolution, education transmission declined to the same level. In the 40 years of the reform era, China has returned to the level of Western Europe and the United States, which is above the world average. As in many other social arenas, China resembles a typical country of market economy.

Rural–urban disparities

One of the most significant forms of inequality in China is the rural–urban divide. Urban per capita income reached 3.3 times that of rural per capita income before the GFC. There has been substantial decline in more recent years, but it was still 2.7 times greater in 2016. The educational gap between the city and countryside is also large. In breaking up the data from Figure 7.1 into urban and rural sub-samples, Figure 7.6 reveals a sharp contrast. The divide started with people born in the 1930s, but was narrowed for people born in the 1950s and early 1960s. Educational expansion in the Cultural Revolution lifted the educational achievements in cities and the countryside, but had a larger impact on the countryside. Divergence began, however, soon after college admission was resumed in 1977. More and more urban youths began to attend college and, when the 1985 birth cohort reached the age of higher education, more than half of urban youths attended college. In contrast, the figure was barely above 10 per cent in the countryside.[2] Yet the divergence did not stop at the higher end of education. Among the 1985 cohort, there was almost no urban resident who did not finish elementary school, but nearly 10 per cent of rural residents did not. Close to 80 per cent of the rural residents in the 1985 cohort did not have high school or higher levels of education, while 75 per cent of their urban counterparts did.

---

2   This contrast may be exaggerated, though, because many rural youths who have a college education stay in the city. The results would be neater if individuals could be categorised by their parents' Hukou (household registration system that identifies an individual as a rural or urban resident). Unfortunately, CFPS does not request this information.

Education trend: Rural

Education trend: Urban

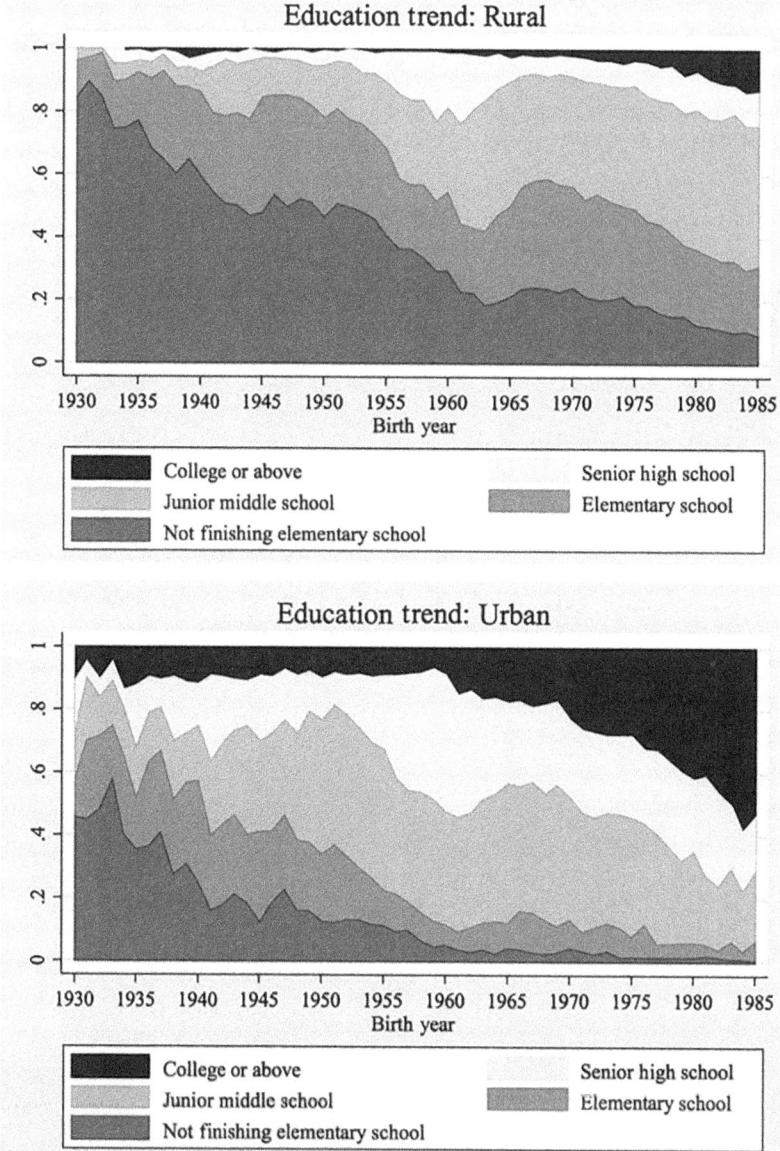

Figure 7.6. Education trend by Hukou

Source. CFPS 2010

Intergenerational transmission may have enlarged the rural–urban divide. Figure 7.7 presents the rural and urban transmission coefficients against the national coefficients. In the birth cohorts of the 1930s, urban and rural transmission coefficients were about the same size. For people born in the 1940s, however, the countryside had smaller coefficients than the city. Literacy programs were a central component of the CCP's modernisation drive, even before it controlled the whole country in 1949. Those programs had more significant effects in the countryside, and the birth cohorts of the 1940s benefited the most from them. As a result, their educational achievements diverged from their parents. Starting from the birth cohorts of the early 1950s, the transmission coefficient began to increase in both the countryside and the city, and the gap between the countryside and the city was not large. There is, however, one period that is worthy of attention. While the coefficient was generally larger in the countryside than in the city, the countryside had a smaller coefficient than the city for people born in the 1960s. Clearly, the broad effect of educational expansion in the Cultural Revolution was to break up intergenerational transmission in the countryside more than in the city, mostly because the countryside started from a much lower basis than the city.

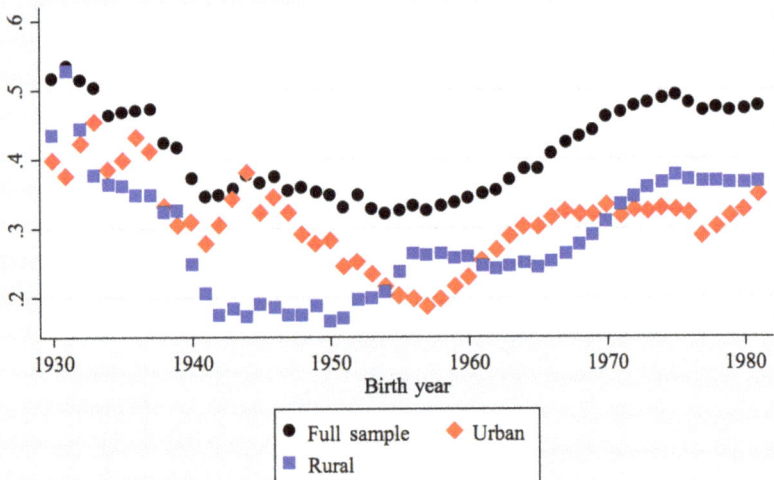

Figure 7.7. Transmission coefficient by Hukou

Note. 1. Education is measured in units of five

2. Each point is estimated using a five-year moving sample

3. X-axis indicates the starting year of each sample window

Source. CFPS 2010

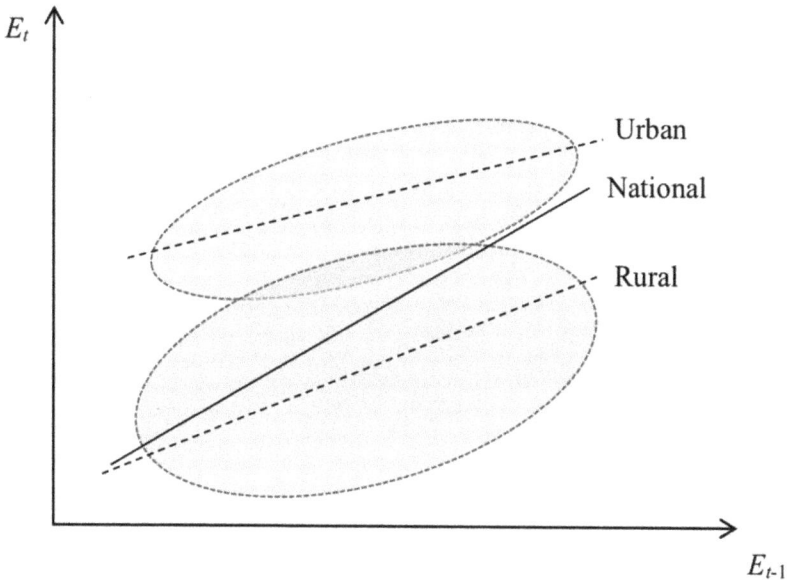

Figure 7.8. An illustration of decomposition
Source. Authors' illustration

Figure 7.7 also shows that the national transmission coefficients were much larger than those of either the countryside or the city. Because the gap between the city and the countryside was not large in most time periods, we have reason to believe that the higher national coefficients were a result of between-group variations of educational level. Figure 7.8 illustrates the idea. In the figure, the horizontal axis represents the highest educational achievement of parents (E_{t-1}), and the vertical axis is the highest educational achievement of children (E_t). The two shaded ovals indicate the urban and rural samples, respectively. To reflect the reality that urban educational levels were higher than rural educational levels, the urban sample is drawn to lie above the rural sample. The two dashed lines are the respective regression lines for the two samples. The slopes, which are the transmission coefficients for the city and the countryside, are not markedly different. The national transmission coefficient is the slope of the regression line for the two samples combined. Because the urban sample lies above the rural sample, the national regression line is steeper than either the rural or the urban regression line. In the Appendix, we develop a decomposition method to separate the national transmission coefficient into three parts: the contribution of urban transmission coefficient, the contribution of rural transmission coefficient, and the contribution of urban–rural educational gaps. The size of the first two components depends on the size of the respective transmission coefficient and the share of the sum of variations of the correlation between parents' and children's education in the urban and rural samples, and the size of the third component depends on the urban–rural gap of education and the urban–rural gap of transmission coefficient weighted by the share of the sum of variations of the correlation between parents' and children's education.

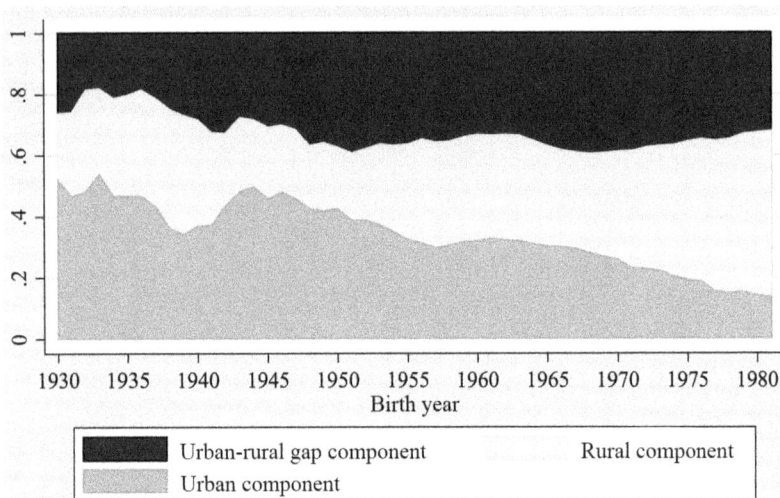

Figure 7.9. Decomposition of transmission coefficient

Note. 1. Education is measured in units of five

2. Each point is estimated using a five-year moving sample

3. X-axis indicates the starting year of each sample window

Source. CFPS 2010

Figure 7.9 presents the shares of contribution of the three components and shows three regularities. First, the contribution of the urban transmission coefficient declined over time, particularly since the cohort of 1945. Because the urban transmission coefficient increased for the more recent cohorts, this result is caused by the shrinking share of variations in the correlation between urban parents' and urban children's educational achievements in the national total variations. Second, the contribution of the rural transmission coefficient increased substantially since the 1950s. For the more recent cohorts, it became the largest contributor. Because the rural transmission coefficient was not substantially larger than the urban transmission coefficient, its larger contribution was created by its larger share of the variations of the correlation between parents' and children's educational achievements. Third, the contribution of the urban–rural gap of education experienced a U–shaped curve, with its lowest points located between the 1950 cohort and the 1965 cohort. This is a surprising result because the urban–rural divide declined the quickest for those cohorts. One explanation is that improvements in urban education were more dynamic and diverse than in rural education in this period of time, so the urban sample contributes a larger share of variation to the estimation. It is likely that the decline in the contribution of the urban–rural gap in more recent history probably was caused by the shrinking gap between the urban and rural transmission coefficients.

Conclusion

The twentieth century witnessed dramatic changes in Chinese society. Ending a long history of stagnation, the start of the century saw China begin a journey of social transformation that was greatly accelerated by the communist revolution. The first 30 years of the People's Republic marked Chinese society with equality. Most significantly, the rural educational level was dramatically raised and, as a result, intergenerational educational mobility increased. This process has reversed since 1978, when the CCP turned its focus to economic growth and spent less effort on social transformation. Improvements in rural education have been left behind and educational achievements no longer keep pace with urban areas. Consequently, intergenerational mobility has been dragged back.

Although the Chinese Government has increased fiscal spending on nine years of compulsory education, investment in high school and college education has been left largely to families. In the countryside, several reasons have contributed to a decline in families' investment in their children's education. First, the high demand for labour in coastal cities has raised the opportunity cost of education. With a middle school diploma, a rural youth can easily find a reasonably paid job at the coast. Second, good high schools are more concentrated in the city and out of the reach of rural youths. As a result, rural youths often end up attending third-tier universities, even if they finish high school. Third, China has a regressive tuition system in its higher education sector and lower quality universities charge higher tuition than better universities (e.g. the tuition of Peking University, which is 5,000 yuan per academic year, has not changed over the last 20 years, but some private universities in Beijing charge 40,000 yuan for an academic year). Rural youths thus have to face two disadvantages: poor quality university education and high tuition cost.

To prevent history from repeating itself, China must reintroduce some of the progressive programs that the government abandoned over the last 40 years. New measures include, but are not limited to, allocating more educational resources to the rural areas (including teacher subsidies), extending compulsory education to 12 years, and allowing elite universities to charge higher tuitions and sparing government finance to support ordinary universities/colleges. This requires that the government put social progress as one of its priorities. During 40 years of relentless economic growth, the Chinese Government and Chinese society have been pre-occupied by a single-minded belief in economic efficiency. Now that China is moving towards a more affluent society, it is time for the government to reintroduce social progress into its programs.

References

Azomahou, T & Yitbarek, E (2016). *Intergenerational education mobility in Africa: Has progress been inclusive?*, Policy Research Working Paper, No. 7843. Washington, DC: World Bank.

Hertz, T, Jayasundera, T, Piraino, P, Selcuk, S, Smith, N & Verashchagina, A (2008). 'The inheritance of educational inequality: International comparisons and fifty-year trends', *The B.E. Journal of Economic Analysis and Policy*, 7(2), 1775–75.

Liang, C, Lee, J, Zhang, H, Li, L, Ruan, D, Kang, W & Yang, S (2012). 'A silent revolution: Research on family backgrounds of students of Peking University and Soochow University (1952–2002)', *Social Sciences in China (Zhongguo Shehui Kexue)*, 1, 98–118.

Yao, Y & Cui, J (2015). 'Estimation of China's human capital stock', *Chinese Journal of Population Science (Zhongguo Renkou Kexue)*, 1, 70–78.

Yao, Y & You, W (2018). 'Women's political participation and gender gaps of education in China: 1950–1990', *World Development*, 106, 220–37.

Appendix

The regression is as follows:

$$y_i = \alpha + \beta x_i + u_i$$

So the OLS estimator is formulated as

$$\hat{\beta} = \frac{\sum_i (x_i - \overline{x}) y_i}{\sum_i (x_i - \overline{x})^2} = \frac{\sum_{i\in urban}(x_i - \overline{x}) y_i}{\sum_i (x_i - \overline{x})^2} + \frac{\sum_{i\in rural}(x_i - \overline{x}) y_i}{\sum_i (x_i - \overline{x})^2}$$

We further denote the means of x in urban and rural samples as x_u and x_r, and let $x_u = x_r + \delta$, where δ represents the urban–rural education gap. Meanwhile, we denote the total/urban/rural number of observations as $N/N_u/N_r$. So we have

$$\overline{x} = \overline{x}_u \frac{N_u}{N} + \overline{x}_r \frac{N_r}{N} = \overline{x}_u - \delta \frac{N_r}{N} = \overline{x}_r + \delta \frac{N_u}{N}$$

So

$$
\begin{aligned}
\hat{\beta} =& \frac{\sum_{i\in urban}(x_i - \overline{x}_u) y_i}{\sum_{i\in urban}(x_i - \overline{x}_u)^2} \frac{\sum_{i\in urban}(x_i - \overline{x}) y_i}{\sum_{i\in urban}(x_i - \overline{x}_u) y_i} \frac{\sum_{i\in urban}(x_i - \overline{x}_u)^2}{\sum_i (x_i - \overline{x})^2} \\
&+ \frac{\sum_{i\in rural}(x_i - \overline{x}_r) y_i}{\sum_{i\in rural}(x_i - \overline{x}_r)^2} \frac{\sum_{i\in rural}(x_i - \overline{x}) y_i}{\sum_{i\in rural}(x_i - \overline{x}_r) y_i} \frac{\sum_{i\in rural}(x_i - \overline{x}_r)^2}{\sum_i (x_i - \overline{x})^2} \\
=& \hat{\beta}_u \frac{\sum_{i\in urban}(x_i - \overline{x}) y_i}{\sum_{i\in urban}(x_i - \overline{x}_u) y_i} \frac{\sum_{i\in urban}(x_i - \overline{x}_u)^2}{\sum_i (x_i - \overline{x})^2} \\
&+ \hat{\beta}_r \frac{\sum_{i\in rural}(x_i - \overline{x}) y_i}{\sum_{i\in rural}(x_i - \overline{x}_r) y_i} \frac{\sum_{i\in rural}(x_i - \overline{x}_r)^2}{\sum_i (x_i - \overline{x})^2} \\
=& \hat{\beta}_u \frac{\sum_{i\in urban}(x_i - \overline{x}_u + \delta\frac{N_r}{N}) y_i}{\sum_{i\in urban}(x_i - \overline{x}_u) y_i} \frac{\sum_{i\in urban}(x_i - \overline{x}_u)^2}{\sum_i (x_i - \overline{x})^2} \\
&+ \hat{\beta}_r \frac{\sum_{i\in rural}(x_i - \overline{x}_r - \delta\frac{N_u}{N}) y_i}{\sum_{i\in rural}(x_i - \overline{x}_r) y_i} \frac{\sum_{i\in rural}(x_i - \overline{x}_r)^2}{\sum_i (x_i - \overline{x})^2} \\
=& \hat{\beta}_u [1 + \delta\frac{N_r}{N} \frac{\sum_{i\in urban} y_i}{\sum_{i\in urban}(x_i - \overline{x}_u) y_i}] \frac{\sum_{i\in urban}(x_i - \overline{x}_u)^2}{\sum_i (x_i - \overline{x})^2} \\
&+ \hat{\beta}_r [1 - \delta\frac{N_u}{N} \frac{\sum_{i\in rural} y_i}{\sum_{i\in rural}(x_i - \overline{x}_r) y_i}] \frac{\sum_{i\in rural}(x_i - \overline{x}_r)^2}{\sum_i (x_i - \overline{x})^2} \\
=& \hat{\beta}_u [1 + \delta\frac{N_r}{N} \frac{\sum_{i\in urban} y_i}{\sum_{i\in urban}(x_i - \overline{x}_u) y_i}] \frac{SST_{x,u}}{SST_x} \\
&+ \hat{\beta}_r [1 - \delta\frac{N_u}{N} \frac{\sum_{i\in rural} y_i}{\sum_{i\in rural}(x_i - \overline{x}_r) y_i}] \frac{SST_{x,r}}{SST_x}
\end{aligned}
$$

Rearranging the equation, we shall have

$$\hat{\beta} = \hat{\beta}_u \frac{SST_{x,u}}{SST_x} + \hat{\beta}_r \frac{SST_{x,r}}{SST_x}$$
$$+ \delta[\hat{\beta}_u \frac{N_r}{N} \frac{\sum_{i \in urban} y_i}{\sum_{i \in urban}(x_i - \overline{x}_u)y_i} \frac{SST_{x,u}}{SST_x} - \hat{\beta}_r \frac{N_u}{N} \frac{\sum_{i \in rural} y_i}{\sum_{i \in rural}(x_i - \overline{x}_r)y_i} \frac{SST_{x,r}}{SST_x}]$$

where $\frac{SST_{x,r}}{SST_x} = \frac{\sum_{i \in rural}(x_i - \overline{x}_r)^2}{\sum_i(x_i - \overline{x})^2}$. And in the graphs, we denote $\hat{\beta}_u \frac{SST_{x,u}}{SST_x}$ as the urban component, $\hat{\beta}_r \frac{SST_{x,r}}{SST_x}$ as the rural component and the remaining as the urban–rural gap component.

8

INEQUALITY AND INTERGENERATIONAL MOBILITY IN INDIA

Himanshu

Introduction

Given the large number of India's poor, the focus of policy and academic debates has largely been on poverty reduction. Discussions on inequality have been rather muted. But another reason has also been the lack of good quality data measuring inequality and, more so, on the impact of inequality on growth, mobility and human development. Nonetheless, recent years have seen a rise in interest in measuring inequality and how it affects social and economic outcomes (Sen & Himanshu 2004; Subramanian & Jayaraj 2006; Himanshu 2007, 2015; Sarkar & Mehta 2010; Chancel & Piketty 2017; Mazumdar et al. 2017). While there is no data after 2012, analysis of trends based on income, consumption and assets suggests that inequality is high in India when compared to other countries with a similar level of economic development. This has now been confirmed economically, considering aspects of income, consumption and assets, but also human development, such as education, health and nutrition. The human development indicators reveal that India suffers from the twin problem of high levels of deprivation and low achievement on most indicators, but also from inequalities of access and achievement. More worrying than this are the trends over time that suggest a secular rise in inequality in almost all dimensions, with only some moderation in the most recent period. These inequalities are now clearly established and no longer a matter of debate.

The analysis also suggests that the rise in inequality coincides with the beginning of the economic reform period that occurred from 1991. Unlike the 1980s, which saw growth accelerate in the economy along with declining inequality, in the period after 2004–05 inequalities grew more slowly, but continued to rise. Incidentally, the period after 2004–05 also saw the fastest decline in poverty in the last three decades. While a more full analysis of the reasons for changes in inequality is beyond the scope of this paper, preliminary analysis suggests that the role of a sectoral pattern of growth, the changing nature of employment and workforce structure and rising unemployment have contributed to a worsening of income distribution. Poor working conditions, low wages and lack of job creation have been a feature of the Indian economy for the last three decades, but these trends have intensified in the last decade. The fact that this period of 'jobless growth' coincided with the period of fastest economic growth raises further questions on the nature of growth but also on inequality of outcome and opportunity. Moreover, there are concerns that employment quality has deteriorated in existing jobs, with a majority having been generated either in the unorganised[1] sector or as informal jobs in the organised sector. With the rise of the unorganised sector and informal work, harsh working conditions without adequate pay or social security are being normalised.

On the other hand, increasing instances of crony capitalism obtaining a rising share of profits and squeezes in wage share have unambiguously contributed to increasing inequality. The mechanism of capital benefiting from a disproportionately large share of growth at the cost of labour is similar to the mechanism Piketty (2014) refers to in the case of developed countries during the same period. While the Indian Government's pro-poor initiatives have contributed to a faster reduction in poverty, they have also contributed to a moderation of the inequality increase.

The rise in inequality needs to be analysed not just in terms of its impact on future economic growth and distribution but also in terms of social and political stability in a country, like India, where horizontal inequalities

---

1   Unorganised sector enterprises are tiny enterprises with less than 10 workers or enterprises that lack electricity and employ less than 20 workers.

based on caste, class, religion, race, gender and location prevail.[2] Much of the discussion on inequality in India has, however, centred on economic inequality, with little focus on aspects of horizontal inequalities. Horizontal inequalities are embedded in social and political structures and affect citizens' access to basic services. Inequality in India is as much about rising income inequality as it is about inequality in education, health, nutrition, sanitation and opportunities. Although difficult to quantify, available evidence suggests a similar rise in inequality in these areas. The burden of these disparities is not borne uniformly across groups or generations. Historically marginalised groups such as Dalits (scheduled castes[3]), tribal groups (scheduled tribes[4]) and Muslims are disadvantaged in access to wealth and employment opportunities but also in access to basic services, which leads to lower levels of health, nutrition and education. Even within these disadvantaged groups, patriarchal norms and social structures have led to women being further excluded from access to basic services. Women also suffer from intra-household discrimination and discrimination in the labour market and opportunities to pursue a livelihood. The existence of wage gaps and the low female workforce participation rate is a known feature of the Indian economy. These aspects worsened during 2004–11, when the economy grew at its highest rate but a decline in female workforce participation was also recorded.

Changes in the labour market and persistent horizontal inequality also affect future mobility of individuals and households by denying them access to basic skills and opportunities. The purpose of this paper is to document and analyse the trends in inequality in India, particularly in the last three decades. The paper also seeks to understand the role of inequality in relation to mobility of households and individuals. I begin by examining the trend in inequality in India in recent decades using standard indicators of income, consumption and assets, where available. I also include dimensions of inequality from village surveys. The next

---

2   Stewart (2002) defines horizontal inequalities as inequalities arising out of an individual's social position based on caste, race and gender.
3   Scheduled castes are the lowest group in the caste hierarchy. Previously described as untouchables, they have been victims of discrimination over centuries. Apart from untouchability, they have systematically been denied access to equal education and employment opportunities. The introduction of the post-independence reservation system improved these circumstances as it demands access to public education and employment proportional to the scheduled caste population.
4   Scheduled tribes are groups notified by the constitution. Historically excluded from mainstream society, they have also been disadvantaged in terms of access to education and employment. Similar to the scheduled castes, they are also beneficiaries of reservation in public education and employment proportional to their population share.

section examines some of the reasons for the changing nature of inequality in India. I go on to consider the impact of inequality on mobility, using available secondary evidence and analysis of mobility using Palanpur surveys, which are perhaps the only longitudinal surveys (covering seven decades) with detailed information on individuals and households in a north Indian village. The paper concludes by presenting some issues for further research.

Inequality in India

Inequality in India has generally been analysed using consumption expenditure data. As is well-known, these underestimate the extent of inequality in the economy. Because these have been available since independence, however, they continue to be the major data source for tracking inequality over time. The information on income inequality is supplemented here with income surveys undertaken by the Indian Human Development Survey (IHDS), which are collected by the National Council of Applied Economic Research (NCAER) and University of Maryland and were conducted in 2005 and 2012 to provide information on consumption as well as income. While the IHDS surveys are only available for two time periods, they offer hitherto unavailable insight into income inequality. These suggest a higher level of inequality than previously assumed but also show a trend in inequality that is similar to that revealed by the consumption surveys. The data on wealth inequality, although not strictly comparable to income or consumption surveys, also supplement the information on inequality at the national level. We use the nationally available National Sample Survey Office (NSSO) surveys on debt and assets to compute measures of asset inequality. The data on taxes and top incomes made available by the World Inequality Database are useful indicators of income inequality at the top level of income distribution and highlight the extreme nature of that inequality. Finally, village surveys are used to examine the nature of inequality at the micro level. Despite issues of comparability and lack of data over time, these also confirm the high level of inequality in India. Not surprisingly, all the data sources broadly confirm the fact that inequality in India has been high during the last two decades, and continues to rise further, at a time when the economy has also been growing at its highest rate.

Consumption inequality

The most accepted measure of inequality in India is based on the consumption expenditure surveys of the NSSO. Available since the 1950s, these have been the primary source for tracking inequality in the country. The data is considered to be a reliable source to study changes in the level of and trends in poverty, inequality and wellbeing. Although these are available for smaller annual rounds, the quinquennial surveys, which are based on a large sample size, have been used to analyse the trend in consumption inequality.

Table 8.1 provides estimates of measures of inequality from the NSSO consumption surveys. Inequality as measured by the Gini of consumption expenditure has seen a rising trend since 1993–94. Other measures of inequality confirm this finding. For example, the ratio of average consumption expenditure of the urban top 10 per cent to the rural bottom 10 per cent was stable between 1983 and 1993–94 but has since then increased.[5]

Consumption inequality as measured by Gini coefficient is shown in Figure 8.1. The all-India consumption Gini coefficient has increased from 0.3 in 1983 to 0.36 in 2011–12. While the rural Gini has seen a modest increase from 0.27 in 1983 to 0.29 in 2011–12, it is the urban Gini that is driving overall inequality. The urban Gini has seen a rapid rise from 0.31 in 1983 to 0.38 in 2011–12. However, the two periods of growth acceleration, first in the 1980s and then after 1991, show contrasting trends. The acceleration in growth rate in the 1980s was accompanied by stagnant inequality and a decline in rural inequality. This trend reversed after 1993–94, however, following the introduction of economic reforms in 1991. The rise in inequality was seen in rural and urban areas and, while this moderated after 2004–05, it continued to show a rising trend, except for a marginal decline in the case of urban areas between 2009–10 and 2011–12.

---

5   An analysis of decile-wise monthly per capita expenditure (MPCE) growth and share of each decile shows that only the top 10 per cent has increased its share in consumption expenditure in the last three rounds. The share of the bottom 90 per cent has gone down over the years. The top 1 per cent now has a share of around 9 per cent in the total consumption expenditure.

Table 8.1. Estimates of consumption inequality from NSSO consumption surveys

	1983	1993–94	2004–05	2009–10	2011–12
Share of various groups in total national consumption expenditure					
Bottom 20%	9.0	9.2	8.5	8.2	8.1
Bottom 40%	22.2	22.3	20.3	19.9	19.6
Top 20%	39.1	39.7	43.9	44.8	44.7
Top 10%	24.7	25.4	29.2	30.1	29.9
Ratio of average consumption of various groups					
Urban top 10% / Rural bottom 10%	9.53	9.43	12.74	13.86	13.98
Urban top 10% / Urban bottom 10%	6.96	7.14	9.14	10.11	10.06
Urban top 10% / Rural bottom 40%	6.47	6.84	9.40	10.11	10.16
Gini of consumption expenditure					
Rural Gini	27.1	25.8	28.1	28.4	28.7
Urban Gini	31.4	31.9	36.4	38.1	37.7
All India Gini	29.8	30.0	34.7	35.8	35.9

Note. All estimates are based on mixed recall period (MRP) estimates of consumption expenditure.

Source. Author's computation from NSSO unit-level data

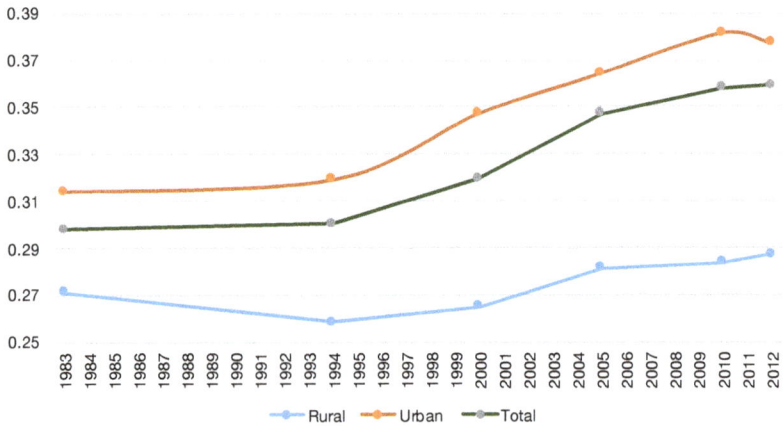

Figure 8.1. Gini coefficient of consumption expenditure (NSSO)

Note. All estimates are based on MRP estimates of consumption expenditure.

Source. Author's computation from NSSO unit-level data

The analysis of the growth incidence curve using monthly per capita expenditure (MPCE) figures confirms the steep rise in inequality after 1993–94. Figure 8.2.1 and Figure 8.2.2 present the growth incidence curve using real MPCE by deciles adjusted for inflation using Consumer Price Index for Agricultural Labourers (CPI AL) for rural areas and Consumer Price Index for Industrial Workers (CPI IW) for urban.[6] While urban MPCE growth outpaced rural MPCE growth, it was the upper deciles of MPCE within rural and urban areas that saw faster growth after 1991 as against the 1980s, when lower deciles saw faster growth.

The growth incidence curves confirm that it was the higher growth during the period of bottom deciles that contributed to a decline in overall inequality during the 1980s. This was true for both rural and urban areas, which saw higher growth of consumption expenditure among the lower deciles compared to the richer deciles in the 1980s. But we see a reversal of the trend after 1993–94, with lower consumption deciles growing slower than the richer deciles. This trend has continued after 2004–05 with a higher rate of growth of consumption across all deciles consistent with the high growth of economy achieved during this period.

Figure 8.3 presents the index of MPCE by rural and urban population groups. While there is not much divergence in the MPCE of various population groups between 1983 and 1994, the gap between various groups starts increasing after 1993–94. Between 1983 and 2012, while the urban bottom 40 per cent witnessed an increase of real MPCE by 51 per cent, the urban top 20 per cent witnessed an increase of 98 per cent. This confirms a faster rise in inequality in urban areas compared to rural areas.

6   The overall real MPCE grew at the rate of 1.72 per cent per annum in rural areas between 1983 to 1993–94 and an almost similar rate of growth at 1.74 per cent per annum occurred in the urban areas. However, the growth rate of urban MPCE was higher in both 1993–94 to 2004–05 and 2004–05 to 2011–12. The growth rate of rural MPCE was 1.28 per cent between 1993–94 and 2004–05 and increased to 4.08 per cent per year between 2004–05 and 2011–12. The corresponding growth rates for urban areas were 1.51 per cent and 4.62 per cent per year.

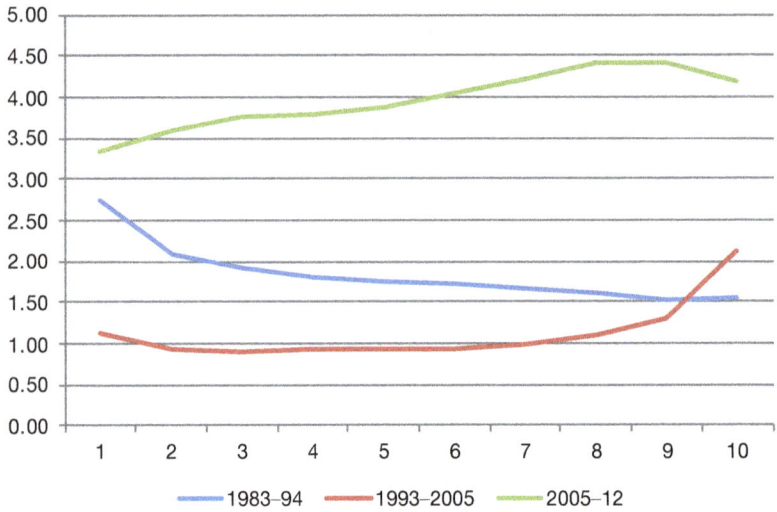

Figure 8.2.1. Growth rate of real MPCE by MPCE deciles (rural)

Note. All estimates are based on MRP estimates of consumption expenditure.

Source. Author's computation from NSSO unit-level data

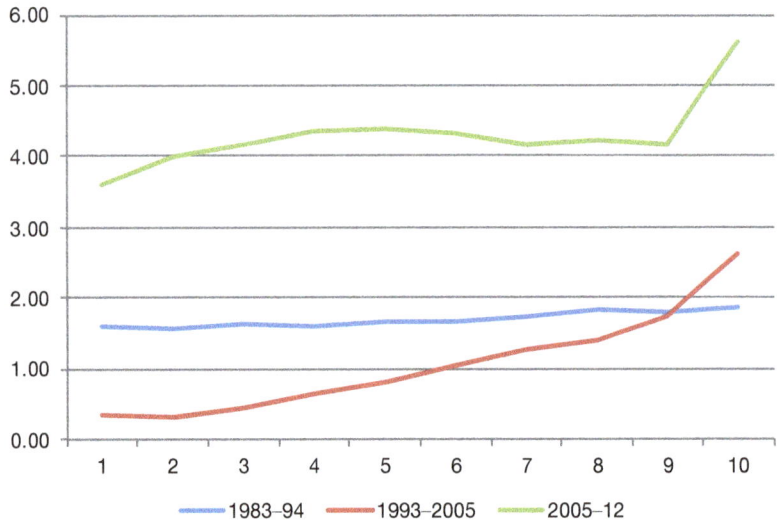

Figure 8.2.2. Growth rate of real MPCE by MPCE deciles (urban)

Note. All estimates are based on MRP estimates of consumption expenditure.

Source. Author's computation from NSSO unit-level data

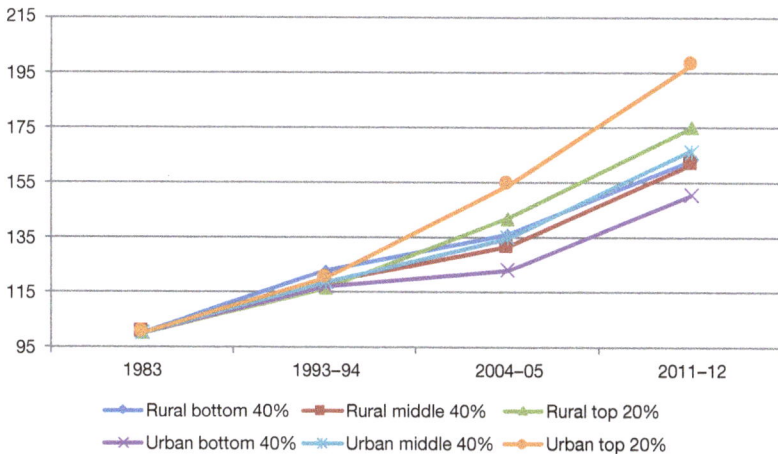

Figure 8.3. Index of MPCE by groups (1983=100)
Note. All estimates are based on MRP estimates of consumption expenditure.
Source. Author's computation from NSSO unit-level data

The pattern of growth across deciles is largely a reflection of the occupational profile of the households in each decile. Vulnerable categories of households, such as agricultural and other labouring households, have seen a lower increase in consumption expenditure than those in regular employment. Casual labour households in urban areas have also witnessed lower increases than the overall increase in consumption expenditure. One way to analyse these is to look at the ratio of consumption expenditure of these households compared to overall consumption expenditure. Table 8.2 presents these ratios for 1993–94, 2004–05, 2009–10 and 2011–12.

Table 8.2. Ratio of average MPCE of some occupation groups to average MPCE of all population

	Rural		Urban	
	AL/All	OL/All	CAS/All	CAS/REG
1993–94	0.78	0.95	0.61	0.54
2004–05	0.75	0.93	0.54	0.47
2009–10	0.77	0.91	0.54	0.46
2011–12	0.78	0.85	0.57	0.48

Note. AL – agricultural labour, OL – other labour, CAS – casual labour, REG – regular workers.
Source. Author's computation from NSSO unit-level data

Although improvement in the ratio of MPCE of agricultural labour households compared to all households is evident after 2004–05, it has worsened for other labour households. While average MPCE of other labour households was 95 per cent of all households' MPCE in 1993–94, this ratio was down to 85 per cent in 2011–12. Similarly, in urban areas, MPCE of casual labour households was 61 per cent of all households' MPCE but declined to only 54 per cent by 2009–10, although it improved marginally to 57 per cent in 2011–12. Also, MPCE of regular worker households has increased faster than MPCE of casual labour households in urban areas as reflected by the ratio of MPCE of casual to regular workers households.

Income inequality

Even though the consumption inequality estimates suggest a rising trend, there is a general belief that the level of inequality in India is low by international standards.[7] Part of the reason for such an understanding is due to the fact that inequality in India is usually measured on consumption expenditure, which is not comparable to inequality in most countries where it is measured on income dimension. While there is no one-to-one correspondence between income and consumption inequality, evidence across countries suggests that consumption inequality is in general lower than income inequality. This is largely because consumption as measured in India by the NSSO tends to underestimate the consumption of the wealthy, but it is also because consumption is a smoothed measure unlike income.[8] On comparable measures of consumption inequality, however, inequality in India is not low.

While there is comparable data over a long period of time on consumption distribution in India, there are a limited number of sources available as far as income inequality estimates are concerned. Those that are available are privately collected data sources and lack official estimates of income inequality. There is now, however, some information available from IHDS

---

7   According to the World Bank's world poverty and inequality databases, the consumption Gini for India was 33.4 for 2004–05 whereas comparative Gini coefficients for selected countries were: Brazil (56.9), China (42.5), Malaysia (37.9), Mexico (46.05), Russia (40.8), South Africa (67.4 in 2006), United Kingdom (37.6), United States (40.6) and Vietnam (36.8).
8   Li, Squire and Zhou (1998) find that consumption inequalities are systematically lower compared to income inequality. Although they suggest that the gap between income and consumption inequality is around 6.6 Gini points, evidence from India on this count suggests that this gap may be anywhere close to 15 points.

surveys that has been used to study inequality in household incomes. The Gini coefficient for household income in India, based on IHDS data, also shows an increase in inequality from 0.54 in 2004–05 to 0.55 in 2011–12. Figure 8.4 presents the Gini coefficient by sector. However, unlike trends reported in the case of consumption and assets, IHDS reports higher inequality in rural areas compared to urban areas although both show a rise in inequality between the two surveys. The income Gini of 0.55 in 2011–12 puts India alongside the most unequal countries in the world. While the level of inequality in itself is worrying, the fact that it has increased since the previous period is more so.

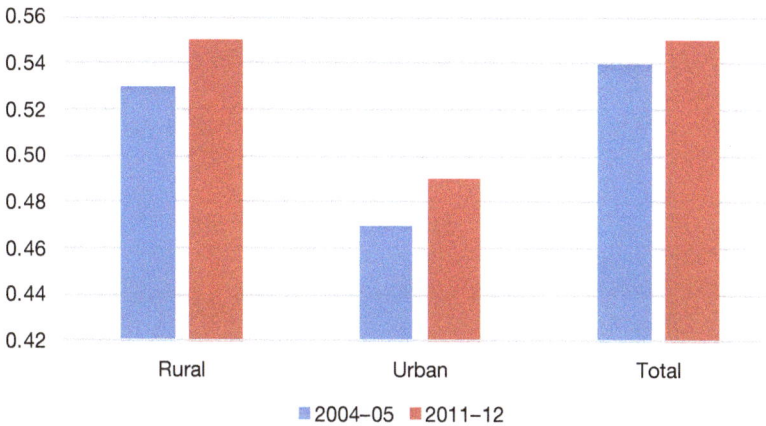

Figure 8.4. Income inequality (IHDS)
Source. Author's computation from IHDS unit data

Despite the fact that the IHDS is the only source of information on income inequality, its use is limited partly because of the longitudinal nature of data with a base of 2004–05. There are concerns that 2011–12 income inequality estimates from IHDS may not be the true income inequality measure for the country as a whole.[9] There are also valid concerns on the quality of income data, particularly variation across states and across sectors over time.

---

9   Since IHDS-2 uses a panel of households with the sampling frame of IHDS-1, there are concerns that it may not be a representative sample for the country in 2011–12. Such concerns are usual with panel data.

Asset inequality

Another dimension of inequality that has increased in recent decades is inequality in assets. These decadal data are available from the All-India Debt and Investment Survey (AIDIS) of the NSSO and are based on a large sample survey of household assets such as land, buildings, agricultural machinery, vehicles; and financial assets such as shares, debentures, and amounts outstanding. AIDIS also collects information on household debt, credit agencies and terms of debt. The survey provides information on physical quantities of assets and their present value in monetary terms. While the AIDIS gives a reasonable estimate of household wealth, it does not have information on corporate wealth. Equally, self-reported surveys are known to contain underestimates in valuations of household wealth in the form of land, buildings and jewellery. Therefore, the extent of inequality based on AIDIS data is, at best, at the lower scale of wealth inequality.

The AIDIS surveys were conducted in the 48th round (1991), 59th round (2002) and 70th round (2012) of the NSSO surveys. While the basic AIDIS questionnaire has remained the same, some changes have been made over the years. The 1991 surveys did not carry a question on household religion nor did they have the other backward class (OBC) category for social group. In the 70th round, the AIDIS survey did not collect information on household durables. To compare total wealth, the value of durables for 1991 and 2002 has been excluded. Another problem is the lack of suitable deflators for inter-temporal comparison. Despite these obvious limitations, the AIDIS data provides evidence of extremely high levels of wealth inequality and a deterioration of wealth distribution over the years.

The fact that wealth inequality estimates tend to be higher than consumption and income inequality is well known. This has also been confirmed in the case of India by earlier studies on wealth inequality (Vaidyanathan 1993; Subramanian & Jayaraj 2006; and Jayadev et al. 2007). Subramanian and Jayaraj (2006) and Jayadev et al. (2007) analysed wealth inequality disaggregated by caste, occupation and states and highlighted the large discrepancy in wealth-holding across caste groups, occupational groups and across states. The level of wealth per capita was found to be similar to the hierarchy of the caste structure and occupational groups. Recent evidence based on the 2012 round of AIDIS by Anand and Thampi (2016) and Sarma et al. (2017) confirms the trend observed in the case of consumption and income inequality. Inequality based on assets has not only increased since 1991 but it has also been accompanied by increasing divergence in assets held by disadvantaged groups such as Dalits, tribal groups and Muslims. Analysis by Credit Suisse as part of its Global Wealth Report (GWR) (2017), which provides annual estimates of wealth inequality for a number of countries, also confirms the finding of a rapid rise in wealth inequality in the last two decades.[10]

Table 8.3 presents the share of wealth held by each decile. The bottom 50 per cent of the population held 9 per cent of total assets in the country in 1991, but that share has declined by one third to only 5.3 per cent by 2012. As against this, the share of wealth held by the top 1 per cent has increased from 17 per cent in 1991 to 28 per cent by 2012. The top 10 per cent held more than 50 per cent of the wealth in all the survey years reported here, with the share rising from 51 per cent in 1991 to 63 per cent in 2012. Since estimates from the AIDIS exclude information on bullion and durables, the share of wealth held by the top 1 per cent and top 10 per cent is likely to be higher. Also, without data on corporate wealth, in all likelihood the share of the top 1 per cent is underestimated

Table 8.3. Decile-wise wealth share

Wealth decile	Percentage share of total wealth		
	1991	2002	2012
1	0.16	0.06	0.03
2	0.85	0.60	0.41
3	1.66	1.32	0.92
4	2.59	2.15	1.56
5	3.75	3.22	2.41
6	5.24	4.67	3.58
7	7.25	6.75	5.31
8	10.41	10.21	8.29
9	16.48	17.15	14.97
10	51.61	53.87	62.52
Top 1%	16.94	17.06	27.60

Source. Author's computation from AIDIS unit data

10 The annual Global Wealth Report bases its wealth data for India on the AIDIS survey but is further refined using regression techniques to fill the gap for intervening years. It also uses external data to rescale the wealth estimates.

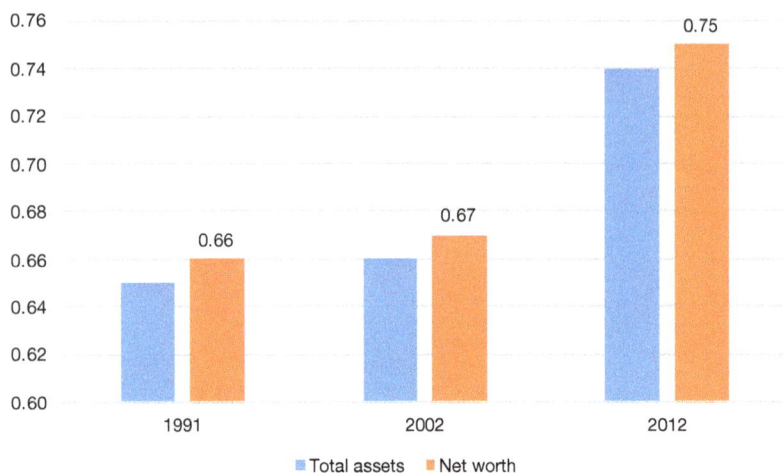

Figure 8.5. Gini coefficient of wealth (AIDIS)
Source. Author's computation from AIDIS unit data

The Gini wealth coefficients are presented in Figure 8.5. These are not only higher than the corresponding estimates of inequality based on income or consumption but also show an increase in the last two decades. While the increase was marginal in the 1990s, it has increased sharply in the last decade. Figure 8.5 also shows that, accounting for debt, net worth inequality is higher than asset inequality. Wealth inequality is in fact similar to estimates of inequality of land holding. Rawal (2008) reports the Gini of land ownership at 0.76 in 2003.

The 2017 GWR measures the Gini coefficient of wealth inequality in India at 0.83. The GWR's corresponding estimate of Gini for wealth in 2011 reports it at 0.804, which suggests an increase by 0.3 percentage points in the next six years. According to the GWR, the bottom 50 per cent of the Indian population held 8.1 per cent of total wealth in 2002, and this declined to 4.2 per cent by 2012. In contrast, the top 1 per cent of the population held 15.7 per cent of total wealth in 2002, and this increased to 25.7 per cent of total wealth by 2012. Among the countries for which GWR gives figures, only the top 1 per cent in Indonesia and the United States have a higher wealth share than India.

Micro-level income inequality

While aggregate inequality estimates are useful in tracking trends in income distribution, they mask regional-level variation. This is particularly so for village-level inequality, which is an important source of data, particularly for the rural economy. Wherever available, this data suffers from problems of comparability across villages and over time. While few surveys have time series longitudinal data spanning decades, the estimates available from village surveys for recent years confirm that the level of inequality at village level is also high. Most village surveys report estimates of inequality based on detailed calculation of income and, despite the methodological differences, suggest a high level of inequality consistent with other sources of information. Estimates of inequality in more recent village studies by the Foundation for Agrarian Studies (FAS) between 2005–08 show Gini coefficients ranging between 0.5 to 0.7 (Rawal & Swaminathan 2011). FAS arrived at these estimates from data collected as part of the Project on Agrarian Relations in India (PARI) and report Gini for eight villages, three from Andhra Pradesh, two each from Uttar Pradesh and Maharashtra and one from Rajasthan. This range provides a general snapshot of villages based in different agro-climatic zones of the country and the results show an extreme concentration of wealth in the top decile. The share of the top income decile for per capita income from pooled data of all villages is reported as 48.06 per cent.

Swaminathan and Rawal (2011) also report a tendency for inequality to be higher among villages with higher per capita income (with the exception of two villages from Maharashtra). They also report the presence of negative income, primarily owing to losses in crop production. In an analysis of income by caste, the authors point to the absence of Dalit households from the top income quintile in all villages but one, and an over-representation in bottom quintiles. Despite the large variation in income inequality reported by most of the village surveys, there is some consensus that inequality has risen, rather than diminished, over time.[11]

---

11 Despite the wealth of information available across states and over time, these village surveys are not utilised as measures of inequality because of the inherent difficulty in comparability across village surveys. The variation is partly due to the difference in time period covered and the local context, but also the methodology used, with each survey having its own methodology of estimation of incomes. This is further compounded by the fact that most of the village surveys are based largely on agricultural incomes. On the other hand, very few have non-agricultural incomes included to the extent that secondary sources suggest may be relevant. For recent changes in income distribution through village surveys, see, Himanshu, Joshi & Lanjouw (2016).

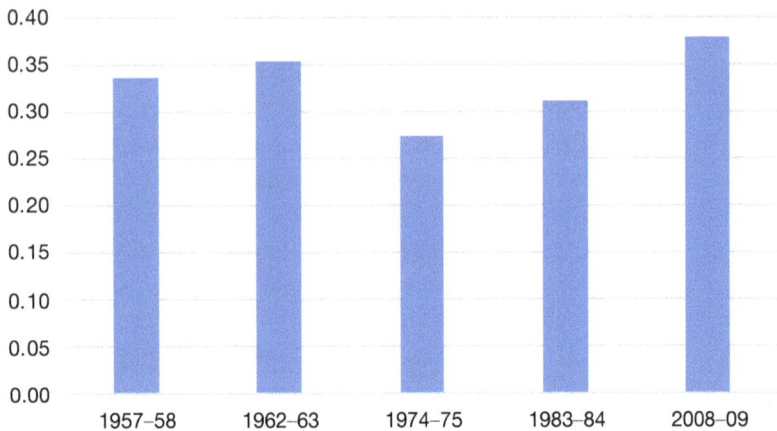

Figure 8.6. Inequality in Palanpur
Source. Himanshu, Joshi & Lanjouw (2016)

While estimates of inequality reported by village surveys are similar to those reported by large-scale surveys, they are slightly higher than estimates reported by national surveys. Similar to national surveys, however, most longitudinal village surveys that have tracked inequality in villages over time report an increase in inequality in recent decades. Swaminathan (1988) reports a rise in inequality in Gokilapuram (Tamil Nadu) from 0.77 in 1977 to 0.81 in 1985. Among the major longitudinal village surveys, Palanpur, a village in the north Indian state of Uttar Pradesh has been surveyed once in each decade, beginning in 1957–58. Figure 8.6 shows the reported Gini coefficient for incomes over the survey years for Palanpur. While inequality declined until 1974–75, which is similar to the national trend, the village has seen a steady rise in inequality since then, reaching the highest level in 2008–09. Between 1983–94 and 2008–09, inequality has increased despite a fall in poverty.

The broad picture emerging from secondary and primary surveys confirms not only that income inequality is high in India, but also that inequality during the last three decades has risen. While the evidence presented here suggests a trend of rising inequality in income and assets, inequality in terms of human development outcomes also suggests a widening of these disparities.

Inequality in income/consumption and assets are as much a measure of inequality of opportunity as they are outcomes of economic processes. These are further compounded, however, by other inequalities that have a role in shaping inequality of opportunity. Individual/household mobility is also stimulated by access to education and healthcare. These in turn are also determined by an individual's/household's position in the social hierarchy. When access to opportunities is shaped by an individual's place of birth, caste, community, religion and gender, the social structure is more critical than access to assets and income because social inequality leads to marginalisation, exclusion and disadvantage. This inequality can be mediated by political and economic institutions, but also by the government, which has a democratic mandate to provide equal opportunities to all.

What explains rising inequality in recent decades?

The rise in inequality over recent decades has been among the fastest in the seven decades since independence, however, it has not attracted policy attention. This is partly because of the belief that increasing inequality is a necessary by-product of growth.[12] But, in India's case, the two phases of growth acceleration, first in the 1980s and then again in the decade after 2004–05, do not justify that assumption. Most indicators suggest that the growth acceleration in the 1980s was accompanied by declining or stable inequality. The trends after the 1990s, however, suggest that the period after the economic reforms of 1991 has unambiguously led to increased inequality in multiple dimensions. Accelerated growth after 2004–05 has been accompanied by a moderate rise in inequality and more rapid reduction in poverty than earlier periods. Based on the trends reported above, there is evidence of three phases of inequality. The 1980s was a period of reduced inequality followed by a sharp rise in the 1990s following the economic reforms. This increase was moderated in the third phase after 2004–05.

---

12   This has some justification in the Kuznets curve argument that posits rising inequality as a result of rapid growth driven by growth in the industrial sector. Inequality reduces when growth broadens to encompass rural areas.

Sectoral pattern of growth

Income distribution outcomes are strongly linked to outcomes in the labour market and the sectoral pattern of growth. The 1980s were a period of accelerated growth led by growth in non-farm and agricultural sectors. This growth rate from 1970 to 1980 of 1.5 per cent compares unfavourably with the 3.4 per cent growth recorded in the 1980s. Figure 8.7 presents the agricultural and non-agricultural growth rate since the 1980s. The post-1991 acceleration was led by growth in the non-agricultural sector, with secular rise in non-farm growth rates. Agricultural growth rates, however, which were rising in the 1980s, declined at the beginning of the 1990s and only showed a trend to increase after 2004–05. Both periods of agricultural growth were accompanied by a decline in inequality as against the 1990s, which witnessed rising inequality. Agricultural growth leads to better returns to farmers, who are among the poorest in society, but it also contributes to rising wages for the casual workers.

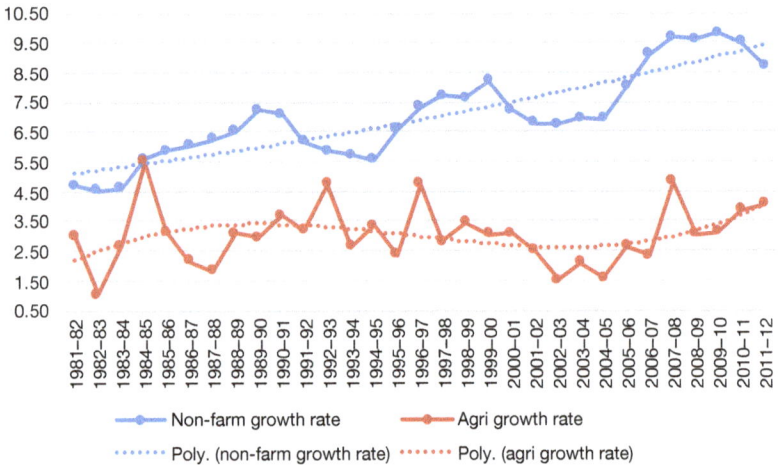

Figure 8.7. Growth rate in the agricultural and non-agricultural sectors (constant 2004–05 prices)
Source. National Accounts of India

While sectoral distribution of growth matters, inequality is also determined by the distribution of the benefits of growth among the various factors of production. As mentioned earlier, agricultural growth contributed to rising rural incomes and wage rises. But it also contributed to an increase in the pace of non-farm diversification. The 1980s witnessed the first wave of non-farm diversification in rural areas, with employment in the non-farm sector rising faster than the agricultural sector. Non-farm diversification was also a result of increased public spending, which contributed to the bottom deciles benefiting from access to non-farm jobs.

The trend of declining inequality was reversed, however, after the economic reform of 1991. The decline in subsidies and opening up of the economy affected job creation but also affected growth in the agricultural sector. The crisis in agriculture during 1997–2003, when growth decelerated to less than the rate of population growth affected a majority of the rural population. The agricultural sector also suffered from an increase in suicides by farmers as a result of economic changes. The period between 1991 and 2004–05 was clearly a period of rising inequality, including interpersonal and regional inequality.

Inequality and labour market outcomes

Policy and academic discourse has been concerned for some time at India's lack of job creation, even when the economy has been growing relatively rapidly (Figure 8.8). This has been a feature of economic growth since the 1990s, but has been accentuated since 2004–05, with job growth virtually collapsing. While almost 10 million working-age people enter the labour force annually, job creation stagnates at 2 million workers. Between 1993–94 and 2004–05, the annual addition to the workforce was 7.6 million per year. This fell to 2 million between 2004–05 and 2011–12. While recent estimates are not available from NSSO Employment-Unemployment Surveys (EUS), Abraham (2017) reports a net decline in the number of workers after 2014 based on Labour Bureau employment surveys. The extent of job losses after 2014–15 has also been confirmed by the Centre for Monitoring Indian Economy (CMIE).

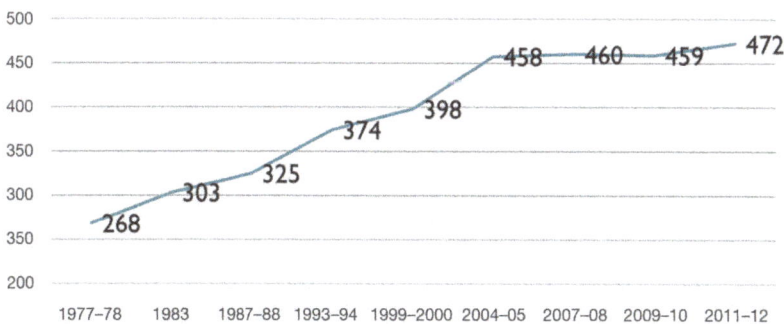

Figure 8.8. Number of workers

Source. Employment–unemployment surveys of NSSO

Inequality in the labour market also arises from the skewed distribution of workers across sectors. Around half of India's workforce is employed in the agricultural sector, despite the sector's falling share in gross domestic product (GDP). The growth of the agricultural sector has remained less than 2 per cent on average since 1991, with employment in agriculture increasing during the same period. A large share of the workers is also employed in the unorganised sector, even though its share of GDP has been falling. On the other hand, the sectors that have grown the fastest, such as finance, insurance, real estate and IT-related services and telecommunications, employ less than 2 per cent of the workforce. This has led to increasing divergence between per-worker productivity in agriculture and construction, which are sectors with the lowest productivity, and workers in the fast-growing sectors. The ratio of labour productivity in the non-agricultural to agricultural sectors has increased from 4.46 in 1993–94 to 5.52 in 2011–12 (Dev 2017).

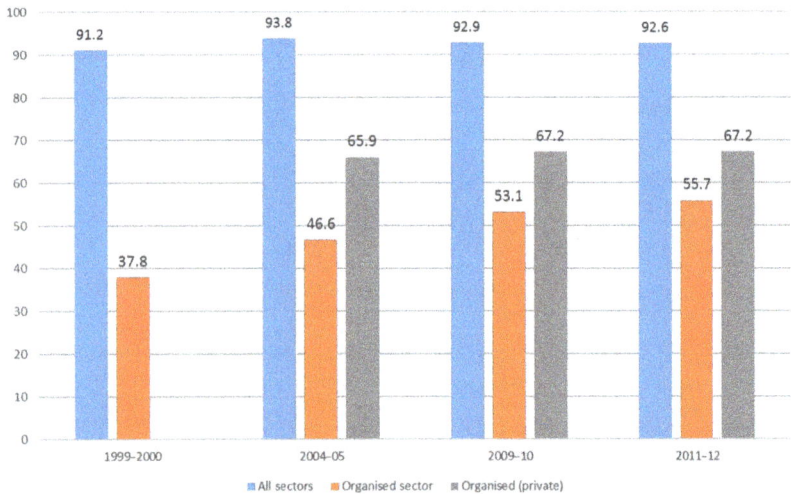

Figure 8.9. Percentage of informal workers by type of employment
Source. NSSO

Another aspect of labour market inequality exists among those who are employed. While a large majority of workers are employed in the informal sector, with no social security, the organised sector has also seen a decline in employment quality over the years. Figure 8.9 gives the distribution of workers by type of employment. At the national level, 93 per cent of all workers are employed as informal workers. These are distributed throughout the unorganised sector where almost all the workers are informal, but also in the organised sector where the percentage of workers employed as informal workers has increased in recent years. A striking trend in recent decades has been the rise in informal workers in the organised sector. Compared to only 38 per cent of workers employed as informal workers in the organised sector in 1999–2000, there were 56 per cent of workers employed as informal workers in the organised sector by 2011–12. Further disaggregation in the public and private sector suggests that it is the private organised sector that employs a significant number of the informal workers, where the rate is almost two-thirds of all workers.

Uneven distribution of the gains from growth

Labour market outcomes are primarily a result of gains from growth being unevenly distributed. Some attribute this to the pattern of capital accumulation during the post-reform period, which has not generated the required structural changes in the economy. Chandrasekhar and Ghosh (2014) characterise the Indian system of capital accumulation as one of 'exclusion through incorporation', particularly in the neo-liberal period. The growth strategy has not included measures to enable mass consumption of goods. In the absence of sufficient measures, inequalities in the system have persisted and even intensified. Financial institutions, input and product markets and insufficient access to credit also intensify this problem. Social institutions and political forces allow discriminatory labour practices to continue, and legal and regulatory institutions enhance the bargaining power of capital. Governments have aided the existing capital accumulation process by allowing corporate tax exemptions, appropriation of land and natural resources and by lax implementation of regulations.

The Annual Survey of Industries (ASI) reveals the emoluments received by various categories of workers. Figure 8.10 presents the wages of production workers, supervisors and managerial staff in the organised manufacturing sector. While workers' wages and the emoluments of managerial staff moved in tandem until the 1980s, they have diverged since the early 1990s. By 2012, the last year for which data is available, managerial emoluments increased by more than 10 times, while worker's wages have increased by less than four.

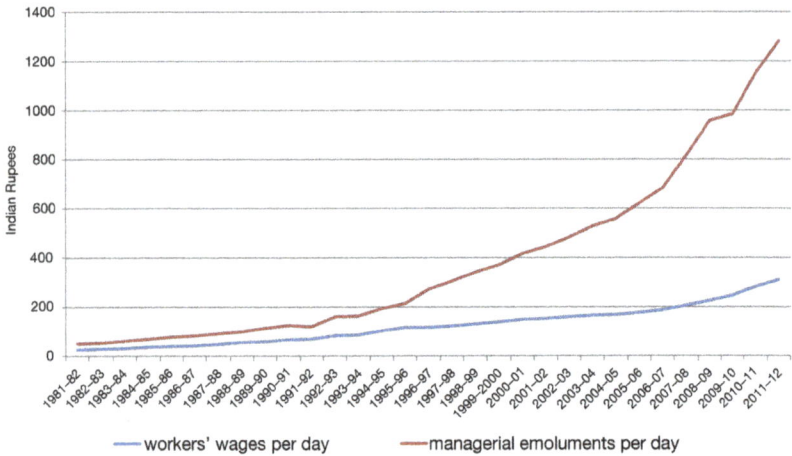

Figure 8.10. Workers' wages and managerial emoluments in organised manufacturing

Source. Author's computation from ASI data

The ASI data also sheds light on the fact that increased productivity has not improved the circumstances of workers. Workers' share in net value added has been suppressed at the cost of profits. Figure 8.11 illustrates the share of wages and profits out of net value added in organised manufacturing. While wage share was higher in the early 1980s, at around 30 per cent with profit share at only 20 per cent, the share changed after the 1990s. In recent years, the share of profits in net value added has increased to more than 50 per cent, reaching a peak of more than 60 per cent in 2007–08. While it declined after the financial crisis, it continues to be above 50 per cent of net value added in organised manufacturing. During the same period, the share of wages in value added declined to 10 per cent and has remained thereabout in recent years. The compression in wage share was accompanied by taking recourse to contractualisation and casualisation of the organised manufacturing workforce.

While increased inequality among workers in the organised sector is only a small component of overall inequality, it emphasises the changing nature of production in the organised sector.

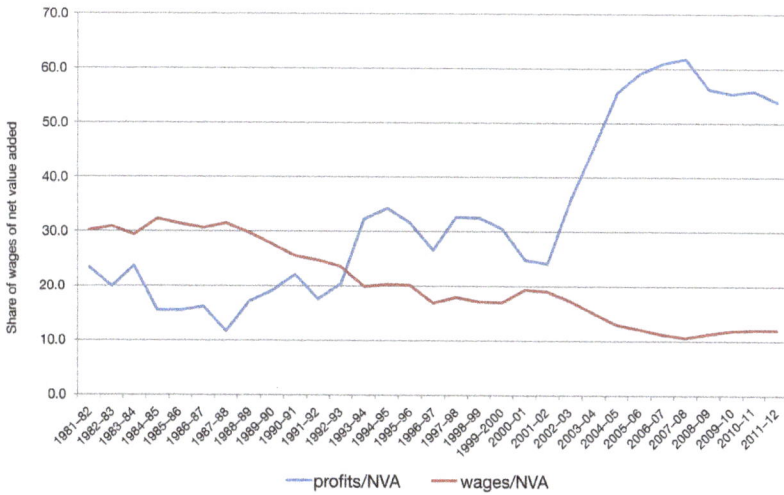

Figure 8.11. Share of profits and wages out of net value added (NVA) in organised manufacturing (ASI)

Source. Author's computation from ASI data

Pro-poor policies

While the post-1991 policies of structural adjustment and liberalisation of the economy undoubtedly saw the fastest rise in inequality, they also contributed to unprecedented distress in the rural economy. The ruling National Democratic Alliance (NDA) government, which sought votes in the name of 'India Shining', lost the election in 2004 because of unrest and distress in rural areas.[13] A renewed focus on rural areas introduced by the new government of 2004–05 alleviated the unrest to an extent. While the overall direction of the economy did not change compared to the post-1991 period, inequality increased more slowly due to a shift towards pro-poor policies. A massive increase in spending on rural areas resulted in most rural poor benefiting from expansion of the Public Distribution System (PDS) and other food-related schemes (Himanshu & Sen 2013). This was also the case with other measures such as the Mahatma Gandhi National Rural Employment Guarantee Scheme (MGNREGS), which contributed to increasing the demand for non-farm labour. Farmers, on the other hand, benefited from generous increases in minimum support

13 While it is simplistic to argue that the rise in inequality contributed to the downfall of the NDA government, the claims of 'India Shining' certainly did not find favour with the rural population, which saw the slogan as an affront to their misery.

191

prices (MSP) and loan waivers that contributed to the raising of real incomes. The cumulative impact of the MGNREGS and MSP increase saw a significant increase in casual wage rates in rural areas, which later spilled over to urban areas. Figure 8.12 gives the real casual labour wages at 2011–12 prices. The period between 2008 and 2013 saw real wages increase at more than 6 per cent per annum, which was faster than the growth of average per capita incomes. While income concentration at the top continued to rise, and this period was also characterised by a rise in crony capitalism, the rise in inequality was moderated by the shift in policy that benefited the bottom half of the population.

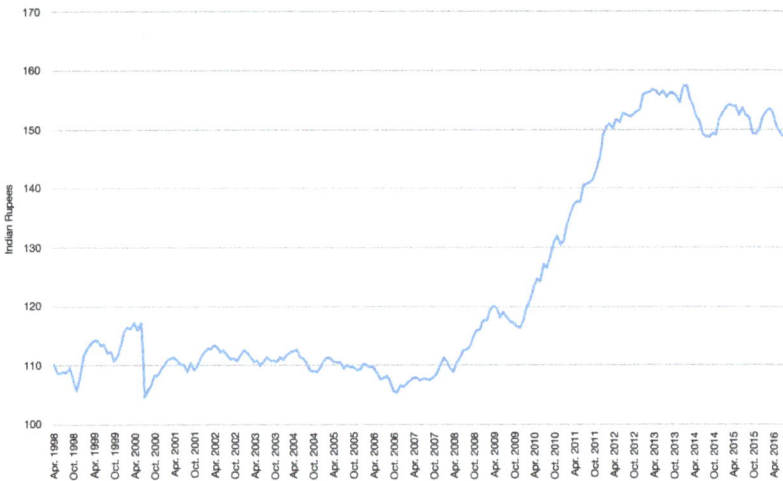

Figure 8.12. Real wages of unskilled labour, 2011–12 prices
Source. Labour Bureau

While government policies contributed to the rise in household incomes at the bottom end of the distribution, it did not result in a significant decline in inequality, unlike in the 1980s in rural areas. This is partly because the inequality that exists in the labour market has seen workers lose on account of a lack of jobs but also due to worsening employment quality. While the pro-poor orientation of the government contributed to moderating the rise in inequality, it was assisted in this by the speed of economic growth that, at 8.5 per cent per annum between 2004–05 and 2011–12, provided revenue for the government to undertake these fiscal measures.

Inequality and intergenerational mobility

Three conclusions can be drawn from the preceding analysis, 1) India is among the countries with the highest level of inequality; 2) inequality in India has been rising over the last three decades, in contrast with most countries that have experienced a decline in inequality; and 3) two episodes of growth acceleration have produced different outcomes as far as inequality is concerned, with the economic acceleration in the 1980s accompanied by declining or stagnant inequality but a sharp rise in inequality post-1991.

What does this mean for individual mobility? Outcomes are determined not only by the existing state of income distribution, but are more dependent on inequality of opportunity. Inequality of opportunity is not an outcome of access to employment and assets alone. Horizontal inequalities, based on where an individual is born and to which caste, community, religion, region and gender, also affect equal access to opportunities (Stewart 2002), due to prejudice, marginalisation and discrimination. Horizontal inequalities affect an individual's participation in the labour market in isolation but also in conjunction with other identities such as caste, which can determine occupational choices. While these barriers have weakened, evidence points to a perpetuation of certain caste groups being employed in certain occupations. Most workers performing menial and dirty jobs come from among the scheduled castes and there are few employed in higher education, the judiciary, media or professional occupations. This is similarly the case with segregation on the basis of religion and gender when inequality manifests itself in access to employment opportunities and in wage gaps across caste or gender.

Intergenerational mobility in India

There is limited information available on intergenerational mobility in India. This is partly because data that can track changes in the economic fortunes of households/individuals over generations is also limited. Some research, however, has utilised the repeated cross-sectional nature of consumption surveys to identify trends in intergenerational mobility, and panel data from IHDS has also been used to arrive at estimates of intergenerational mobility.

Using IHDS (2004–05) data, Rama et al. (2015) report mobility of fathers and sons for a broad range of occupations including unskilled workers, farmers, skilled or semiskilled workers, and white-collar workers.[14] They report substantial mobility in occupations across generations with over 40 per cent of the children of unskilled workers and 36 per cent of the sons of farmers engaged in occupations other than their fathers'. They also break down the fathers' age by 10-year cohorts and report increased mobility over generations. Their review of mobility by caste and religious groups finds no difference between mobility of Muslims and Hindus, but higher mobility among disadvantaged caste groups such as scheduled castes (SC) and scheduled tribes (ST) compared to forward castes.

These findings are confirmed by other studies. Using NSSO surveys, Hnatkovska et al. (2013) reported higher mobility among disadvantaged groups compared to general castes and found this to be true for occupational transition and educational attainment. Their finding is similar to work by Dang and Lanjouw (2015) who created a longitudinal panel to analyse change in poverty levels among households using NSSO consumption surveys. On the other hand, using the IHDS data, Motiram and Singh (2012) report considerable persistence of occupations across generations and low-paying jobs among the SC/ST groups.

Azam (2016), Mohammed (2017) and Chakraborty et al. (2016) use the panel data from NCAER surveys to examine intergenerational mobility. Azam finds considerable difference between mobility of forward (higher) castes versus lower castes (SC/ST) and, using data from 1993–94, 2004–05 and 2011–12, he reports the highest upward and lowest downward mobility among the forward castes and the reverse for the ST. He also reports the lowest mobility among Muslims in the 2004–11 period. On the other hand, using the same data set, Mohammed reports estimates of intergenerational elasticities that lie between 0.28 and 0.37, which is lower than estimates from other countries. While within-group mobility among SC/ST households is found to be high, Mohammed reports low between-group convergences. Chakraborty et al. (2016) use the Rural Economic and Demographic Survey (REDS) data to analyse the role of formal networks in intergenerational mobility. They report an 11.5 per cent increase in mobility among sons compared to fathers due to the presence of formal networks. Similarly, mobility away from traditional

---

14 The occupation of fathers is reported by sons and is subject to biases and recall errors.

occupations is 31.1 per cent in the presence of formal networks. Thorat et al. (2017) use IHDS data to analyse the relative probabilities of falling and escaping poverty. They report that all groups have done well in terms of escaping poverty between 2004 and 2011, but SC and ST groups have less chance of escaping poverty compared to forward castes. Ranganathan et al. (2016) also use IHDS data to conclude persistence in lower quintiles among backward castes and higher quintiles among forward castes. They also report higher intertemporal mobility among SC and backward castes.

The broad conclusion of these studies points towards a rise in intergenerational mobility although SC/ST groups continue to face disadvantage. While most of these studies have used occupation as the proxy for mobility, it is difficult to obtain information on earnings from different occupations for different generations.

Intergenerational mobility from Palanpur surveys

While the evidence on intergenerational inequality from large surveys is mixed, there is no study that has attempted an analysis of inequality and intergenerational mobility. This is understandable given the lack of long-time series data, including availability of income distribution across generations. Krueger (2012) and Corak (2013) point out that countries with high inequality are associated with relatively low intergenerational income mobility. Using the elasticity of a son's lifetime earnings with respect to his father's lifetime earnings, Corak (2013) introduces the idea of the 'Great Gatsby curve' to plot the relationship between intergenerational elasticity of income and a cross-sectional measure of income inequality, the Gini coefficient.[15]

The mobility of individuals and households is not just dependent on individual effort, talent and assets but also depends on social identity, horizontal inequalities, public policy and the social and political environment. A consequence of high inequality is its impact on public services. In societies where inequality is high, the wealthy can often buy

---

15 The Great Gatsby curve shows a positive relationship across countries, where higher inequality in a given country at a given point in time is associated with lower intergenerational mobility (a higher intergenerational elasticity of earnings).

basic services and leave the public services for the poor[16]. But even in a case of individual effort, talent and assets, the acquisition of these depend on the relative position of the father.

While cross-country studies confirm such a relationship, its mechanism is more likely to operate at the micro level. The effect of inequality at village or town level is likely to be more pronounced since what matters for individuals is their close surroundings and the availability of public services and employment opportunities.

An examination of the relationship between income inequality and intergenerational mobility can be usefully undertaken in the case of rural India, specifically through the surveys of Palanpur, a small village in western Uttar Pradesh. It is not representative of India's half a million or so villages in its social and economic structure, but it is uniquely endowed with data suited to the study of intergenerational mobility over a long period of time. There have been seven rounds of Palanpur surveys, once in each decade starting from 1957–58, with the last being 2015. It has been surveyed in 1963, 1974, 1983, 1993, 2008–10 and 2015. The uniqueness arises also from the close attention to data quality paid by successive researchers who undertook a complete census of the village in each survey round. Some of these survey rounds have involved long stays in the village, with the 2008–10 survey lasting a full two years.

For all the survey rounds except 1993 and 2015, meticulously collected income estimates for all the resident households of the village are available.[17] These have now been made comparable and consistent with a common definition. The longitudinal nature of the data collection allows one to compare the income, occupation and other characteristics of children with fathers for two generations.[18]

Between 1957–58 and 1963, there was a marginal increase in inequality in the village, with the Gini coefficient rising from 0.336 to 0.353. But it declined to 0.272 in the next round of 1974, the lowest inequality ever in

16   See Sinha (2016) and Sinha et al. (2016) for inequality and collective action for public services.
17   Unlike most empirical analyses of distributional change at the village level, the Palanpur study has taken as its reference domain not just a sample of households in a particular village or locality, but the entire population of the village. All houscholds in the village were surveyed and interviewed, and income data were collected for the entire population for five out of the seven survey years.
18   See Himanshu et al. (2013) for details on inequality trends and decompositions.

the village.[19] Between 1975 and 1983 inequality increased, but remained lower than its 1957–58 and 1963 levels.[20] The survey conducted in 2008–10, the Gini index, at 0.379, is at its highest level compared to all other survey years. The rise in inequality since the late 1970s mirrors the rise in inequality reported earlier for all India. The increase in inequality after 1983 is largely driven by the non-farm sector but inequality has also risen within caste groups. While within-group differences are large and have increased over time in Palanpur, there has been a decline in income differences between caste groups. This observation applies even when the population is divided into two groups, Jatabs – historically the most socially and economically disadvantaged group in the village – and the rest of the village. Using classical inequality decomposition as well as the Elbers, Lanjouw, Mistiaen, Özler (ELMO) decomposition,[21] there is strong evidence of an improvement in the condition of Jatabs as a group, relative to the rest of the village population. The improvement in the condition of Jatabs is a result of improved incomes in agriculture, which has allowed some of them to lease land, and the availability of non-farm jobs. Expansion of non-farm job opportunity has allowed individuals belonging to various groups to look beyond their historical agricultural occupations and to explore new ventures.

The unique Palanpur data, with income data available for more than two generations, permits examination of intergenerational mobility across generations in the village. The long period of surveys allows tracking and

---

19 The remarkable decline between 1963 and 1974 was the consequence of three principal factors. First, with the investment in irrigation in the 1960s and the advent of green revolution methods in the late 1960s and 1970s there was a significant expansion in the use and application of modern agricultural technologies, introduction of newer farming practices and better irrigation devices. The distributional 'incidence' of the expansion of irrigation was particularly progressive in that, whereas previously only a few, better-off, farmers were in a position to irrigate their land (using 'Persian wheel' lifting technologies that required the digging and maintenance of a large well and complementary draught animal power), this period saw the expansion of irrigation to all farmers. By 1974–75, all village land was irrigated. Second, that year was also a particularly good agricultural year in terms of harvest quality in Palanpur. As a result, those who had spent less on inputs were less at risk from lower or negative incomes in the face of a bad harvest. And 'errant' farming practices (e.g. late sowing, poor weeding) tended to be less severely penalised. The third factor to contribute towards an equalisation of income in 1974–75 was that the distribution of land cultivated in Palanpur was more equal in 1974–75 than in other years.

20 The increase in inequality in 1983–84 can be attributed to the emergence of new, non-farm employment opportunities that were taken up mostly by villagers from economically better-off backgrounds. Also, 1983–84 was a bad agricultural year that led to further widening of the income gaps between those who derived some earnings from outside and those who were entirely dependent on agriculture.

21 The ELMO method offers a reinterpretation of sub-group inequality following the method suggested in their paper. For details see, Elbers, Lanjouw, Mistiaen and Özler (2008).

assessing of *changes* in intergenerational elasticity over two generations. Intergenerational elasticity in income can be calculated for two periods, 1957–58 to 1983–84 and 1983–84 to 2008–10, each with a gap of 25 years. Father–son pairs can be identified for each period, with sons in the latter period being 25–35 years of age. The per capita income of the household in the initial period is assumed to be the father's income.[22] The following model is estimated:

$$\log (\text{income}_{son}) = \alpha + \beta \log (\text{income}_{father}) + \varepsilon$$

Where income_{son} is the per capita household income in the latter period and income_{father} is the per capita household in the former period. Table 8.4 reports the estimated elasticities.

Table 8.4. Intergenerational elasticity in earnings and inequality (1958–2009)

	1958–84 (1)	1984–2009 (2)	1958–74 (1984) (3)	1974 (1983)–2009 (4)
Number of observations (in the age group 25–35 years)	58	100	58	100
Gini coefficient in terminal year	0.336	0.379	0.235	0.379
Intergenerational elasticity	0.328	0.396	0.294	0.441

Note. Columns 3 and 4 represent the elasticity replacing the income for 1983–84 by an average of 1974–75 and 1983–84 because 1974–75 was a good agricultural year and 1983–84 was a bad year.

Source. Author's computation from Palanpur survey data

Higher income inequality is observable as being associated with higher intergenerational income elasticity (and thus lower mobility), which is consistent with Corak (2006). An increase in intergenerational elasticity over time is also observable, as is a rise in overall inequality as measured by the Gini coefficient. Alternative estimates confirm the robustness of the result by taking the average of incomes of 1974–75 and 1983–84, since 1983–84 was a bad year in terms of agricultural production. The increase in intergenerational elasticity is even more pronounced in this case. Interestingly, the estimates of intergenerational elasticity are not very different from 0.396 and are 0.441 for the 1983/84 – 2008/09 period are broadly in line with the findings from Mohammed (2016) using IHDS

---

22   In other words, if the son lies in the working age group of 25–35 years and is part of the household in 2008–09, then the per capita income of the household in 1983–84 is considered as his father's income.

data for the later period. Even earnings elasticity reported by Atkinson et al. (1983) between sons and fathers of 0.436 in the town of York over the period 1950 to 1975–78 is similar.

One of the possible routes through which intergenerational elasticity is presumably influenced is inheritance passed on to successive generations, and more so in an agrarian economy like Palanpur. The emergence of non-farm labour as an alternative source of income should, however, break the rigidities in income and wealth transmission. While this is the case in Palanpur, the nature of non-farm diversification has been such that access to these jobs has varied across caste and income strata for different non-farm jobs. Jatabs and households at the lower end of the income strata have mostly been restricted to manual casual labour when accessing non-farm jobs. On the other hand, the expansion of non-farm opportunities has not led to a weakening of the role of education and networks, which played a role in non-farm diversification during earlier surveys. These were more important for accessing regular, well-paying, non-farm jobs, which remain concentrated amongst Thakur and other advantaged households that have better access to networks and can finance 'entrance fees' or bribes. Networks are important in the case of casual jobs and there is evidence of them playing an important role for Jatabs in accessing non-farm jobs. The new non-farm opportunities create possibilities for upward mobility and, within any group, some move to take these opportunities more quickly than others. Nevertheless, income and social status increase the likelihood of obtaining these non-farm jobs, and this effect becomes more important in overall structures as the number of non-farm opportunities rise.

Intergenerational mobility in Asia

Although important, studies on intergenerational mobility are rare. Part of the problem is the availability of data that allows tracking of individual/ households over a period of time. This is particularly so for developing countries but, even for developed countries, few studies are available.[23] How does India and Palanpur compare to other countries in Asia? Most Asian countries, except Japan, have moved from developing into the category of developed countries. Each has followed its own path of national transformation and is beset with social and political issues that define the nature of intergenerational mobility.

---

23   See Atkinson (1981); Aaronson and Mazumder (2008); Björklund and Jäntti (1997); Corak (2011); Lefranc and Trannoy (2005); Leigh (2007); and Solon (2002).

Among the Asian countries, India and China are often compared for the size of their populations, but also because of the complexity of their social structures. The recent rise of China has attracted attention to the issue of inequality and intergenerational mobility. Similar to India, China also experienced rising inequality during the period of growth acceleration after the 1980s. Fan et al. (2015) examine the issue of intergenerational mobility in China using data from the Chinese Household Income Project (CHIP). They conclude that the rise in Gini coefficient of income from 0.26 in 1980 to 0.43 in 2010 has been accompanied by a decline in intergenerational mobility in income and education. The intergenerational income elasticity increases from 0.315 to 0.442 between cohorts born before and after 1970. They also report a significant decline in elasticity in the case of females and residents in economically disadvantaged regions within China. The cross-sectional analysis of intergenerational mobility and income inequality confirms the presence of a Great Gatsby curve. Deng et al. (2013) also confirm the lack of intergenerational mobility in the case of China.

On the other hand, Lam and Cuong (2017) show high mobility across income quintiles in the case of Vietnam. Using data from the Vietnam Household Living Standard Surveys (VHLSS), they also find the degree of mobility declining over time but still at a high level. The intergenerational elasticity of earnings for parents and children at around 0.36 is, however, stable over 2004 and 2014. Kim (2015) reports a high degree of mobility in South Korea and, in Asia, South Korea and Japan are seen as examples of countries with high income and occupational mobility along with low inequality. In fact, in both these countries the level of inequality is similar to the Nordic countries of Denmark, Finland, Norway and Sweden. South Korea and Japan are also examples of countries that have seen rapid growth in per capita income without a rise in income inequality. Using the Japan Household Panel Survey (JHPS), Ueda (2015) estimates intergenerational income elasticity among fathers and sons to be in the range of 0.32–0.34. Another country that shows stable intergenerational mobility is Taiwan. Despite high economic growth, Chu and Lin (2016) report stable intergenerational income elasticity in Taiwan between 1990–94 and 2005–10.

In most cases, the estimates of intergenerational elasticity in Asian countries are broadly in the range for India that is reported using the national surveys and Palanpur surveys. This is so except in the case of China, which shows a decline in intergenerational mobility, whereas most others show stable elasticities and high intergenerational mobility.

Conclusion

The debate on the performance of the Indian economy in recent decades has moved away from the concerns of an economy trapped in low-growth equilibrium to one among the fastest growing economies. Although growth has slowed in recent years, India continues to be among the countries with a reasonably high rate of growth. The issue that needs to be debated, however, is whether the growth is sustainable or not.

These concerns are not just academic but are being debated politically as well. The growth of the economy in the last three decades has coincided with a period of jobless growth and acute farm crisis, which continues to remain an economic and political challenge. The pattern of growth has increased incomes and reduced poverty but also led to an increasing gap between a majority of labourers stuck in farming and the informal sector with poor working conditions. The livelihood and wellbeing of these individuals are also affected by the persistence of inequalities of caste, religion, region and gender, all of which contribute to exclude and marginalise a large segment of the population. These issues are appearing as political fissure points, with anger among the Dalits (SC) leading to demands for community-based reservation.

Inequality has largely been driven by changes in the labour market, with an increasing share of capital reserved for the cost of labour. The rise in profit rate has accompanied the decline in wage share. But it has also been accompanied by rising inequality in access to public services such as health and education. This has also led to concerns of crony capitalism. But whether the process of growth is sustainable depends not just on economic policies but also policies on human development and inclusion. The evidence from intergenerational mobility provides a mixed picture, with the poor and the disadvantaged experiencing an overall increase in access to non-farm jobs but it also shows persistence of caste-based rigidities. In the long run, inequality is not just a matter of moral and philosophical concern but is also instrumental in sustaining the growth of the economy through allowing the disadvantaged to participate in and benefit from the growth process.

References

Aaronson, D & Mazumder, B (2008). 'Intergenerational economic mobility in the United States: 1940–2000', *Journal of Human Resources*, 43(1), 139–72. doi.org/10.3368/jhr.43.1.139.

Abraham, V (2017). 'Stagnant employment growth: Last three years may have been the worst', *Economic and Political Weekly*, 52(38), 13–17.

Anand, I & Thampi, A (2016). 'Recent trends in wealth inequality in India', *Economic & Political Weekly*, 51(50), 59–67.

Atkinson, A (1981). 'On intergenerational income mobility in Britain', *Journal of Post-Keynesian Economics*, 3, 194–218. doi.org/10.1080/01603477.1980. 11489214.

Atkinson, AB, Maynard, AK & Trinder, CG (1983). *Parents and children: Incomes in two generations*. London: Heinemann.

Azam, M (2016). *Household income mobility in India: 1993–2011*, IZA Discussion Papers, 10308. Institute for the Study of Labor (IZA).

Banerjee, A & Piketty, T (2005). 'Top Indian incomes, 1922–2000', *The World Bank Economic Review*, 19(1), 1–20. doi.org/10.1093/wber/lhi001.

Björklund, A & Jäntti, M (1997). 'Intergenerational income mobility in Sweden compared to the United States', *American Economic Review*, 87(5), 1009–18.

Chakraborty, T, Mukherjee, A, Sahaz, S & Shekhawat, AS (2016). 'Formal institutions, caste network and occupational mobility', conference paper, 12th Annual Conference on Economic Growth and Development, ISI Delhi.

Chakravorty, S, Chandrasekhar, S & Naraparaju, K (2016). *Income generation and inequality in India's agricultural sector: The consequences of land fragmentation*, No. 2016-028. Mumbai: Indira Gandhi Institute of Development Research.

Chancel, L & Piketty, T (2017). *Indian income inequality, 1922–2014: From British Raj to Billionaire Raj?*, No. 12409, CEPR Discussion Papers.

Chandrasekhar, CP & Ghosh, J (2014). *Growth, employment patterns and inequality in Asia: A case study of India*, ILO Asia-Pacific Working Paper Series.

Chu, Y-WL & Lin, M-J (2016). *Economic development and intergenerational earnings mobility: Evidence from Taiwan*, working paper, Department of Economics, National Taiwan University, www.econ.ntu.edu.tw/uploads/asset/data/58325b6248b8a17a8b03f89f/hist_1051208.pdf.

Corak, M (2006). 'Do poor children become poor adults? Lessons from a cross-country comparison of generational earnings mobility', *Research on Economic Inequality*, 13, 143–88. doi.org/10.1016/S1049-2585(06)13006-9.

—— (2011). *Generational income mobility in North America and Europe*. Cambridge University Press.

—— (2013). 'Income inequality, equality of opportunity, and intergenerational mobility', *Journal of Economic Perspectives*, 27(3), 79–102. doi.org/10.1257/jep.27.3.79.

Credit Suisse (2017). 'Global Wealth Report', November 2017. www.credit-suisse.com/articles/news-and-expertise/2017/11/en/global-wealth-report-2017.html.

Dang, H-A & Lanjouw, PF (2015). *Poverty dynamics in India between 2004 and 2012: Insights from longitudinal analysis using synthetic panel data*, World Bank Policy Research Paper, 7270. doi.org/10.1596/1813-9450-7270.

Deng, Q, Gustafsson, B & Li, S (2013). 'Intergenerational income persistence in urban China', *Review of Income and Wealth*, 59(3), 416–36. doi.org/10.1111/roiw.12034.

Dev, MS (2017). 'Inequality, employment and public policy', Presidential address, Indian Society of Labour Economics, 2017.

Elbers, C, Lanjouw, P, Mistiaen J & Özler, B (2008). 'Reinterpreting between-group inequality', *The Journal of Economic Inequality*, 6(3), 231–45. doi.org/10.1007/s10888-007-9064-x.

Fan, Y, Junjian Y & Zhang, J (2015). 'The Great Gatsby curve in China: Cross-sectional inequality and intergenerational mobility', conference paper, Asian Bureau of Finance and Economic Research, Singapore.

Himanshu (2007). 'Recent trends in poverty and inequality: Some preliminary results', *Economic & Political Weekly*, 42(6), 497–508.

—— (2015). 'Inequality in India', *SEMINAR*, August, www.india-seminar.com/2015/672/672_himanshu.htm.

Himanshu & Sen, A (2013). 'In-kind food transfers – I: Impact on poverty', *Economic and Political Weekly*, 48(45/46), 46–54.

Himanshu, Jha, P & Rodgers, G (eds) (2016). *The changing village in India: Insights from longitudinal research*. Oxford University Press. www.oxfordscholarship. com/view/10.1093/acprof:oso/9780199461868.001.0001/acprof-9780199 461868.

Himanshu, Joshi, B & Lanjouw, P (2016). 'Non-farm diversification, inequality and mobility in Palanpur', *Economic and Political Weekly*, 51(26 & 27), 43–51. doi.org/10.1093/acprof:oso/9780199461868.003.0011.

Himanshu, Lanjouw, P, Murgai, R & Stern, N (2013). *Non-farm diversification, poverty, economic mobility and income inequality: A case study in village India*, Policy Research Working Paper Series, 6451. The World Bank.

Hnatkovska, V, Lahiri, A & Paul, SB (2013). 'Breaking the caste barrier: Intergenerational mobility in India', *Journal of Human Resources*, 48(2), 435–73. jhr.uwpress.org/content/48/2/435.short.

Jayadev, A, Motiram, S & Vakulabharanam, V (2007). 'Patterns of wealth disparities in India during the liberalisation era', *Economic and Political Weekly*, 42(38), 3853–63.

Kim, T (2015). 'Intergenerational economic mobility in Korea: Assessment, drivers, and lessons'. In T Kim & A Mulakala (eds), *Social mobility: Experiences and lessons from Asia* (pp 7–21). Korea Development Institute and The Asia Foundation, South Korea.

Krueger, A (2012). 'The rise and consequences of inequality in the United States', 12 January, speech, Center for American Progress, Washington D.C.

Lam, NT & Cuong, NV (2017). *Intragenerational and intergenerational mobility in Viet Nam*, ADBI Working Paper, 722. Tokyo: Asian Development Bank Institute.

Lefranc, A & Trannoy, A (2005). 'Intergenerational earnings mobility in France: Is France more mobile than the US?', *Annales d'Economie et de Statistique*, 78, 57–77. doi.org/10.2307/20079128.

Leigh, A (2007). 'Intergenerational mobility in Australia', *The B.E. Journal of Economic Analysis and Policy*, 7(2), Article 6. doi.org/10.2202/1935-1682.1781.

Li, H, Squire L & Zhou, H-F (1998). 'Explaining international and inter-temporal variation in income inequality', *The Economic Journal*, 108(446), 26–43. doi.org/10.1111/1468-0297.00271.

Mazumdar, D, Sarkar, S & Mehta, BS (2017). 'Inequality in India – I', *Economic and Political Weekly*, 52(30), 47–56 and 'Inequality in India – II: The wage sector', *Economic and Political Weekly*, 52(32), 58–66.

Mohammed, ARS (2017). 'Does a good father now have to be rich? Intergenerational income mobility in rural India', SSRN, www.isid.ac.in/~epu/acegd2016/papers/ShariqMohammed.pdf.

Motiram, S & Singh, A (2012). 'How close does the apple fall from the tree? Some evidence from India on intergenerational occupational mobility', *Economic and Political Weekly*, 47(40), 56–65.

Piketty, T (2014). *Capital in the twenty-first century.* Harvard University Press.

Rama, M, Béteille, T, Li, Y, Mitra, PK & Newman, JL (2015). *Addressing inequality in South Asia*, South Asia Development Matters. Washington, DC: World Bank.

Ranganathan, T, Tripathi, A & Pandey, G (2016). *Income mobility among social groups in Indian rural households: Findings from the Indian Human Development Survey*, IEG Working Paper, No. 368.

Rawal, V (2008). 'Ownership holdings of land in rural India: Putting the record straight', *Economic and Political Weekly*, 43–47.

Rawal, V & Swaminathan, M (2011). 'Income inequality and caste in village India', *Review of Agrarian Studies*, 1(2), ras.org.in/income_inequality_and_caste_in_village_india.

Rodgers, G & Soundarajan, V (2015). *Patterns of inequality in India, 1983–2011/12: project paper D (India).* Institute of Human Development.

Sarkar, S & Mehta, BS (2010). 'Income inequality in India: Pre- and post-reform periods', *Economic and Political Weekly*, 45(37), 45–55.

Sarma, M, Saha, P & Jayakumar, N (2017). *Asset inequality in India: Going from bad to worse*, SSER Working Paper, 17/1.

Sen, A & Himanshu (2004). 'Poverty and inequality in India – II: Widening disparities during the 1990s', *Economic and Political Weekly*, 39(39), 4361–75. www.epw.in/journal/2004/39/special-articles/poverty-and-inequality-india-ii.html.

Sinha, D (2016). *Women, health and public services in India: Why are states different?* Routledge. doi.org/10.4324/9781315626512.

Sinha, D, Tiwari, DK, Bhattacharya, R & Kattumuri, R (2016). 'Public services, social relations, politics, and gender: tales from a north Indian village'. In Himanshu, P Jha & G Rodgers (eds), *The changing village in India: Insights from longitudinal research.* Oxford University Press. doi.org/10.1093/acprof:oso/9780199461868.001.0001.

Solon, G (2002). 'Cross-country differences in intergenerational earnings mobility', *Journal of Economic Perspectives*, 16, 59–66.

Stewart, F (2002). *Horizontal inequalities: A neglected dimension of development*, QEH Working Paper Series, No. 81.

Subramanian, S & Jayaraj, D (2006). *The distribution of household wealth in India*, research paper, No. 2006/116. UNU-WIDER, United Nations University (UNU).

Swaminathan, M (1988). 'Growth and polarisation: Changes in wealth inequality in a Tamilnadu village'. *Economic and Political Weekly*.

Swaminathan, M & Rawal, V (2011). 'Is India really a country of low income inequality? Observations from eight villages', *Review of Agrarian Studies*, 1(1), ras.org.in/is_india_really_a_country_of_low_income_inequality_observations_from_eight_villages.

Thorat, A, Vanneman, R, Desai, S & Dubey, A (2017). 'Escaping and falling into poverty in India today', *World Development*, 93, 413–26. doi.org/10.1016/j.worlddev.2017.01.004.

Ueda, A (2015). *An empirical analysis on intergenerational persistence of income in Japan*, WINPEC Working Paper Series, No. E1511. Waseda Institute of Political Economy, Waseda University, Tokyo, Japan.

Vaidyanathan, A (1993). 'Asset holdings and consumption of rural households in India: A study of spatial and temporal variations'. In Indian Society of Agricultural Economics, *Agricultural development policy: Adjustments and reorientation*. New Delhi & Oxford: Indian Society of Agricultural Economics.

9

INTERGENERATIONAL EQUITY UNDER INCREASING LONGEVITY[1]

Sumio Saruyama, Saeko Maeda, Ryo Hasumi
and Kazuki Kuroiwa

Introduction

The Japanese population is ageing faster than any other population in the world. Data from the Organisation for Economic Co-operation and Development (OECD) show that the ratio of persons aged 65 and older to the overall population in 2013 was highest in Japan at 25.1 per cent. According to Japan's National Institute of Population and Social Security Research (NIPSSR), this ratio will rise to 38.1 per cent by 2060. The number of seniors aged 75 and over and who use medical and nursing-care services with increasing frequency, is rising at a fast pace. By 2060 the share of late-stage elderly aged 75 and over will reach 25.7 per cent of the population, or one in four persons (Figure 9.1).

1   In preparing this paper, the authors have received important insights from Masaaki Kawagoe, Specially Appointed Fellow of the Japan Center for Economic Research (JCER). JCER President Kazumasa Iwata also provided advice and comments on the research overall. At the PAFTAD (Pacific Trade and Development) Conference in Tokyo in February 2018, we received very helpful comments from participants including Naohiro Yashiro, Showa Women's University Professor; and Shiro Armstrong, Director of the Australia–Japan Research Centre at The Australian National University, who were both discussants in our presentation. The authors would like to express their gratitude to all of them. Any errors that remain are solely those of the authors.

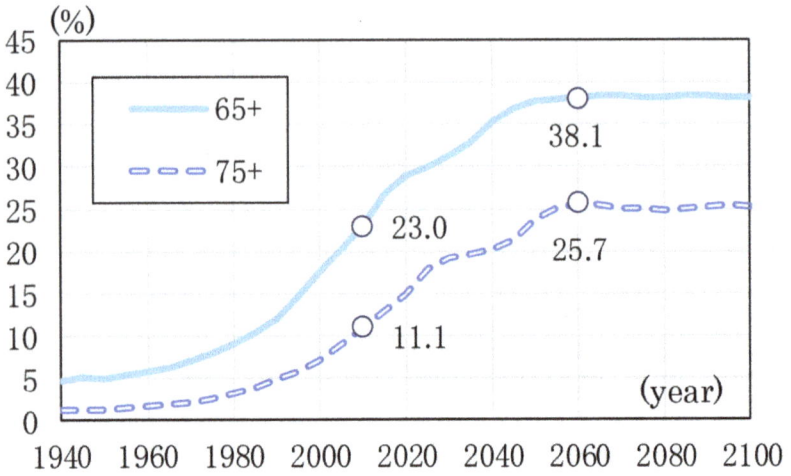

Figure 9.1. Ratio of the elderly in the population

Source. Population Census, Statistics Bureau of Japan. From 2020 onward, projections by NIPSSR

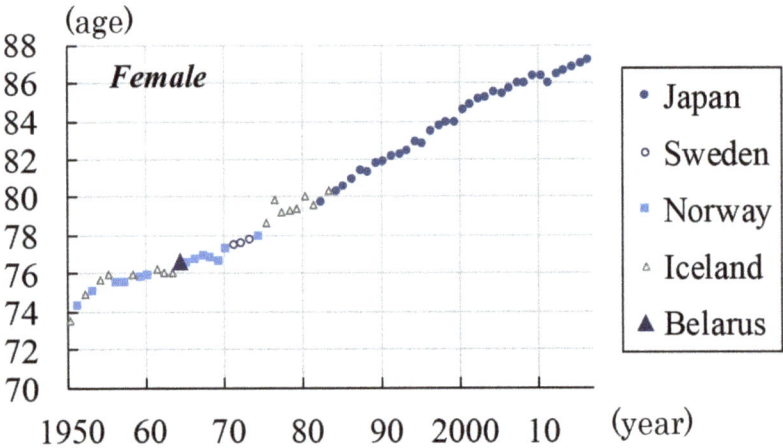

Figure 9.2. Best-practice life expectancy

Source. Human Mortality Database, University of California, Berkeley, United States, and Max Planck Institute, Germany, www.mortality.org

At the same time, lifespans are lengthening. A look at 'best-practice life expectancy', or the maximum life expectancy observed among nations in a given year, shows that female life expectancy over the last 160 years has increased by 40 years at nearly a linear rate of more than two years every decade (Oeppen & Vaupel 2002). Since the 1980s, moreover, Japan has occupied the top position (Figure 9.2). For males, Japan ranks second after Hong Kong. Some observers also believe that generations born in the twenty-first century will live past the age of 100 as a matter of course (Gratton & Scott 2016).

The increase in the old-age dependency ratio means that there is greater need for society to provide for the cost of living longer. Through public pensions and medical and nursing-care benefits, the government is providing for the lion's share of the expenses required in old age. The bulk of these expenses is financed through taxes and social-insurance premiums paid by the working generations.

'Generation accounting', investigated typically by Auerbach et al. (2011), is an attempt to clarify the balance of benefits and burdens on taxes and social security by generation. A previous study that applied the generation accounting method to Japan found the net burden ratio is higher for younger generations (Masujima et al. 2010, Suzuki et al. 2012). Among the countries in which generation accounting research was conducted, Japan is the country that burdens future generations the most (Auerbach et al. 1999).

The news is not all bad, however. By living longer, people can enjoy the positive aspects of a longer life. Becker's (2007) theoretical model translates increased lifespan into economic value. Based on a model of overlapping generations, Becker derives the value of a longer lifespan from a willingness to pay for the cost of a longer life. According to Kawagoe (2018), who applied the same model to Japan, the drop in the death rate in Japan that occurred between 1970 and 2005 can be valued roughly at 165 trillion yen annualised.

The aim of the present study is to assess aspects of ageing by incorporating the economic value following from longer life into generational accounting, which measures the disparities between the generations. We regard the value of living longer as the additional consumption one is able to enjoy. We estimate the extent to which recently born generations will be economically prosperous by having longer lifespans.

If people live longer, it would be natural for them to keep working longer in order to support themselves. We highlight longer working careers as one of the changes that societal ageing would produce. Japanese people presently begin receiving their public pension (the basic pension) from the age of 65, the general target age for exiting the workforce. In view of the lengthening of lifespans, however, pulling out of the workforce at 65 is too early.

In 1961, when universal pension coverage was first established in Japan, average male life expectancy was 66 years, and payment of pension benefits began at the age of 60. Benefits were received for less than 10 years on average. In 2015, average male life expectancy was 81 years, yet the age at which benefit payments begin has been raised just five years to age 65. This means that the period over which benefits are received has grown to 16 years. If the average lifespan increases further along the recent trend, it is likely that Japanese people will receive benefits for more than 20 years in 2050.

In January 2017, the Japan Gerontology Society and the Japan Geriatrics Society proposed that the term 'elderly', which now refers to people aged 65 and older, be redefined to mean persons aged 75 and older. They also proposed that the term 'early stage elderly', which currently refers to those aged 65 to 74, be regarded as meaning 'semi-elderly', indicating that such persons are still able to contribute to society. The recommendations were based on the judgement that advances in medical care and improvements in the living environment now mean that the physical mobility and intellectual capacity of early stage elderly are at a more youthful level than before.

In the present study as well, we consider career prolongation and raising of the starting year for paying pension benefits as promising options. The government would gain latitude in its financial balance relative to gross domestic product (GDP) from (1) a reduction in pension benefits, (2) an improvement in revenues from taxes and insurance premiums and (3) an improvement in GDP following an expansion of the working population. If these strategies can be mobilised to lighten the burden on the working generations, it could have the effect of reducing the disparity between the burdens of each generation.

We focus on three representative generations: the population born in 1950[2] (Generation 1), the children of this generation born in 1980 (Generation 2), and the generation born 30 years later in 2010 (Generation 3). We have selected 1950 as the starting year because underlying data with a firm statistical basis is readily available for the following years.

In estimating the generational accounting and the consumption that each generation can enjoy under certain macro-economic assumptions about the future, we found that Generation 3, the youngest generation, will see its lifetime consumption expand by 9–13 per cent thanks to the longer lifespans obtained after Generation 1. If the age at which workers leave the workforce can be raised by 10 years over the present while other conditions remain constant, national and local governments would see a 6–7 per cent improvement in their primary balance relative to GDP. The resulting financial surplus could then be applied to lightening the net burden on the younger generation with respect to the balance of benefits and burdens relating to taxes and social security. The younger the generation, the heavier is the net burden and the greater the disadvantages from societal ageing. If, however, account is taken of the increase in consumption that follows from longer lifespans and the expansion in labour force participation, the inevitability of the younger generations being hit hardest by societal ageing will for the most part be avoided.

In an age when people live to 100, withdrawal from the workforce at the age of 65 is too early. Japan needs to forge a system under which people work an additional 10 years. Lengthening healthy lifespans will also be important so people can better enjoy the additional consumption that longer lifespans will make possible.

Ageing will also accelerate in other Asian countries (Figure 9.3). According to the UN population forecast, the proportion of people aged 65 and over will grow in every country at different rates. Life spans will also be longer and, by 2060, the average life expectancy of women will exceed 90 in Korea and be around 85 in Thailand, China, Vietnam and Malaysia. As Asian countries improve their social security for the elderly, the burden on active workers may increase, and there is a possibility that the inter-generational disparity in fiscal burden will occur as it has in Japan. This analysis, therefore, has important implications for Asian countries.

---

2   The generation born in Japan after World War II is known as the baby boomer generation, however, the number of births most notably increased in the three years between 1947 and 1949.

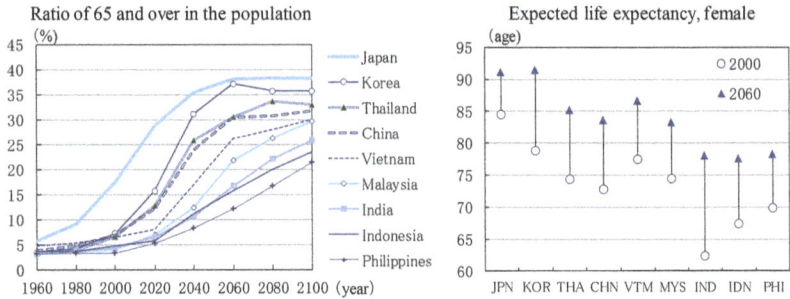

Figure 9.3. The ratio and life expectancy of the elderly in Asian countries

Source. United Nations, World Population Prospects, 2017, population.un.org/wpp/; NIPSSR, Population Projection for Japan, www.ipss.go.jp/index-e.asp

The following section explains the analytical framework on which the study is based. This is followed by an introduction to the data used for the analysis and the several assumptions we have made concerning such factors as the macro-economic outlook, taxes and social security. The next section on consumption, benefits and burden profiles examines how the three generations evolve over time with the data we identified and this is followed by our estimation of the impact that longer lifespans (the survival rate) will have on each generation, taking into account the greater number of years spent in the workforce.

Analytical framework

Our study focuses on the disparities between the generations. The elements used in our assessment are (1) consumption, (2) generational accounting, (3) government finances, (4) households, (5) GDP, and (6) discount rates.

Consumption

We define lifetime consumption for generation i as follows,

$$\hat{C}_i = \sum_{t=1}^{Z} s_{i,t}\beta^{t-1}C_{i,t}$$

Here, $C_{i,t}$ refers to the per capita real consumption in the period t for generation i. $s_{i,t}$ is the survival rate in the period t with period 1 of generation i set as 1, β being the discount factor. If the discount rate per year is set at ρ, then we may write $\beta = 1/(1 + \rho)$. Z is the upper limit of the period, set at 100 years in the present study. Here, we do not consider the disutility from labour. We assume consumption is the only source to affect welfare.

Generational accounting

Generational accounting refers to the balance between the benefits of government services and the tax and social security premiums paid for those services. In Figure 9.4, $B_{i,t}$ indicates the benefits received in period t by generation i while $T_{i,t}$ indicates the associated tax and social security premium burden. The net benefit is $B_{i,t} - T_{i,t}$ (omitted from the figure). The generational accounting value $\hat{G}_i$ for generation i is, as with lifetime consumption, defined as follows,

$$\hat{G}_i = \sum_{t=1}^{Z} s_{i,t}\beta^{t-1}(B_{i,t} - T_{i,t})$$

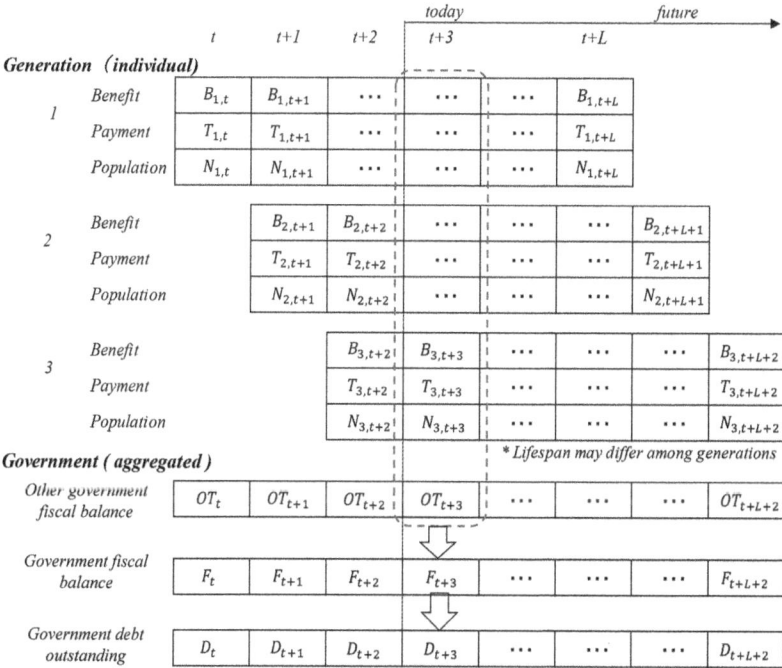

Figure 9.4. Benefits and payments by generations and government finance

Source. Figure compiled by the authors

213

$B_{i,t}$ and $T_{i,t}$ comprise the following factors, respectively:

$$B_{i,t} = BP_{i,t} + BM_{i,t} + BE_{i,t} + BC_{i,t}$$
$$T_{i,t} = TP_{i,t} + TM_{i,t} + TD_{i,t} + TC_{i,t}$$

where $BP_{i,t}$ represents pension benefits, $BM_{i,t}$ represents medical and nursing-care in-kind benefits, $BE_{i,t}$ represents education in-kind benefits, while $BC_{i,t}$ represents other cash benefits. $TP_{i,t}$ represents premiums for pensions and $TM_{i,t}$ represents premiums for medical and nursing-care insurance. $TD_{i,t}$ represents income tax and $TC_{i,t}$ indicates the consumption tax burden. Educational benefits are financed through taxes, so their cost payments are not indicated here explicitly as a separate burden. Individual co-payments for medical and nursing care and education constitute a portion of consumption.

The generational accounting approach taken here differs from the traditional generational accounting used by Auerbach et al. (2011) in three ways.

First, we do not take into consideration 'future generations'. Under traditional generational accounting, the youngest of existing generations is deemed the zero-age generation, and the generations to be born after that are together treated as future generations. Future generations serve as the funding source for ultimately repaying the currently outstanding government debt in full. We include the generations to be born in the future in our calculation, but do not assign to them the task of having to repay the entirety of the government debt.

The second point on which the present analysis differs from traditional generational accounting is related to the first point, but instead of setting the full repayment of the government debt as the criteria for balancing future benefits and burdens, we set the condition as maintaining the government debt-to-GDP ratio at a fixed-target level of about 250 per cent. Japan's combined central and local government debt to GDP ratio is about 190 per cent in 2016. It would not be realistic to place the entire burden of repaying this debt on a particular generation. By taking the individual's benefits and burdens as well as the government financial balance (explained in the next section) into account, we have computed the extent of the net burden that it would be appropriate to require from individuals.

Third, we have incorporated an assessment of the past into our analysis. Traditional generational accounting focuses primarily on comparing the youngest of presently living generations (the zero-age generation) with future generations. If the net impact on future generations is found to be large, it indicates that a fiscal deficit exists, including a portion that will arise in the future. This excludes from consideration past benefits and burdens, so when making comparisons between the elderly and the present working generation, for example, there is no thought of comparing what their respective benefits and disadvantages may have been in the past. A study by Masujima et al. (2009) attempted to include this past assessment in the methodology by using a generational accounting formula that assessed the future with survival rates and discount rates taken into account but applied it retroactively to the past to estimate the net burden for generations grouped into five-year cohorts between the age of zero through 90. We adopt this same methodology to make generational comparisons. We look at generations separated by 30 years, or those born in 1950, 1980 and 2010 among others.

Government finances

As noted in the previous section, we derive the government's fiscal balance by aggregating individual benefits and burdens. The fiscal balance F_t is defined by the following expression,

$$F_t = \sum_i \left(T_{i,t} - B_{i,t} \right) N_{i,t} - (1 + r_t) D_t + OT_t$$

The first term is the product of the per capita net burden and the population by generation $N_{i,t}$ and indicates the government's tax and social security balance with respect to households. D_t is the government debt outstanding, while r_t is the interest rate paid. OT_t indicates other fiscal surpluses. Included in OT_t are corporate income taxes and property taxes from tax revenue, and, among expenditures, general administration and public works spending. The fiscal balance less interest payments yields the primary balance. The debt outstanding in period $t + 1$ declines (or expands if a deficit) only to the extent of the fiscal balance (surplus) in period t.

$$D_{t+1} = D_t - F_t$$

The fiscal variables are linked by the above identities, but in actual calculation we control the household burden so that the government debt converges to a certain level of GDP (about 250 per cent). We adjust the consumption tax and medical and nursing-care premiums in the baseline. In order to obtain the macro-aggregated total, generations other than generations 1, 2 and 3 are factored into the estimates.

Households

Budget constraints for households are considered as follows,

$$C_{i,t} + TC_{it} = [W_{i,t} - (T_{i,t} - \tilde{B}_{i,t})] \cdot PC_{i,t}$$

$W_{i,t}$ represents wages and $T_{i,t} - \tilde{B}_{i,t}$ is the tax and social-insurance net burden. In-kind benefits (medical treatment, nursing care, education) are excluded from benefits. The terms within the brackets represent disposable income, while $PC_{i,t}$ represents the propensity to consume. The term TC_{it} on the left side of the expression is the consumption tax burden, meaning that consumption expenditures, including the portion expended for consumption tax, are factored into the above expression. In one sense, households will seek to spread their consumption evenly over their life cycle, but here we assume instead that consumption is linked simply to disposable income in the period.[3] $PC_{i,t}$ is assumed to be exogenous. The wages $W_{i,t}$ earned on average by generation i at time t are influenced by the labour force participation rate $F_{i,t}$.

$$W_{i,t} = \bar{W}_{i,t} \cdot RLF_{i,t}$$

The term $\bar{W}_{i,t}$ represents the wage level when all workers in the same generation are working.

GDP

The health of government finances can be judged via the ratio to GDP of parameters such as the primary balance or the outstanding balance of government debt. We therefore need to derive GDP. To simplify the analysis, we abstract the capital stock and define real GDP (Y) in terms of the following production function,

$$Y = AL$$

---

3   Consumption remained weak even after the initial pullback that followed the consumption tax hike in 2014. This implies that many households are under income or liquidity constraints.

The term L represents the labour force population while A is labour productivity. L is the sum of the five-year-old population of men and women in production age multiplied by their labour participation rates. If RLF_i is deemed the labour force participation rate for each cohort 15 years and over, we have,

$$L = \sum_i RLF_i \cdot N_i$$

As the labour participation of the elderly rises in tandem with increasing lifespans, Y will rise owing to RLF_i. Nominal GDP $\tilde{Y}$ is the product of real GDP and the deflator P (an exogenous variable):

$$\tilde{Y} = PY$$

Discount rates

When assessing the value and benefit of social welfare and long-term public works projects, cultural properties, environmental protection and other policies extending over the long term and over multiple generations, one important question is how to weight the benefits that arise at different times. Discount rates using a given coefficient to discount values arising in the future can be understood in different ways.

Discounting can arise from, for example, (i) time preference and opportunity costs involved in investments, (ii) future uncertainty and value change, (iii) growth rate (productivity) due to capital accumulation and technological progress, and (iv) depreciation of capital stock and consumption goods.

Previous studies of generational accounting often used discount rates of 3–4 per cent per year. Masujima et al. (2010) adopted variable rates that add a premium on top of the growth rate. Suzuki et al. (2012) used the pension yield. Auerbach et al. (2011) ran simulations under various discount rates including $\rho = 3$ per cent based on past real interest rates and then attempting to verify the robustness of the results.

In the present paper, we adopted three options, namely using zero per cent (no discount rate), using the rate of 3 per cent, and using the productivity growth rate. Productivity is the approach of using labour expended as a standard for obtaining economic value and, in a practical sense, it is close to the per capita growth rate. Figure 9.5 is a graphic illustration of our adopted discount rate of ρ and β^{t-1}, which is the cumulative value of β. As indicated below, future productivity is assumed to grow at an annualised rate of 1 per cent. The base year for discounting is 2010.

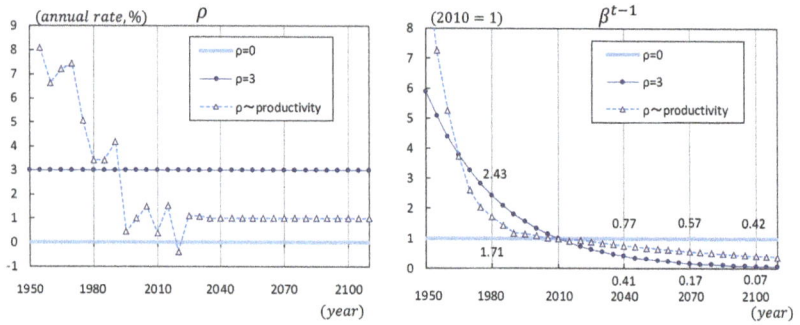

Figure 9.5. Discount rates
Source. Figure compiled by the authors

Data and assumptions

In this chapter, we explain the data used in the analysis and our assumptions about the future (including the macro-economic outlook, calculation of taxes and social security rates, and survival rates).

Data

One contribution of the present study is careful estimation of each generation's consumption on top of the components of generational accounting.

We divide generations into 21 cohorts of five years from age zero through four up to age 100 and over. The basic statistics used in our estimates are from sub-sectoring household accounts in the System of National Accounts (SNA) and the National Survey of Family Income and Expenditure (NSFIE),[4] which constitute the basic data for the above, supplemented by medical and nursing-care and educational data. Since data from NSFIE are originally based on households, we convert them

---

4   Stiglitz et al. (2010) have pointed out that 'Aggregate data is insufficient to recognize how distributional policy works'. The OECD provided guidelines for sub-sectoring of SNA. Estimates are made in conjunction with the NSFIE released in Japan every five years. See Kawagoe and Maeda (2017) for more details.

into individual amounts (equivalent values) using the household-member ratio from the population census. Children are responsible for a portion of household consumption, while the head of household is considered to bear the tax and social-insurance burden.

Consumption is defined as including the individual's co-payment less in-kind medical and nursing-care and education benefits, and subtracting imputed rent. Imputed rent is usually a portion of consumption, but the SNA also regards it as a household operating surplus. We avoid complexities by omitting imputed rent. Also, using data on the elderly from the NSFIE (households of single females aged 80 through 84), we incorporate into our analysis a declining consumption with advancing age.[5]

Among benefits, medical, nursing-care and educational in-kind benefits comprise a single component of generational accounting. In-kind benefits correspond to costs covered by public insurance in the case of medical and nursing care and expenses of the government for compulsory education and grant assistance for private schools in the case of education. Co-payments for education (including tuition and other such expenses for private schools) are included in consumption. 'Other In-kind Benefits' refers to forms of public assistance, such as the one-time allowance for childbirth and maternity benefits, childcare leave benefits, the childcare allowance, unemployment benefits and welfare benefits. The consumption tax burden is estimated simply as the product of consumption and the consumption tax rate.

We estimate values for the above variables by age (not cohort) in five-year intervals over the period from 1994 through 2014 and, for the past, applied the data retroactively using relevant macro-economic indicators. Time series data by cohort could be obtained by tracing and linking values by age using cohort age. For converting nominal and real values, we used the private consumption deflator. Real variables are based on 2011 prices.

---

5   Female data is used because figures on males are easily confused with residents of specified facilities, making it difficult to ascertain the actual numbers.

Macro-economic assumptions

We have formulated a number of future values based on macro-economic assumptions (Table 9.1). For the years through 2030, we base our assumptions on the Japan Center for Economic Research (JCER) Medium-Term Economic Forecast. For the years after 2030, we have extrapolated from that forecast to formulate an outlook along the lines of the cautious scenario H described in the Official Fiscal Projections as released by the Ministry of Health, Labour and Welfare (MHLW) in 2014.

Table 9.1. Macro-economic assumptions

(annual rate, %)						
This study				Ministry of Health, Labour and Welfare		
(~2030)		(2035~2115)		(2024~)		
Based on JCER's forecast				F	G	H
1)	Real wage	0.7	1.0	1.3	1.0	0.7
2)	Deflator for consumption	0.6	0.5	1.2	0.9	0.6
3)	Total factor productivity	0.6		1.0	0.7	0.5
4)	Labour productivity	1.0	1.0			
5)	Long-term interest rate	1.4	1.0	4.0	3.1	2.3

Note. a) Figures up to 2030 by JCER's forecast are those for 2025–30.

b) Long-term interest rates are yields on 10-year government bonds, while those of MHLW are returns on financial investment.

c) Deflator for GDP is assumed to be identical to that for consumption.

d) F, G, H are scenarios presented by MHLW as alternatives. A–E are more optimistic.

Source. Authors' assumptions based on JCER's Medium-Term Economic Forecast and MHLW's Official Fiscal Projections

Our principal assumptions for the years 2035 and after include the following:

1. per capita labour productivity and real wages will grow at an annual rate of 1 per cent

2. prices (the consumption deflator and the GDP deflator) will rise at about 0.5 per cent annually

3. the long-term interest rate (gauged by the yield on 10-year Japanese Government bonds) will hover at about 1 per cent.

Assumptions regarding tax and social welfare

One important factor concerns the social welfare benefits and burdens slide rule (or the link to the macro-economic indicators). In our study, we have assumed that medical and nursing-care premiums and the consumption tax rate will be raised with a view to maintaining the government debt-to-GDP ratio at about 250 per cent. This is just one of the stabilised levels of debt that we reach by gradually closing the deficit of primary balance, and does not have specific meaning.

1. consumption will be linked to the disposable income with consumption tax deducted

2. income taxes will be linked to the wages for the working population and pensions for the elderly

3. the social-insurance premium burden:

    a. pension premiums (imposed on the working population) will be linked to wages

    b. as for medical and nursing care (the working population), premiums will be raised in line with aggregate benefits up to a ceiling of about 20 per cent of wages through 2065

4. social welfare benefits:

    a. the 'macro-economic slide' will be implemented with regard to pensions through 2045. The macro-economic slide serves to cap the growth rate of benefits in periods when the growth rate of the elderly is high. Since the projected inflation rate is low, we have assumed zero growth in the amount of benefits for both new recipients receiving pension benefits for the first time and existing recipients already receiving benefits during this period

    b. thereafter, benefits for new recipients would in principle be linked to wages and benefits for existing recipients would be linked to the price level. However, we have raised the growth rate for existing recipients slightly above the price level so that the difference between new and existing recipients does not widen

    c. we assume that medical and nursing-care benefits will be linked to wages.

Survival rate projections

Our projections for survival rates are based on MHLW Life Tables. These data measure factors such as mortality rates (i.e. the likelihood of dying within the next year) of persons at every age covered by the Life Table. In our present analysis, we have linked in order Life Tables already released and then projected survival rates for cohorts by birth year. Since all generations covered by our analysis have remaining life as of 2017, we need to establish certain assumptions regarding future mortality rates. We have applied mortality-rate projections used in the Population Projections for Japan released by NIPSSR through 2065. Since there are no mortality-rate projections from and after 2066, we have extrapolated for future years based on the projection for 2065.[6]

Based on the above projections, the likelihood of surviving to an age, which we refer to as the survival rate, of each generation would be at age 70: (i) 76.3 per cent for Generation 1, which is influenced by a high mortality rate during childhood; (ii) 88.6 per cent for Generation 2; and (3) 90 per cent or more for Generation 3. The median lifespans for each cohort are estimated to be 85.8 years for Generation 1, 90 years for Generation 2, and 93.2 years for Generation 3 (Figure 9.6).

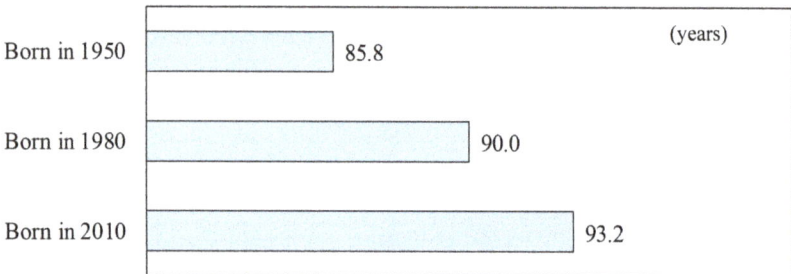

Figure 9.6. Expected lifespan of each cohort (median)
Source. Estimation using NIPSSR's Japanese Mortality Database, www.ipss.go.jp/p-toukei/JMD/index-en.asp

---

6   With regard to the generation born in 2010, we assume a 0.1 per cent annual erosion in mortality rates based on the lowest mortality rate in 2065.

Consumption, benefits and burden profiles for the three generations

Figure 9.7 shows consumption and generational accounting age trends in a baseline case for the three generations (those born in 1950, 1980 and 2010) respectively, based on the above premises. All values are presented in 2011 prices. The △ symbol indicates the status of each generation as of 2015. It should be noted that all values after that year are projections.

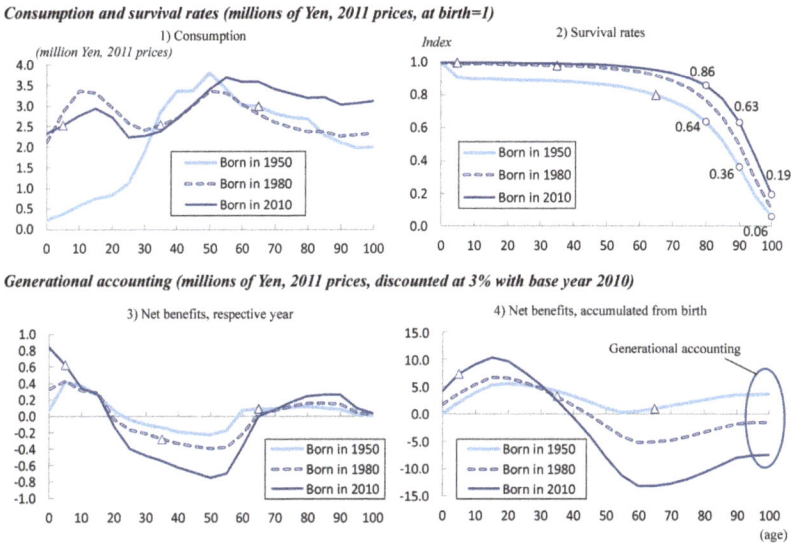

Consumption and survival rates (millions of Yen, 2011 prices, at birth=1)

Generational accounting (millions of Yen, 2011 prices, discounted at 3% with base year 2010)

Figure 9.7. Consumption and generational accounting

Note. Benefits–Premiums (pension, medical and elderly care) + education benefits – income tax – consumption tax.

Source. Authors' calculation

A look at consumption (panel 1) in Figure 9.7 reveals that the consumption level of Generation 1 during its youth is low. This generation was born shortly after the war and did not benefit early on from the subsequent economic growth. In contrast, Generation 2 enjoyed a high level of consumption during youth. The level of household consumption rose in the period of the economic bubble, part of which was enjoyed during childhood. The values for Generation 3 are for the most part projections.

Until approximately 2070, this generation will feel the impact of the rising burden caused by the need to stabilise government finances through increases in the consumption tax and medical and nursing-care premiums. Their consumption during midlife (up to 2060s) will therefore be lower than that of Generation 2. Generation 2, which is 35 years old in 2015, will face a rising burden in almost all parts of their remaining lives, and their consumption growth rate will consequently be low. In the second half of life for Generation 3, the burden increase will run its course and, although the rate of growth will be slow (about 1 per cent per capita in real terms), their consumption level will be highest among the three generations thanks to steady economic growth. The consumption levels of the three generations will be about the same at age 50, but if per capita wages for Generation 1 are set at 1, per capita wages will be 1.25 for Generation 2 and 1.69 for Generation 3. Owing to this rising burden, later generations will be unable to enjoy the benefits suggested by economic growth. The consumption that Generation 3 can enjoy can be further reduced if we discount the future.

Panel 2 shows survival rates by cohort. In contrast with Generation 1, which has a 64 per cent survival rate at age 80, the survival rate for Generation 3 is 86 per cent at the same age.

Panel 3 shows net benefits, the basis of generational accounting, shown for each respective year. Data are adjusted using a discount rate of 3 per cent. There are disparities in benefits during childhood because allowances for childbirth and child rearing have been increasing in recent years. Generation 1 did not have the opportunity to benefit from such family allowances. From the age of 20, when people enter the workforce, the burdens begin to exceed the benefits. Thereafter, the burden gets larger for each successively older generation and it rapidly expands when individuals reach their 40s and 50s. The consequences of adopting a transferable financing scheme, which requires the current working generation to bear social security expenses as societal ageing progresses, are evident here. Benefits in old age are marginally greater for later generations. Panel 4 shows the cumulative net benefits of panel 3 through age. Net benefits are positive for Generation 1 throughout life, but Generations 2 and 3 begin experiencing a net burden from around age 40, a situation that continues for life. The cumulative total lifelong value on the far right is equal to that under generational accounting. The later the generation, the larger is the net burden.

The components of general accounting are shown in Figure 9.8.1 (benefits) and in Figure 9.8.2 (payments). A look at panel 1 of Figure 9.8.1 shows that Generation 1, which will be subject to the macro-economic slide (through the 2040s), will see a gradual decline in the amount of benefits in real terms. Generations 2 and 3 will experience a rising trend in receipts because they will begin receiving pensions after the macro-economic slide is no longer applied but also because existing pensions are expected to see a slightly higher growth than the price level in our setting.

Medical and nursing-care benefits are higher the later the generation because we assume that medical and nursing-care remuneration will be linked to wages, which is also assumed to be faster in growth rates than the price level. 'Other cash benefits' of panel 3, as mentioned above, reflect the fact that benefits paid during childhood, such as childbirth benefits and child allowances, are higher in recent years. Values for education in-kind benefits are influenced, for example, by the fact that personnel expenses for teachers differ in each period and that, in recent years, grant programs have been created for high school tuition costs.

Benefits (millions of Yen, 2011 prices) – individual basis

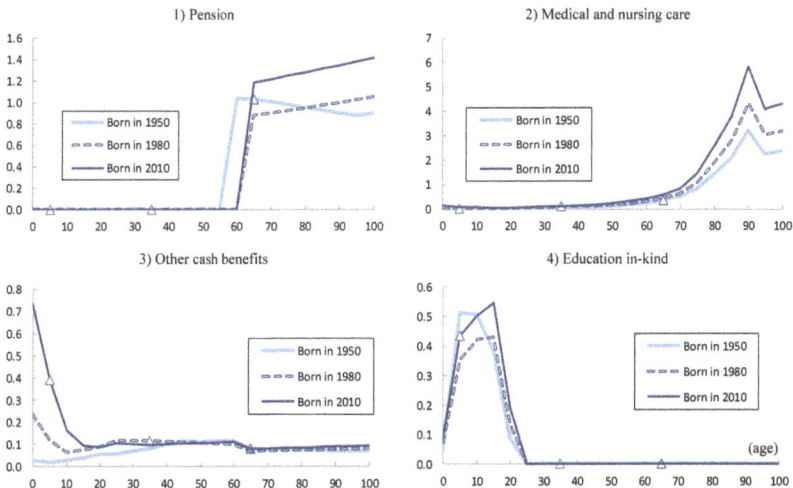

Figure 9.8.1. Components of generational accounting – benefits
Source. Authors' calculation

Taxes and premiums (millions of Yen, 2011 prices) – imposed on the head of the household except consumption tax

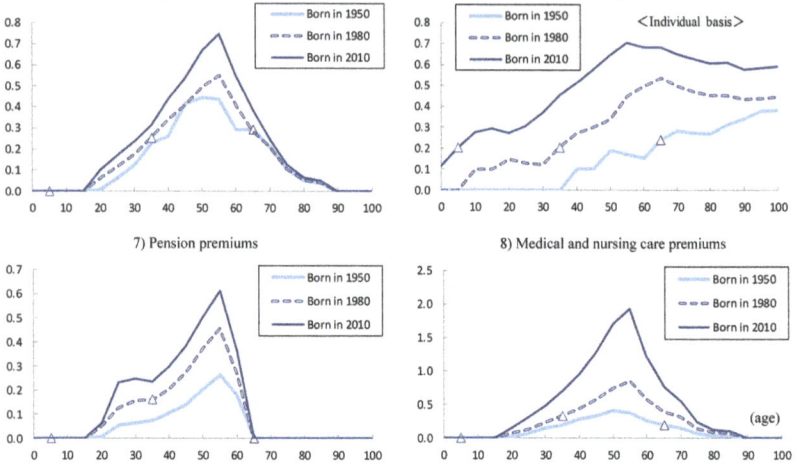

Figure 9.8.2. Components of generational accounting – payments
Source. Authors' calculations

As for the payment components, burdens become heavier the later the generation. This reflects the assumption that consumption tax, medical and nursing-care insurance premiums will be raised through the 2060s. When we compare the burden of each generation at the age of 50, Generation 3 will bear 2.5 times more burden than Generation 1, and Generation 3 cannot make the most of the increase in wages from economic growth.

Next let us examine how macro-economic aggregates evolve (Figure 9.9). The GDP growth rate will be slightly negative in real terms. We expect per capita labour productivity to remain steady at 1 per cent per annum, as the labour force population will decline by just over 1 per cent per year starting in the 2040s. Nominal GDP will grow at a pace of just under 0.5 per cent. We see the long-term interest rate (the yield on the benchmark 10-year Japanese Government bonds) at 1 per cent, exceeding the nominal growth rate. In the government financial balance, the government debt to GDP ratio will be held to about 250 per cent, in which case it will be necessary for the central and local governments to maintain approximately a 1 per cent surplus in their primary balance to GDP ratio.

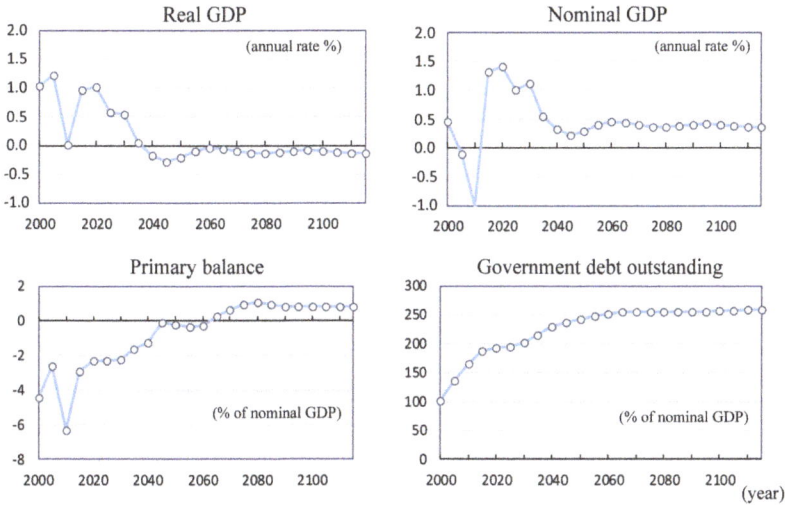

Figure 9.9. Macro-economic indicators
Source. Authors' calculations

Simulation

Additional consumption obtainable from living longer

First, we derive the benefits that arise from longer life in terms of the increase in consumption that longer life makes possible. We assume for simplicity that the survival rates for generations 2 and 3 were as low as those for generations born in 1950, and see how much more consumption the later generations secure with longer survival rates. Our findings are shown in Figure 9.10. The upper and middle panels show lifetime consumption, the upper panel being the baseline case and the second panel being the case with the survival rates assumed equivalent to that of Generation 1. The bottom panels are the difference between the two ΔC_1 and its ratios to the baseline.

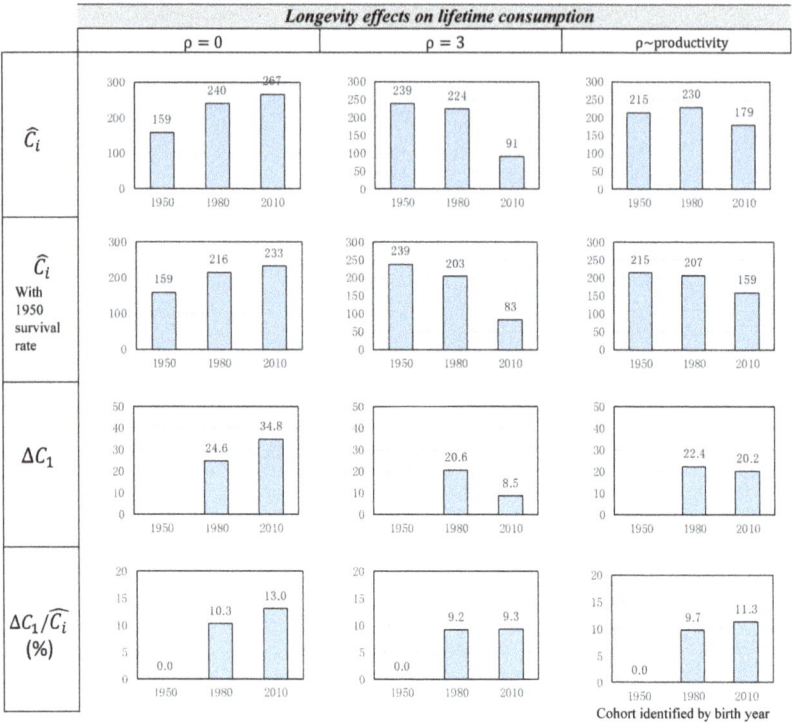

Figure 9.10. Lifetime consumption $\hat{C}_i$ and its increase from longevity ΔC_1 (millions of yen, 2011 prices)

Source. Authors' calculations

Let us first consider lifetime consumption $\hat{C}_i$. The findings differ according to the discount rate setting. If we focus on the difference between Generation 3 and the preceding generations, the lifetime consumption of Generation 3 is seen to be the lowest, except in the no-discounting case. If we adjust the difference between the generations using either 3 per cent or productivity as discount rates that reflect the difference of economic circumstances where each generation is placed, Generation 3 can be viewed as the poorest. When using productivity, the outcome falls in the middle between no discount and 3 per cent discount.

The rates of increase in the benefits ΔC_1 of longer life for Generation 3 are (reading left to right) 13 per cent, 9 per cent and 11 per cent. In the case of Generation 2 the results are 10 per cent, 9 per cent and 10 per cent, which is not much different from Generation 3. These results are the consequence of a rapid lengthening of lifespans between 1950 and 1980. The differences arising from the discount rate settings are not especially large and we can conclude that the extension of lifespans arising over the past 60 years has given rise to an increase in lifetime consumption of about 10 per cent.

The impact of working longer

When people live longer, it is natural for them to continue working longer too. Japanese presently begin receiving a public pension (the basic pension) from the age of 65, the general target age for leaving the workforce. In contrast with the present practice, we assume that people will work 10 years longer. Our model assumes that the age at which they begin receiving their pension will be rolled back and that they will continue paying pension-insurance premiums as they work.

This will give rise to latitude in the government's financial balance. It might be seen as a financial dividend for the government arising from longer lifespans. The upturn in the government's primary balance relative to the baseline case we will define as the fiscal surplus. We also consider a scenario in which the surplus is restored to households (as through reductions in medical and nursing-care insurance premiums). In view of further life extensions anticipated in the future, we do not see it as overly unrealistic to assume that people will stay in the workforce for an additional 10 years, but given the large differences among the elderly, we have also included estimates envisioning a five-year extension of working life. The cases we envision can thus be summarised as follows,

a. the baseline case

b. extension of work by 10 years

c. extension of work by 10 years (with the financial surplus being restored to households)

d. extension of work by five years

e. extension of work by five years (with the financial surplus being restored to households).

The additional time that we assume the elderly will spend in the labour force is depicted in Figure 9.11. Notwithstanding the retirement age of 65, just under 70 per cent of Japanese men continue working from the ages of 65 through 69 and just over 30 per cent continue working from the ages of 70 through 74. The assumption is that elderly people aged 75 to 79 work as much as their predecessors would have when 10 (or five) years younger. We assumed that the extensions take place after 2035 for 65 through 69 year olds, after 2045 for 70 through 74, and after 2055 for 75 through 79.

Along with the assumption of the labour force rate, wages, taxes, social security payments and propensity to consume of those aged from 65 through 69 to 75 through 79 are set to the same level as those 10 (or five) years younger in the baseline. Elderly Japanese people have a willingness to work and, in terms of health, they are younger than the preceding generations of the same age. It is assumed that it will be possible to obtain higher wages if we have a system to encourage elderly employment.

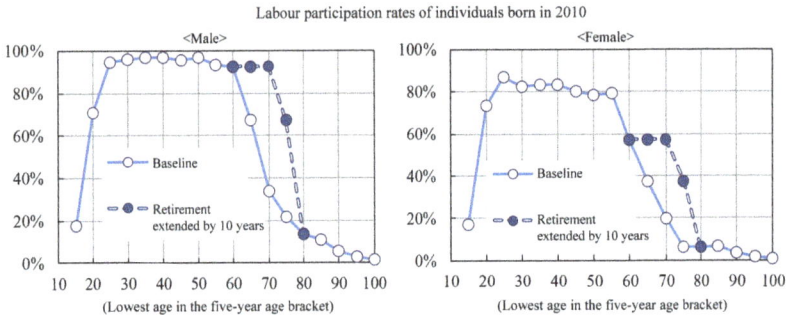

Labour participation rates of individuals born in 2010

Figure 9.11. Assumption of extended retirement
Source. Figure compiled by the authors

The fiscal surplus turns out to be as represented in Table 9.2.

Table 9.2. Fiscal surplus expected from extended retirement

		(percentage of nominal GDP)
10 years longer	case (b)	6.1~6.8
5 years longer	case (d)	3.7~4.1
(Deviation from case (a))		

Source. Authors' calculations

Next, we look at what the impact on consumption and benefits would be for each generation if the fiscal 'dividend' were restored to households (Figure 9.12). The top panel Baseline $\hat{C}_i$ is the same as in Figure 9.10. The generational accounting value $\hat{G}_i$ is identical with the value in the final year of Figure 9.7 (4) for the case of the 3 per cent discounting. Whatever the discount-rate setting, the generational accounting value is positive for Generation 1, about even for Generation 2 and negative for Generation 3. This confirms that the younger the generation, the greater is the net burden.

The term $\hat{G}_i + \Delta C_1$ is the sum of (i) generational accounting balance, or the costs imposed on (or benefits gained by) each generation from the advance of ageing; and (ii) the increase in consumption that constitutes the benefit from longer lifespans. It is the overall assessment indicator for societal ageing. The findings show that the disadvantages for Generation 3 are somewhat alleviated. In the absence of discounting, the value is highest for Generation 3, while valuation based on productivity yields puts Generation 2 and Generation 3 at about the same level.

The bottom panel in Figure 6.14 represents a case in which the fiscal surplus from working longer is restored to households. Evident here is the increase of lifetime consumption $\hat{C}_i$ thanks to wages earned by the elderly who remain in the workforce, which we will label ΔC_2. Generation 1 is at the best advantage in terms of generational accounting $\hat{G}_i$, as in case of the top panel, but Generation 2 and Generation 3 are either at about the same level or, in the case of no discounting or productivity discounting, Generation 3 slightly exceeds Generation 2.

When the increased portion ΔC_1 of direct consumption resulting from longer lifespans and the increased portion ΔC_2 of consumption accompanying the longer period in the workforce are added to generational accounting (bottom panel), the benefit for Generation 3 is seen to be largest in the case of no discounting. In the case of discounting for productivity, it is around the same level as for Generation 1. With discounting of 3 per cent, the benefits for generations 2 and 3 are substantial.

Figure 9.13 shows the case in which the period in the workforce is extended by five years and confirms the same trends. If we factor in the consumption obtainable from living longer and the increased consumption made possible from the elderly working longer, it no longer follows that the youngest are subject to the greatest disadvantages.

In the above calculations, the discount rate can have a decisive influence on the evaluation of the result. It is difficult to make deterministic decisions on what to adopt as the discount rate. In this study, we used three discount rates of zero per cent, 3 per cent, and productivity. Three per cent is the value often used in previous generational accounting studies, including by Auerbach et al. (2011). The reason we added zero per cent and productivity as alternatives, which are lower than 3 per cent in the forecast period, is that the setting of 3 per cent seems to exceed the real interest rate levels since 2000. We assume that the future real interest rate stabilises at 0.5 per cent in the long term. Discount rates by productivity may better match this assumption for the forecast period.

Lifetime consumption $\hat{C}_i$ and generational accounting $\hat{G}_i$
Increase from longevity ΔC_1, and from extended retirement ΔC_2

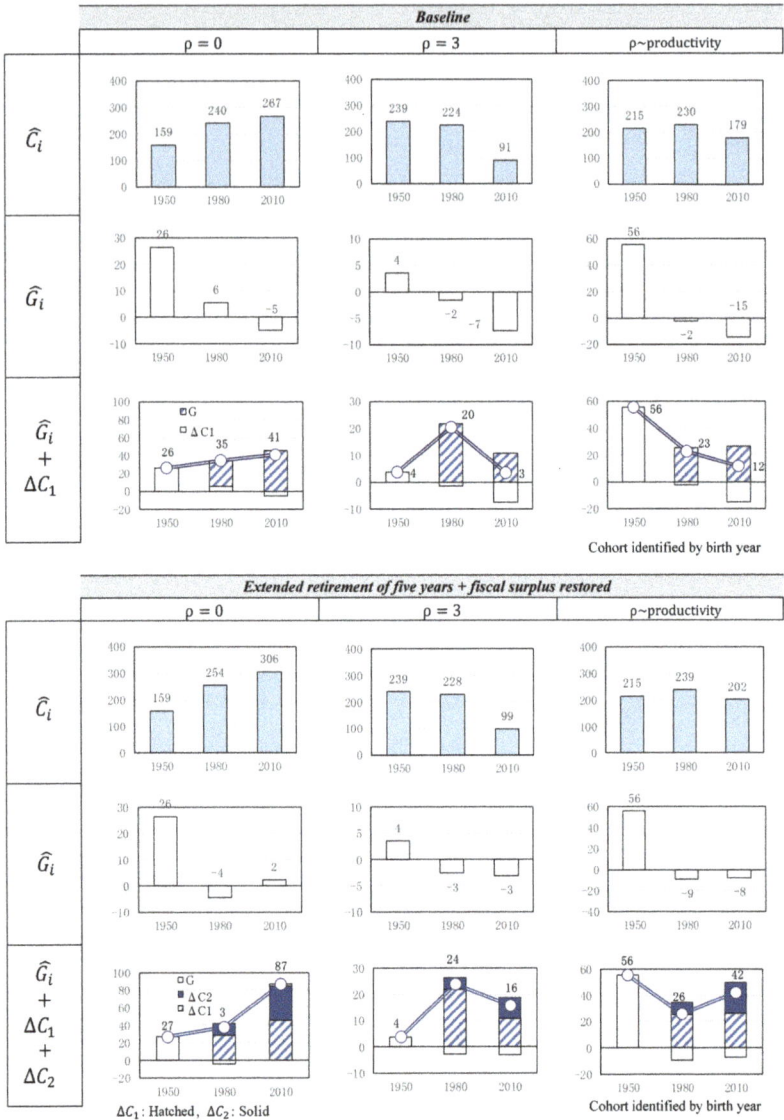

Figure 9.12. Effects of retirement extended by 10 years (millions of yen, 2011 prices)

Source. Authors' calculation

Lifetime consumption $\hat{C}_i$ and generational accounting $\hat{G}_i$
Increase from longevity ΔC_1, and from extended retirement ΔC_2

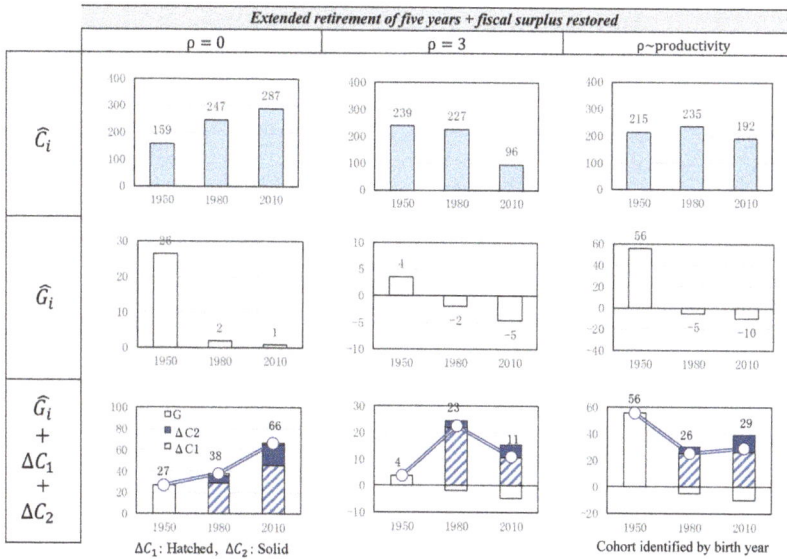

Figure 9.13. Effects of retirement extended by five years (millions of yen, 2011 prices)

Source. Authors' calculation

Considering consumption allocation across multiple periods, the discount rate is approximately the sum of the per capita growth rate and the time preference rate. In this study, per capita output is projected to grow 1 per cent annually. Assuming a discount rate of 3 per cent implies that the time preference rate is 2 per cent. The consequences of climate change influenced the Stern Review to adopt one of the lowest preference rates at 0.1 per cent. Its discount rate is set at around 1.5 per cent (Stern 2015). Different time preference and discount rates may be adopted depending on what we evaluate.

Conclusion and discussion

This study's focus on three generations seeks to identify their net tax and social welfare burden and the additional consumption enjoyed from living longer. In addition to generational accounting as taken up by previous research, we have estimated consumption for each generation.

We confirm the findings of previous research to the effect that, the younger the generation, the greater will be its net burden with respect to tax and social welfare balances (generational accounting) payable to the government. Even if the ratio of government debt to GDP can be held to 250 per cent in a bid to stabilise government finances, the old age dependency ratio will continue to rise until approximately 2060. As a result, and because Japan finances social security costs from tax revenues and social-insurance premiums, the burden on the working generation will continue to rise over this period. Generation 2 will face a rising burden throughout most of their lives while Generation 3 will face it through midlife.

If the survival rate of Generation 1 forms the baseline for measuring the benefits of living longer, Generation 3 will experience a 9–13 per cent increase in lifetime consumption. Generation 2 will see a 9–10 per cent increase.

The elderly's longer participation in the workforce has the effect of ameliorating the need for fiscal belt-tightening. In view of the fact that lifespans will continue to increase, we have assumed that people will work 10 years longer than at present, that the age at which they will begin receiving pension benefits will in principle be raised to 75, and that while working they will continue to pay social insurance premiums. In that case, the primary balance of the central and local governments to GDP would improve by 6–7 per cent over the baseline case.

As noted above, extending people's time in the workforce will even out the disparities between the burdens and benefits of each generation. If the resulting fiscal surplus is then applied to reducing medical and nursing-care premiums, it will be possible to lighten the burden on the younger generations.

What might the implications of the above analysis be? First, it once again highlights the importance of maintaining good health. Maintaining good health is desirable for its own sake. Increasing healthy lifespans makes it possible to preserve quality of life during old age and to fully enjoy consumption. A look at the health status of Japan's elderly as gauged by the ratio of 'Persons with subjective symptoms of physical disorders' in the Comprehensive Survey of Living Conditions published by the MHLW shows that elderly Japanese in 2016 were on average five to 10 years more youthful than they were in 1998 (Figure 9.14). Further efforts to maintain and improve health as well as preventive medical treatment and nursing care are thus important.[7]

Elderly Japanese people also wish to work. According to a survey conducted by the Cabinet Office in 2014, 57 per cent of those aged 60 or over answer the question of 'What age do you want to work to?' with up to 75 or older (in Figure 9.15, these answers varied from 'forever, if I can', 'until about 75 years old' or 'until about 80 years old').

The second implication of this study is the importance of creating institutions to promote self-help efforts. This could also be described as narrowing the scope of public insurance. The future burden is concentrated on the younger generations because most of the cost for medical and nursing care for the elderly is funded through public insurance. The extension of time spent in the workforce discussed in our analysis is one form of self-help. The fact that the age at which Japanese people begin receiving pensions is set at 65 in a sense constrains people over 35 from working. Kitao (2015) estimates that reducing the amount of per capita pension payments by 20 per cent would raise the labour force participation rate among people aged 70 through 90 by from 11.6 per cent to 24.2 per cent. In February 2018, Cabinet met to decide on the general agenda for measures to make it possible for people to begin receiving public pension benefits after the age of 70. In 2013, JCER proposed privatisation of the earnings-related component of public pensions and the use of taxes as a funding source for the basic pension (Iwata & Saruyama 2013). If the social-insurance premiums imposed on employers were eliminated, it would also have the effect of creating jobs and boosting wages. Also important would be the use of technological innovation to enhance the productivity of the elderly and continuing education to enhance the human capital of prime-age and elderly workers.[8]

---

7   The potential contribution that health-promotion expenditures (investment) and health and preventive benefits for medical and nursing care could make toward improving health are described in such health economics studies as Yuda et al. (2013) and Murphy and Topel (2006).

8   For models relating to the falling birthrate and societal ageing, population decline and technological development see Hashimoto and Tabata (2016); regarding the relationship between recurrent education and longer lifespans, see Tanaka (2017).

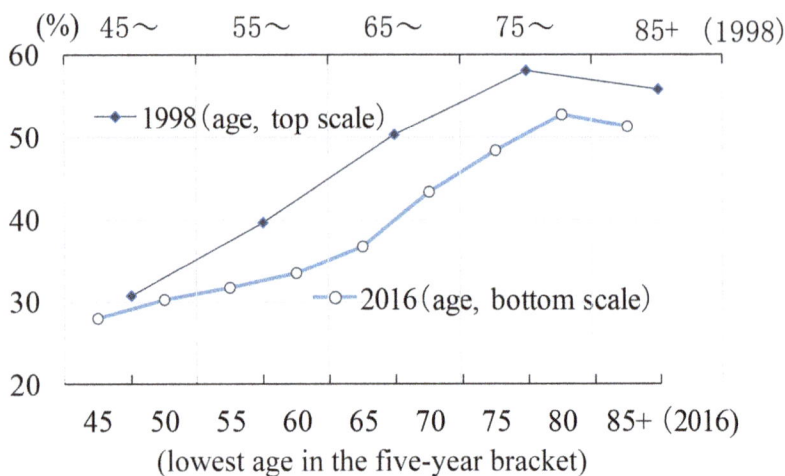

Figure 9.14. Ratio of 'have subjective symptoms of physical disorders'

Source. Comprehensive survey of living conditions, MHLW, www.mhlw.go.jp/english/database/db-hss/cslc-index.html

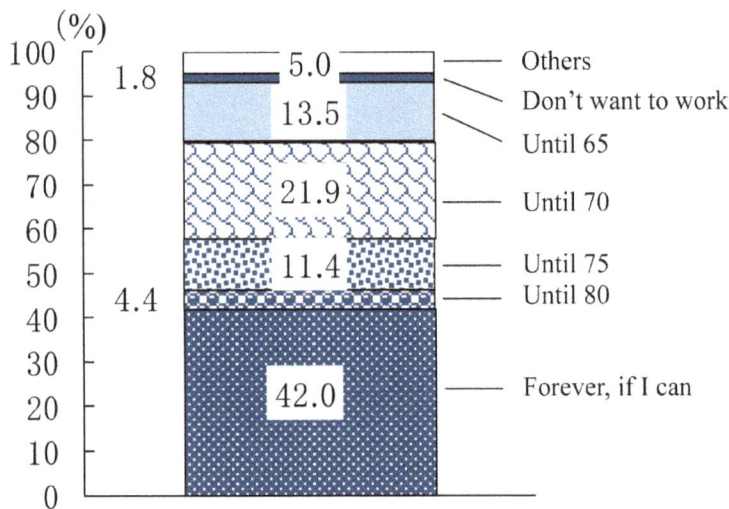

Figure 9.15. What age do you want to work to?

Note. Survey of individuals aged 60 and over who are currently working.

Source. Survey of elderly people's everyday life, 2014, Cabinet Office, www8.cao.go.jp/kourei/ishiki/h26/sougou/zentai/index.html (Japanese)

Self-help also involves the element of saving on one's own. Privatising the public pension system would raise the household-savings rate and, through capital accumulation, would help improve individual utility (Iwata 1997). Birkeland and Prescott (2007) compare alternative modes of operating the social-insurance system by comparing the tax-and-transfer system with an independent savings-for-retirement system, including investment, and argue that adopting a savings-for-retirement system with a sizable government debt would enhance utility. They argue that the optimum size of the government debt relative would be about 4.5 times GDP for the United States and just over twice GDP for Japan. Iwamoto and Fukui (2014) have argued for a funded medical and nursing-care insurance system. They report that it would be possible to even out the burden among the generations by setting the insurance premium imposed on the working generation at a much higher level.

Thirdly, the burden of the 'future generation' is hidden in our calculations. The burdens on the existing generations, especially the younger generation, are relieved to some extent by stabilising government debt at 250 per cent of GDP. The policy to ease the burden for existing generations is a policy to make future generations pay the price. Even under the above conditions, Generation 3's tax and social security burden at the age of 55 will be around three times that of Generation 1 at the same age. Generation 3's consumption level is barely maintained with the condition that per capita productivity grows 1 per cent per year and the long-term interest rate is kept at 1 per cent. In the event of a more severe economic situation, a larger scale debt reduction plan will be required and the disadvantage of the young generation may not be resolved even when extended retirement is enforced.

Japanese societal ageing is only half completed. The most severe stages are yet to come. Japan needs to enhance the sustainability of its social-insurance system and urgently institute reforms to narrow the gaps among the generations regarding the related burdens and benefits.

References

Auerbach, AJ, Gokhale, J & Kotlikoff, LJ (2011 (1991)). 'Generational accounting: A meaningful alternative to deficit accounting'. In V Tanzi & HH Zee (eds), *Recent developments in public finance*, Vol. 2, *Stabilization and growth* (pp 122–77), Elgar Research Collection, The International Library of Critical Writings in Economics, Vol. 250. Cheltenham, UK and Northampton, Mass.: Elgar.

Auerbach, AJ, Kotlikoff, LJ & Leibfritz, W (eds) (1999). *Generational accounting around the world*, University of Chicago Press.

Becker, GS (2007). 'Health as human capital: synthesis and extensions', *Oxford Economic Papers*, 59, 379–410. doi.org/10.1093/oep/gpm020.

Birkeland, K & Prescott, EC (2007). 'On the needed quantity of government debt', *Quarterly Review*, Federal Reserve Bank of Minneapolis, 31(1), 2–15.

Bloom, DE, Canning, D & Fink, G (2010). 'Population aging and economic growth', *Oxford Review of Economic Policy*, 26(4), 583–612. academic.oup.com/oxrep/article-abstract/26/4/583/453716.

Gratton, L & Scott, A (2016). *The 100-year life*. Bloomsbury Information Ltd.

Hashimoto, K & Tabata, K (2016). 'Demographic change, human capital accumulation and R&D based growth', *Canadian Journal of Economics*, 49(2), 707–37. doi.org/10.1111/caje.12211.

Iwamoto, Y & Fukui, T (2014). 'Policy options for financing the future health and long-term care costs in Japan', *Fiscal Policy and Management in East Asia*, 50(3), 324–38.

Iwata, K (1997). 'Privatization of public pension system and its welfare consequence: The case for Japan and the USA', *The Japanese Journal of Social Security Policy*, 33(2), 149–56 (in Japanese).

Iwata, K & Saruyama, S (2013). *Growth friendly reform of tax and social security: Examination with macro-econometric model*, RIETI Discussion Paper Series, 13-J-001 (in Japanese).

Kawagoe, M (2018). 'How can Japanese extended longevity be evaluated? An estimate of a fruit of economic growth', *Keizai Bunseki*, March, 197, 28–52 (in Japanese).

Kawagoe, M & Maeda, S (2017). *What does sub-sectoring household accounts tell us about aging in Japan?*, OHEM Discussion Paper, 2017-E002.

Kitao, S (2015). 'Fiscal cost of demographic transition in Japan', *Journal of Economic Dynamics & Control*, 54, 37–58. doi.org/10.1016/j.jedc.2015.02.015.

Masujima, M, Shimasawa, M & Murakami, T (2009). *Study on generational accounting model with the social security system*, ESRI Discussion Paper Series, No. 217 (in Japanese).

Masujima, M, Shimasawa, M, Tanaka, G, Sugishita, M, Yamamoto, H & Takanaka, M (2010). *Inter- and intra-generational inequality*, ESRI Discussion Paper Series, No. 248 (in Japanese).

Murphy, KM & Topel, RH (2006). 'The value of health and longevity', *Journal of Political Economy*, 114(51), 871–904. doi.org/10.1086/508033.

Oeppen, J & Vaupel, JW (2002). 'Broken limits to life expectancy', *Science*, 296, 1029–31. doi.org/10.1126/science.1069675.

Stern, N (2015). 'The ethics of intertemporal values and valuations'. In *Why are we waiting? The logic, urgency, and promise of tackling climate change* (pp 151–84). MIT Press.

Stiglitz, J, Sen, A & Fitoussi, J-P (2010). *Mis-measuring our lives: Why GDP doesn't add up*. The New Press.

Suzuki, W, Masujima, M, Shiraishi, K & Morishige, A (2012). *Intergenerational inequality caused by the social security system*, ESRI Discussion Paper Series, No. 281 (in Japanese).

Tanaka, M (2017). 'Human capital accumulation through recurrent education', *Economic Analysis*, 196, 49–84 (in Japanese).

Yuda, M, Suzuki, W, Morozumi, R & Iwamoto, Y (2013). 'The effect of introducing prevention benefits on changes in care levels of support-level 1 care receivers', *The Japanese Journal of Social Security Policy*, 49(3), 310–25 (in Japanese).

10

FEMALE LABOUR FORCE PARTICIPATION IN INDONESIA: WHY HAS IT STALLED?

Lisa Cameron, Diana Contreras Suarez
and William Rowell

Introduction

Indonesia now boasts the largest economy in the Association of Southeast Asian Nations (ASEAN) and the 16th worldwide (Asian Development Bank (ADB) 2015). The economy has expanded considerably since the 1970s, except when growth halted temporarily during the East Asian financial crisis of 1997–98. Continued economic development has meant rising average incomes, changes in the sectoral structure of the economy (from agriculture to manufacturing and services) and increasing industrialisation and urbanisation, among other changes (Elias & Noone 2011). Despite the significant changes in the Indonesian economy, the impact on the experience of women in the labour market is muted. The 2014 World Development Indicators show that 51.4 per cent of Indonesian women aged 15 and above participate in the labour force (either working or looking for work). This participation rate has remained largely unchanged over the past two decades and the large gap between female and male labour force participation persists. Female labour force participation in Indonesia remains low relative to countries in the region at a comparable stage of development (see also ADB, International Labour Organization (ILO) & Islamic Development Bank (IDB) 2010).

The aim of this paper is to identify the drivers of female labour force participation (FLFP) in Indonesia and why FLFP has remained unchanged over the period 1996 to 2013. We separate labour force participation into components on the supply and demand sides of the labour market – educational attainment, marital status, fertility, household structure, distance to urban centres, main local industries – and implement a cohort analysis that separates out the effect of life cycle factors (age) on women's labour force participation and cohort effects (changes in participation over time).

Understanding the constraints that women face in the labour market is essential in forming policies aimed at addressing these constraints to encourage FLFP. Previous studies attribute the gender gap in participation to family roles, child-caring and cultural norms in relation to women's traditional roles (Jayachandran 2015). Increases in participation are likely to have flow-on effects through female empowerment that, in turn, may affect other facets of the gender divide – for example, political representation, having greater say over household decision-making and being less accepting of spousal violence. Identifying the drivers of low FLFP is also important to help address constraints facing the Indonesian economy, which is trying to shift from a pattern of economic growth driven by resources and cheap labour and capital to growth based on high productivity and innovation (ADB 2015). Increased FLFP has the potential to be a key contributor to improving Indonesia's productivity, enabling it to avoid the middle-income trap and continue its economic development into the future.

Although the raw figures on women's labour market participation show little change over the last two decades, we show that this masks changes that offset one another in the current population. The analysis produces several key results. First, the main drivers of FLFP appear to be on the supply side – marital status, educational attainment and the number of children aged between 0 and 2 years of age present in the household. On the demand side, the main source of village income (reflecting the local industrial structure) impacts FLFP.

Second, we find higher education is important to increase FLFP at young ages when household responsibilities are the main barrier to women participating. Most single and highly educated women have entered the labour market by age 25 and keep participating almost until retirement age. In contrast, women who are married, less educated and have children only increase their participation rates after age 40.

Third, once we control for individual and household characteristics, we find that the underlying propensity for FLFP has increased over time, despite the lack of change in the aggregate figures. The cohort analysis shows that labour force participation of young females is higher than their older counterparts with similar characteristics at the same age. This is particularly marked in urban areas. If this trend continues, we expect the aggregate level of FLFP to increase over time as the older cohorts exit the labour market – although the changing composition of the economy away from the agriculture sector currently works in the opposite direction.

Even with this increase in younger women's labour market participation, the projections from our model show that, without considerable policy support, it is unlikely that Indonesia will reach its G20 commitment of reducing the gap between male and female labour force participation by 25 per cent by 2025.[1] This implies an increase in FLFP from 51.4 per cent to 58.5 per cent.

Our findings suggest that policy interventions should be aimed predominantly at the supply side. For example, policies aimed at improving access to tertiary education for girls, particularly in rural areas where education levels remain low, would be likely to increase FLFP.

Barriers related to the traditional view of women's role in the household and reflecting expectations that a woman leaves the labour force once she is married or has had children, may be more difficult to overcome. But our results suggest that shifts are occurring in these cultural norms, particularly in urban areas. Policies supporting married women to re-enter the labour market, especially in urban areas, such as through the provision of child care, would improve the likelihood of FLFP increasing in the future. Strategies that support women working while looking after the family, such as the provision of part-time, family-friendly work, are also likely to help.

---

1   Figure 10.A.1 shows G20 FLFP goals for all G20 countries, and the base G20 FLFP measure (defined as labour force participation in 2012).

The next section discusses the relevant literature on FLFP in Indonesia and beyond. This is followed by sections that present the data used and the empirical strategy. We then discuss the findings and use our estimated model to project Indonesia's FLFP into the future. The final section concludes and discusses policy implications.

Literature review

Unchanged and low FLFP despite rapid growth, fertility decline and increased female educational attainment is not a phenomenon unique to Indonesia. Figure 10.1 shows the level of FLFP in the ASEAN+3 countries (ASEAN plus China, Japan and South Korea) and how it changed between 1995 and 2017. Indonesia is among the countries with the lowest level of FLFP and sits in a similar range to Malaysia, Myanmar, the Philippines, Korea and Japan. India has also experienced rapid economic growth and its FLFP has remained low at 18 per cent. Klasen and Pieters (2015) find that the stagnation of FLFP in urban India since the 1980s is largely due to an increase in male education and income, a change in the sectoral structure of the economy where the share of employment in agriculture and manufacturing has decreased (these are the sectors that tend to employ more unskilled women), and a decline over time of the positive effect of secondary and tertiary education. Further, Afridi et al. (2016) and Andres et al. (2017) study the decline in FLFP in India, including rural areas. Using different methodological approaches, both find that increasing education levels for married women and men in their household as well as stability in family income are the major contributors to the decline. Countries in the Middle East and North Africa also have low and constant levels of FLFP despite increases in female education levels. Gaddis and Klasen (2014) suggest that this pattern can be partially explained by conservative social attitudes towards women's work. In contrast, Latin-American countries experienced rapid economic growth during the second half of last century accompanied by significant growth in FLFP. The increase in FLFP has been attributed to women's increased education levels and reductions in fertility rates (Gasparini et al. 2015). Changes in the sectoral structure of the economy minimally affected women's participation. There has, however, been a de-acceleration of FLFP growth in Latin America in the last two decades.

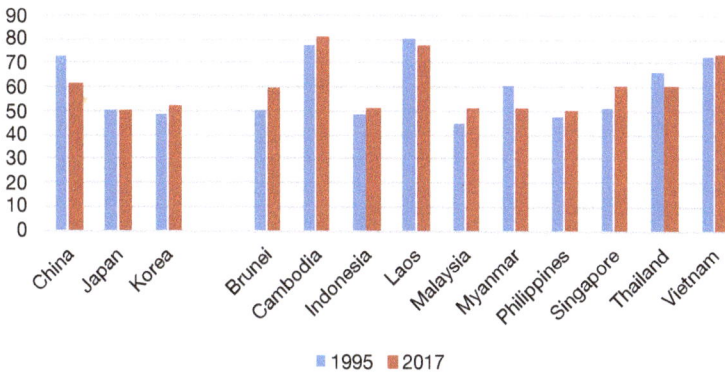

Figure 10.1. ASEAN+3 FLFP, 1995–2017

Source. World Bank 2017, modelled ILO estimates available at: data.worldbank.org/
indicator/SL.TLF.CACT.FE.ZS

The empirical literature that focuses on the drivers of FLFP in Indonesia is relatively sparse. Schaner and Das (2016) use 21 years of the Indonesian National Labour Force Survey (SAKERNAS) to identify the barriers to and drivers of FLFP. They focus on trends by birth cohort, educational attainment, geography and the type of work (e.g. informal sector, self-employed, employee). They also use the 2012 Indonesia Demographic and Health Survey to examine the correlations between female labour market outcomes and proxies of empowerment, household wealth and family structure including fertility. Their main findings are that younger women in urban areas have increased their labour force participation in recent years and this has largely been achieved by wage employment. Younger women in rural areas, however, have reduced their labour force participation largely by opting out of informal/unpaid employment. They also find evidence of within-country U–shaped relationships between FLFP and education and wealth, suggesting that one reason why FLFP has remained constant despite large gains in income and educational attainment is that the growth in FLFP at the top of the income and education distribution has largely been offset by losses at the bottom of the distribution. Child care responsibilities are another factor that limits women's engagement in the labour market. Women with young children are significantly less likely to work relative to their childless peers. Women appear to re-enter the labour force as their children get older either by performing family work or being self-employed but there is no re-entry into wage employment as children age. Finally, they find that wage jobs are preferred among women, but they are predominantly held by highly educated women in urban areas.

Feridhanusetyawan and Aswichayono (2001) use SAKERNAS data to examine the changing patterns of male and FLFP and earnings in Indonesia from 1986 to 1997. Their main finding is that, with time, women stayed in the labour market longer over this period. They find an inverse U–shaped relationship between labour force participation and age. While at the beginning of the period the participation turning point for women was earlier than for men, by the end of the 1990s the peak-ages for males and females were similar. Education played a significant role in determining labour force participation especially in urban areas, and the effects were stronger for females than males early in the period. But, by the late 1990s, the effects were similar for males and females. They found that the probability of a woman entering the labour market declines significantly if she is married or has more dependent children in the family. But for men, being married and having more dependent children increases the probability of entering the labour market.

Comola and de Mello (2009) examined the determinants of employment and earnings for the Indonesian labour market. They use a multinomial logit model to estimate labour market status (e.g. unemployed, employed in the formal sector, or employed in the informal sector) on SAKERNAS data for 1996 and 2004. Their focus is not explicitly on gender but they find that women living in a household with a high dependency ratio are less likely to have a formal-sector job and more likely to be inactive than those in a low dependency household. Women's labour force participation declines during their most fertile years. Van Klaveren et al. (2010) show that, while male labour market participation is highest in the age range of 35–49 years, for females it is highest in the post-child-rearing years (ages 45–59).

Cepeda (2013), in an analysis for the World Bank, uses information from the 2009 SAKERNAS to show that single women aged 15 to 24 have the highest rate of participation compared to other marital categories in this age range. The aggregate drop in participation on marriage in this age range is an enormous 37.7 percentage points. Interestingly the biggest drop is among married women without children and, after the first child, the reduction decreases per each additional child. One of the suggested explanations for this is an anticipatory effect. As women get married they expect to have children immediately, so they stop working even before pregnancy. From age 25 to 64, divorced and widowed women with children are the ones with the highest labour force participation.

Alisjahbana and Manning (2006) show that women's labour force participation decisions reflect a combination of marital and socio-economic status. Poorer married women are more likely to participate than married women in non-poor households.

Data

The data used in this paper come from two sources – the National Socioeconomic Survey (SUSENAS) and the Village Potential Statistics (PODES).

The SUSENAS is a nationally representative survey conducted annually and typically covering about 200,000 households. Each survey contains a core questionnaire that consists of a household roster listing the sex, age, marital status, and educational attainment of all household members.[2] It also includes questions on labour market activity, health, fertility, and other household characteristics.

One of the advantages of the SUSENAS data set (over the more widely used SAKERNAS) is that it collects information on household composition, which allows us to explore the role of child-raising and the availability of alternative child-carers in the household (primarily grandparents and other women who could act as babysitters) in the decision to participate. We supplement the SUSENAS data with data from the PODES, which is a three-yearly census of all villages across Indonesia (approximately 65,000). We use the PODES for information on some demand-side characteristics of the labour market, such as the distance to the nearest district office (to act as a proxy for access to jobs) and the main source of income of the village.[3]

---

2   This core questionnaire is supplemented by modules covering about 60,000 households that collect additional information, such as health care and nutrition, household income and expenditure, and labour force experience.

3   We extract the distance to the nearest district office from the 2011 PODES. The main source of village income is likely to change over time due to the changing composition of the Indonesian economy, so for this PODES variable we merge the PODES data to the closest year of the SUSENAS data. For 1996, 2000 and 2011 we match the PODES with the corresponding year of the SUSENAS. For the 2007 SUSENAS, we merge with the 2008 PODES because there is no PODES for that particular year. In 2013, we use the information from the 2011 PODES as this is the closest year. However, the 2013 SUSENAS does not include the unique village identifiers that are available in other years. District is the smallest geographical unit reported so we calculate the main income source at the district level using PODES 2011 and merge it with the 2013 SUSENAS data. As a robustness check, we re-estimated our main results excluding the 2013 data. The results were similar, so the 2013 data was retained for the estimation.

The available data allow us to control for the following characteristics that could impact on FLFP,

- at the individual level, we control for whether the individual is the head of the household, marital status (e.g. married, divorced, widowed or single), and the level of education completed by the individual (e.g. primary school, lower secondary school, upper secondary school, or tertiary education)
- at the household level, we control for the number of people living in the household, the number of females aged between 45 and 65 years in the household (excluding the female respondent) who are potential babysitters, the number of elderly (defined as greater than or equal to 65 years of age) women and men in the household and the number of children in the household by age (the age groupings are 0–2 years of age, 3–6, 7–11, and 12–17)
- at the village level, we control for distance to the nearest district office and the main source of village income. We also control for provincial unemployment rates (calculated from the SUSENAS) to act as a proxy for the underlying economic conditions at that time.

A disadvantage of the SUSENAS is that it is cross-sectional, so we cannot observe the same individuals or households across time (this is true also of the SAKERNAS). But, by using the SUSENAS from 1996, 2000, 2007, 2011 and 2013 survey years, we can observe how the participation of different birth cohorts (groups of people born in the same years) change over time and life cycle (age) effects.

Methodology

To estimate the determinants of FLFP we regress whether an individual participates in the labour force or not ($y_i=1/0$) on a set of potential drivers (x_j) using a probit model. That is, we estimate:

$$y_i = \beta_0 + \sum_{j=1}^{k} \beta_j x_{ji} + \varepsilon_i \qquad (1)$$

The vector of potential drivers (x_j) includes those discussed above. On the supply side of the labour market we control for marital status, if the individual is the head of the household, the highest level of education achieved, household size, the presence of a babysitter or elderly men or women in the household and the number of children at certain ages. On the demand side, we include distance to the nearest district office and the main source of income in the village. We also control for geographic differences using province dummies and the unemployment rate for each province.

Intuitively, the regression identifies the relationship between the control variable and labour force participation. The magnitude of the effect is captured by the coefficient on the control variable (β_j).

Dummy variables are also included for the age of the individual at the time of the survey and their year of birth. The coefficients (and associated marginal effects) on the age dummies capture how an individual's likelihood of participating varies across the life cycle, irrespective of their year of birth and after controlling for other characteristics. The coefficients on the year of birth dummy variables allow us to compare people born in different years, which identifies whether the younger cohorts behave differently in relation to labour force participation than their older counterparts and the extent to which the propensity to participate in the labour market has changed over time.[4]

We estimate equation (1) separately for men and women and disaggregate by rural and urban status.[5]

Results

Descriptive results

Table 10.1 presents the summary statistics of labour force participation and the explanatory variables for urban and rural areas. At the individual level, there is a substantial gap between female and male labour force participation – FLFP is on average 33 percentage points (approximately 40 per cent) less than male participation (85 per cent compared to 52 per cent). The participation rates also tend to be higher in rural areas

---

4   We use 49 age dummies covering from 15 to 64 years of age (the omitted category is 15 years of age) and 49 cohort dummies – one for each year of birth from 1943 to 1992 (the omitted category is someone born in 1943). See Euwals et al. (2011) for a similar approach in the context of the Netherlands.

5   Separately estimated results for Java–Bali and the outer islands are presented in the appendix.

compared to urban areas for both men and women. Most household heads are males, and most females and males are married. At the household level, there are more potential babysitters in households in urban areas, possibly due to higher housing prices. At the village level, the distances to the nearest district office (a proxy for the distance to the labour market) are unsurprisingly less in urban areas. Agriculture is most prevalent in rural areas compared to urban areas where services and large trade/retail represent income sources.

Table 10.2 disaggregates the summary statistics by survey year. The key results are that the gender gap in labour force participation remains largely unchanged over the period (see also Figure 10.2). Educational attainment has increased over time, with women's educational attainment increasing more than men's. Household size has shrunk over time, and the average number of children per household has declined. Finally, the unemployment rate shows a downward trend from 1996 to 2013.

Table 10.1. Summary statistics of labour force participation and explanatory variables

Variables	Urban		Rural	
	Male	Female	Male	Female
Individual characteristics:				
Labour force participation	0.813	0.475	0.886	0.565
Household head	0.573	0.075	0.621	0.067
Marital status: single	0.371	0.288	0.308	0.199
Marital status: married	0.611	0.634	0.670	0.718
Marital status: divorced	0.009	0.026	0.010	0.026
Marital status: widowed	0.009	0.052	0.012	0.057
Education: primary	0.213	0.237	0.368	0.364
Education: lower secondary	0.231	0.227	0.199	0.170
Education: upper secondary	0.360	0.301	0.159	0.113
Education: tertiary	0.105	0.095	0.028	0.025
Household characteristics:				
Household size		4.810		4.697
Number of women aged 45–65 years		0.313		0.276
Number of elderly females		0.077		0.076
Number of elderly males		0.065		0.071
Number of children: 0–2 years		0.223		0.247

Variables	Urban		Rural	
	Male	Female	Male	Female
Number of children: 3–6 years		0.309		0.364
Number of children: 7–11 years		0.423		0.507
Number of children: 12–17 years		0.663		0.6750
Village characteristics:				
Distance to nearest district office (<100 km)		0.462		0.788
Main income: agriculture		0.309		0.961
Main income: mining/quarrying		0.011		0.004
Main income: processing/industry		0.087		0.008
Main income: large trading/retail		0.243		0.009
Main income: services other than trade		0.350		0.018
Unemployment#		0.039		0.033
Observations	469,157	481,751	681,427	691,280

Notes. # Unemployment rate by region.
Source. Authors' calculations using SUSENAS and PODES

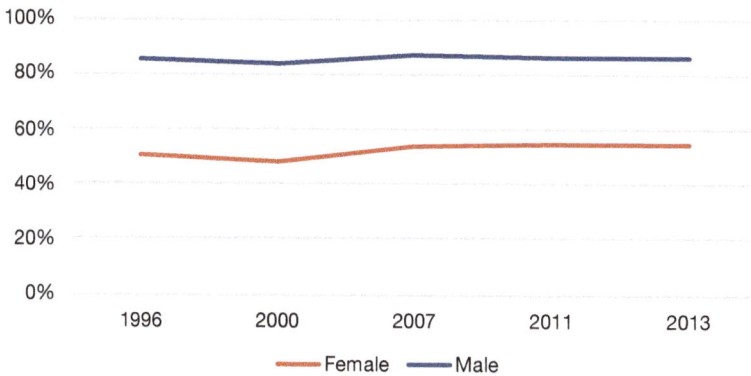

Figure 10.2. Female and male labour force participation over time
Source. Authors' calculations using SUSENAS

Table 10.2. Summary statistics of labour force participation and explanatory variables over time

Variables	1996 Male	1996 Female	2000 Male	2000 Female	2007 Male	2007 Female	2011 Male	2011 Female	2013 Male	2013 Female
Individual characteristics:										
Labour force participation	0.854	0.507	0.832	0.477	0.865	0.542	0.860	0.550	0.857	0.547
Household head	0.572	0.053	0.574	0.061	0.605	0.073	0.625	0.081	0.625	0.084
Marital status: single	0.373	0.274	0.371	0.271	0.328	0.229	0.304	0.206	0.298	0.203
Marital status: married	0.613	0.664	0.613	0.658	0.652	0.683	0.671	0.705	0.674	0.704
Marital status: divorced	0.007	0.025	0.008	0.026	0.009	0.026	0.012	0.026	0.013	0.026
Marital status: widowed	0.007	0.037	0.008	0.045	0.011	0.062	0.013	0.063	0.015	0.067
Education: primary	0.348	0.346	0.327	0.335	0.296	0.308	0.283	0.287	0.273	0.281
Education: lower secondary	0.187	0.159	0.206	0.185	0.224	0.206	0.217	0.206	0.222	0.211
Education: upper secondary	0.194	0.144	0.234	0.182	0.251	0.202	0.256	0.206	0.274	0.222
Education: tertiary	0.039	0.025	0.040	0.026	0.068	0.062	0.070	0.073	0.074	0.081
Household characteristics (per household):										
Household size		5.108		4.814		4.722		4.563		4.456
Number of women aged 45–65 years		0.269		0.283		0.297		0.299		0.311
Number of elderly females		0.078		0.084		0.077		0.071		0.075
Number of elderly males		0.069		0.072		0.070		0.065		0.065
Number of children: 0–2 years		0.260		0.218		0.242		0.233		0.212
Number of children: 3–6 years		0.393		0.324		0.333		0.332		0.310

Variables	1996 Male	1996 Female	2000 Male	2000 Female	2007 Male	2007 Female	2011 Male	2011 Female	2013 Male	2013 Female
Number of children: 7–11 years		0.559		0.449		0.445		0.464		0.437
Number of children: 12–17 years		0.846		0.720		0.633		0.587		0.587
Village characteristics (per village):										
Distance to nearest district office ('100km)		0.647		0.515		0.642		0.726		0.723
Main income: agriculture		0.675		0.674		0.679		0.700		n/a
Main income: mining/quarrying		0.003		0.004		0.007		0.011		n/a
Main income: processing/industry		0.029		0.040		0.043		0.049		n/a
Main income: large trading/retail		0.106		0.121		0.122		0.095		n/a
Main income: services other than trade		0.187		0.161		0.149		0.145		n/a
Unemployment#		0.051		0.040		0.034		0.027		0.027
Observations	219,045	230,355	174,903	179,665	325,065	328,629	345,598	347,342	85,973	87,040

Notes. # Unemployment rate by region.
Source. Authors' calculations using SUSENAS and PODES

Looking at age differences, Table 10.3 shows that labour force participation is lowest in the 15–29 age group. This is likely due to these individuals still being in school or completing higher levels of education. The proportion of those who are household heads follows a similar trend. Nearly half of all women aged 15 to 29 years are married and this increases to around 90 per cent for those aged 30 to 44 years. This decreases to 75 per cent for women aged 45 to 64 years as the proportion of widowers increases by a commensurate amount. Lastly, in terms of educational attainment, while there is a clear gender gap in attainment for the older age groups, there is no gender gap between males and females in the youngest cohorts. There is a greater share of females completing tertiary education than males.

Table 10.3. Summary statistics of labour force participation and individual characteristics by age group

	Male			Female		
Variables	15–29	30–44	45–64	15–29	30–44	45–64
Labour force participation	0.700	0.980	0.938	0.422	0.596	0.610
Household head	0.185	0.841	0.960	0.020	0.056	0.183
Marital status: single	0.741	0.077	0.016	0.519	0.048	0.022
Marital status: married	0.253	0.903	0.939	0.463	0.892	0.753
Marital status: divorced	0.005	0.013	0.012	0.015	0.031	0.037
Marital status: widowed	0.001	0.007	0.033	0.003	0.029	0.188
Education: primary	0.295	0.306	0.320	0.304	0.334	0.292
Education: lower secondary	0.302	0.169	0.120	0.293	0.147	0.089
Education: upper secondary	0.263	0.267	0.163	0.243	0.196	0.088
Education: tertiary	0.035	0.080	0.069	0.049	0.068	0.040
Observations	469,998	406,980	273,606	482,448	418,598	271,985

Source. Authors' calculations using SUSENAS

Estimation results

Table 10.4 presents the results of estimating equation (1) for men and women by rural and urban status. For ease of interpretation we present marginal effects, which are interpreted as the percentage point change in the probability of the individual participating in the labour market associated with a one unit change in that explanatory variable. Marital status is a key driver of labour force participation for women. A married woman in a rural area is 11 percentage points less likely to be working or looking for work than a single woman and this difference is statistically significant. The impact is more pronounced for married women in urban areas as they are 24 percentage points less likely to be participating than single women.

Table 10.4. Marginal effects of pooled sample

Variables	Rural		Urban	
	Female	Male	Female	Male
Household head	0.2109***	0.0565***	0.1143***	0.0370***
	(0.0031)	(0.0015)	(0.0040)	(0.0021)
Marital status: single (omitted)				
Marital status: married	–0.1068***	0.0753***	–0.2430***	0.1589***
	(0.0025)	(0.0016)	(0.0028)	(0.0025)
Marital status: divorced	0.0101**	0.0088***	0.0156***	0.0300***
	(0.0050)	(0.0019)	(0.0058)	(0.0034)
Marital status: widowed	–0.1585***	0.0145***	–0.1525***	0.0493***
	(0.0046)	(0.0016)	(0.0048)	(0.0025)
Education: no schooling (omitted)				
Education: primary	–0.0303***	0.0017**	–0.0215***	0.0160***
	(0.0016)	(0.0007)	(0.0026)	(0.0018)
Education: lower secondary	–0.1101***	–0.0453***	–0.1008***	–0.0558***
	(0.0021)	(0.0011)	(0.0027)	(0.0023)
Education: upper secondary	–0.0313***	–0.0309***	–0.0162***	–0.0382***
	(0.0024)	(0.0012)	(0.0026)	(0.0020)
Education: tertiary	0.2745***	–0.0095***	0.2794***	0.0066***
	(0.0032)	(0.0022)	(0.0030)	(0.0023)
Household size	–0.0160***	–0.0049***	0.0048***	–0.0040***
	(0.0006)	(0.0002)	(0.0006)	(0.0004)
Number of women aged 45–65 years	0.0173***	0.0048***	0.0121***	–0.0059***
	(0.0020)	(0.0005)	(0.0022)	(0.0011)
Number of elderly females	0.0316***	0.0034***	0.0099***	–0.0042**
	(0.0025)	(0.0009)	(0.0029)	(0.0017)
Number of elderly males	0.0244***	0.0088***	0.0206***	0.0065***
	(0.0024)	(0.0009)	(0.0030)	(0.0019)
Number of children: 0–2 years	–0.0797***	0.0104***	–0.0754***	0.0188***
	(0.0016)	(0.0007)	(0.0020)	(0.0014)
Number of children: 3–6 years	0.0056***	0.0083***	–0.0248***	0.0172***
	(0.0013)	(0.0005)	(0.0016)	(0.0011)

Variables	Rural		Urban	
	Female	Male	Female	Male
Number of children: 7–11 years	0.0254***	0.0087***	–0.0043***	0.0153***
	(0.0012)	(0.0004)	(0.0014)	(0.0009)
Number of children: 12–17 years	0.0225***	0.0073***	0.0042***	0.0119***
	(0.0011)	(0.0004)	(0.0012)	(0.0007)
Distance to district office ('100km)	0.0016*	0.0002	0.0173***	0.0065***
	(0.0009)	(0.0003)	(0.0016)	(0.0009)
Main income: agriculture (omitted)				
Main income: mining/quarrying	–0.1186***	–0.0048	–0.0743***	–0.0012
	(0.0103)	(0.0041)	(0.0076)	(0.0051)
Main income: processing/industry	–0.0196***	–0.0039	0.0029	0.0007
	(0.0071)	(0.0028)	(0.0030)	(0.0019)
Main income: large trading / retail	–0.0953***	–0.0294***	–0.0218***	–0.0185***
	(0.0069)	(0.0034)	(0.0021)	(0.0014)
Main income: services other than trade	–0.1328***	–0.0328***	–0.0433***	–0.0319***
	(0.0048)	(0.0025)	(0.0020)	(0.0013)
Unemployment[#]	–0.0083***	0.0029***	–0.0223***	–0.0053***
	(0.0006)	(0.0002)	(0.0007)	(0.0004)
Observations	691,280	681,427	481,751	469,157

Notes. Standard errors in parentheses, *** $p<0.01$, ** $p<0.05$, * $p<0.1$. Estimations include province, age and date of birth fixed effects. [#] Unemployment rate by region.

Source. Authors' calculations using SUSENAS and PODES

Being a household head for both men and women increases the likelihood of labour force participation in both urban and rural areas. But the magnitude of the impact for men is substantially smaller because men are generally the primary income earners, so largely work irrespective of whether they are the household head or not. The level of educational attainment is also a strong driver of FLFP. For women, completing upper secondary school increases the likelihood of participation compared to someone who only completed lower secondary by about 8 percentage points in both rural and urban areas. The magnitude of the impact increases dramatically if women attain the next education level (tertiary education). But for men, there is little variation in the probability of participating regardless of levels of education. Men, as the main breadwinners in Indonesian society, tend to work.

Household size decreases participation for women in rural areas – an increase in household size by one decreases the likelihood of participation by nearly 2 percentage points. But the magnitude of the impact for urban females and males is much closer to zero. The presence of another woman aged 45–65 years in the household or an elderly female or male in the household significantly increases the likelihood of female participation by around 1 to 3 percentage points. This may reflect the ability of the woman to leave children at home with an adult. The magnitude of the impact of these potential childminders is much higher for women than men, for whom the effect is negligible. The presence of children in the household also has markedly different effects for men and women. For women, the presence of young children has a negative effect on the likelihood of participating. The presence of a child under two years of age decreases the probability of participation by 8 percentage points but has only a small (and positive) effect on men's labour market activity.

On the demand side of the labour market, we hypothesised that the coefficient for distance to the nearest district office would be negative as it was intended to capture distance to an active labour market. The coefficient, however, is positive, albeit small. The variable could be positively correlated with agricultural employment in rural areas and the positive coefficient reflecting women's greater involvement in agriculture. The villages' main sources of income variables show that female participation is highest in areas with agriculture and industry (which includes manufacturing). As the economy moves further away from agriculture to other sectors, however, female participation drops.

The results for Java–Bali and the outer islands follow a similar pattern to those presented in Table 10.4 and are presented in Table 10.A.1 in the appendix.

We re-estimate the model for each year of the SUSENAS separately to determine if the drivers of labour force participation have changed across time. The marginal effects for each year are presented in the appendix – see Table 10.A.2. This analysis shows that most of the drivers of FLFP (both the direction and magnitude of their impact) remain largely unchanged over time. These include if the individual is the household head or a widower and if they achieved at least primary level of education, the presence of elderly females and males in the household and the number of young children in the household.

There are, however, several interesting changes in the drivers of FLFP over the period. In 1996, married women were around 23 percentage points less likely to participate than their single counterparts. By 2013, the negative impact of being married for women decreased to around 14 percentage points. The relationship between gender and industrial structure has also changed. Villages that have large trading or retail as their main source of income have become associated with higher levels of FLFP over time. In 1996, villages that had large trading or retail as their main income source had lower female participation than those whose main source of income came from agriculture by about 10 percentage points. But by 2013, the penalty for FLFP of such income sources had decreased to be only around 2 percentage points, suggesting women were starting to be accommodated in these industries.

Age and cohort results

The descriptive results showed that the raw FLFP figures have largely remained unchanged over the survey years. This section examines the results by age and cohort to enable us to understand the extent of changes in participation across the life cycle and/or the changing attitudes of younger cohorts towards participation that may keep the aggregate figures unchanged.

The results for males and females are shown in Figure 10.3.[6] The results of the age analysis are largely as anticipated. Female labour force participation increases quickly up until around 25 years of age before slowing during the years typically associated with child bearing. It peaks at around 45 years of age before starting to decline. The contrast with males shows the extent of the disparity across these years. Men's participation rises sharply to almost 100 per cent once the period of educational attainment is over.

The analysis of age effects shows the extent to which women's decision to work is affected by their child-rearing responsibilities. Figure 10.4 compares the age analysis for Indonesia to a similar analysis conducted for the Netherlands (taken from Euwals et al. 2007). Notwithstanding the cultural and other country differences, the figure shows that there is a much larger decrease in women's labour force participation during the child-bearing years in Indonesia than in the Netherlands (once the

---

6   The sample averages of the explanatory variables are applied to the regression coefficients and added to the age and cohort effects to present the impact of different ages and cohorts on labour force participation.

number of children and other explanatory variables are controlled for). There is no discernible drop associated with the child-bearing years in the Netherlands. Female labour force participation in the Netherlands reaches its peak of about 70 per cent at age 26. In contrast, in Indonesia, women's labour force participation at age 26 is about 15 percentage points below its peak (55 per cent compared to the 70 per cent it reaches at age 45).

The cohort effects plotted in Figure 10.3 reveal some interesting findings. They show that, other things being equal, FLFP has increased from around 40 per cent for those born in the 1940s to around 60 per cent for those born most recently in the 1980s and early 1990s. Male labour force participation has remained at about 95 per cent across the cohorts.

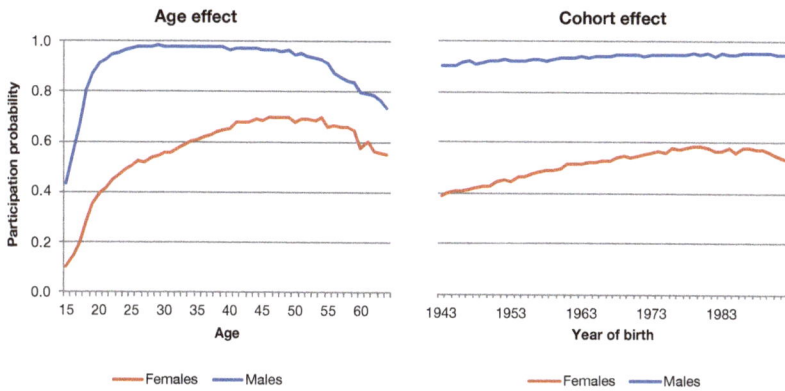

Figure 10.3. Age and cohort effects
Source. Authors' calculations using SUSENAS and PODES

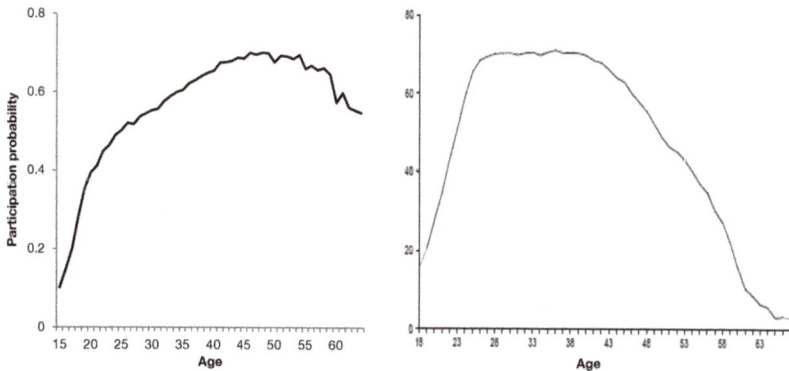

Figure 10.4. Age analysis of FLFP in Indonesia (left-hand side) and the Netherlands (right-hand side)
Source. Euwals et al. 2011 and authors' calculations using SUSENAS and PODES

The cohort analysis thus reveals a large increase in the underlying propensity for women to participate in the labour force. This may reflect changing cultural norms. If this trend continues over time, as the older cohorts exit the labour market, we expect to eventually see an increase in FLFP. This increase seems to level off for the younger cohorts with no increases apparent after the 1973 cohort (aged 40 in 2013) but this may also reflect younger cohorts still completing their education.

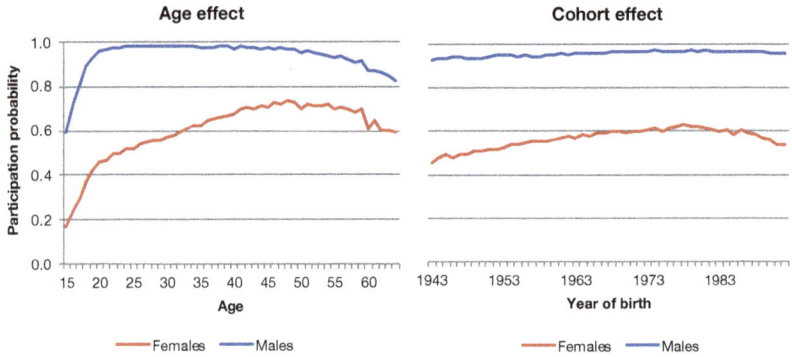

Figure 10.5. Age and cohort effects for rural areas

Source. Authors' calculations using SUSENAS and PODES

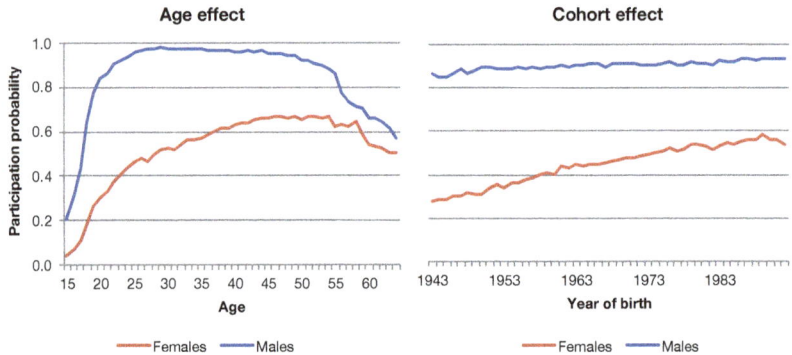

Figure 10.6. Age and cohort effects for urban areas

Source. Authors' calculations using SUSENAS and PODES

Figure 10.5 and Figure 10.6 present the results for rural and urban areas respectively. Some differences emerge. The age profile shows that the probability of participation in the labour market for younger urban females is lower than for their rural counterparts. This probably reflects the higher educational attainment in urban areas delaying their entry into the labour market. There is also a sharp decline in the male age profile at around 55 years of age. Unlike rural areas, where the decline in male labour force participation is gradual, in urban areas this is particularly pronounced. The current legislated retirement age in Indonesia is 55, and its effect is more evident in urban areas as a result of there being more formal sector jobs.

The cohort effects for women show greater differences between rural and urban areas. There have been larger increases in young women's labour force participation in urban areas than rural areas. The labour force participation of the older cohorts in urban areas is estimated at around 28 per cent and more than double to close to 60 per cent for the youngest cohorts. The increase in rural areas is much smaller but starts from a higher base (increasing from 45 per cent to 62 per cent). This is again consistent with changing cultural norms and women beginning to be accepted into non-agricultural employment in urban areas.

Figure 10.A.2 – Figure 10.A.5 in the appendix disaggregate the age and cohort effects further into their respective Java–Bali and the outer islands regions. The findings are largely consistent across the different regions.

The appendix further disaggregates the age and cohort effects for women by marital status, level of educational attainment and the number of children in various age categories in the household and the village's main source of income (see Figures 10.A.6 – 10.A.9). Figure 10.A.6 shows that labour force participation increased for both married and unmarried women in the younger cohorts. This suggests that the change in attitudes towards FLFP is not hindered by traditional roles related to marital status.[7]

Younger cohorts across all levels of educational attainment have increased their labour force participation compared to the older cohorts, except participation by upper-secondary educated women, which has remained constant (Figure 10.A.7). Figure 10.A.8 shows that FLFP increased for all women, regardless of the age of their children (although less for women with children under the age of two, and not much for birth cohorts since the late 1970s). Figure 10.A.9 shows that FLFP among the younger cohorts from villages with processing/industry, large trading/retail and services as their

---

7   The age effect also shows the considerable difference between married and unmarried females – for unmarried females, labour force participation reaches its peak by the age of 25, but for married females it takes until around 50 years of age for labour force participation to reach its peak.

main source of income has increased relative to their older counterparts.[8] Younger cohorts from agricultural villages have also increased their labour force participation but not to the same extent as the other sectors given that FLFP was already quite high in the older cohorts in agricultural villages. This has stalled, however, for cohorts born after 1970.

Female labour force participation projections

The G20 countries' 2014 commitment to decrease the female/male labour market participation gap by 25 per cent by 2025 means that Indonesia will need to increase its FLFP to 58.5 per cent. This goal will be challenging to achieve given that women's labour force participation in Indonesia has remained constant at just over 50 per cent for the last two decades. The analysis above, however, identified an increasing underlying propensity for women to participate in the labour market once other factors, such as changes in industrial structure, education and household composition, are controlled for. This section presents projections of FLFP to 2025.

We first examine how well the model predicts FLFP by comparing its predicted values with the observed levels in the raw data. We then estimate the rate of growth of each of the variables that determine FLFP in our model and use these to project FLFP through to 2025. We examine the sensitivity of our results to alternative scenarios and then conclude.

Using the estimated coefficients in equation (1),[9] we calculate the predicted values of FLFP within the sample period and compare the result to the observed values. Figure 10.7 plots the actual and predicted values of FLFP. The model performs relatively well with the predicted value being close to the observed value, except in 2000 where the actual value dips from trend. The predicted trend between 1996 and 2007 is steeper that the trend after 2007.

---

8   Mining/quarrying also show improvement across the younger cohorts but the variability in these results and the age effect are likely due to the smaller sample size of females in this sector. For example, there are only 7,795 observations for this sector compared to 47,312 observations for the processing/ industry sector or 123,007 observations in the large trading/retail sector.
9   To calculate a national FLFP we estimate the model over both urban and rural samples, including a control for urban areas. Results are presented in Table 10.A.3 in the appendix.

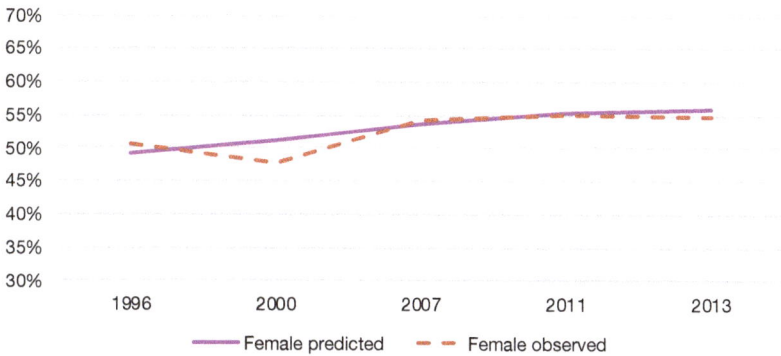

Figure 10.7. Observed and predicted FLFP
Source. Authors' calculations using SUSENAS

In order to predict the values of FLFP up to 2025, we need to make assumptions about the values of the variables that determine FLFP (e.g. level of education, industrial structure, age composition). We use a simple trend-time series model to predict the value of all the determinants up to 20 years ahead following equation (2), which we estimate using data from 1996 to 2013.

$$X_i = \alpha_0 + \alpha_1 t + \varepsilon_i \tag{2}$$

where t takes the value of 1 in 1996, 5 in 2000, 12 in 2007, 16 in 2011 and 18 in 2013; and ε is the random error term. Table 10.5 shows the estimated percentage-point growth for each of the variables. In terms of education, this model predicts that the proportion of women with at least primary school education will decrease each year by 0.0043 percentage points while the proportion of women with tertiary education or more will increase by 0.0032 percentage points annually. The proportion of people living in urban areas is forecast to increase by 0.0073 percentage points each year.

Table 10.5. FLFP determinants' annual growth in percentage points

Variables	Time trend
Household head	0.0020
Marital status: married	0.0022
Marital status: divorced	0.0000
Marital status: widowed	0.0017
Education: primary	−0.0043

Variables	Time trend
Education: lower secondary	0.0040
Education: upper secondary	0.0050
Education: tertiary	0.0032
Household size	–0.0273
Number of elderly females	–0.0004
Number of elderly males	–0.0002
Presence of a potential babysitter	0.0019
Number of children: 0–2 years	0.0004
Number of children: 3–6 years	–0.0028
Number of children: 7–11 years	–0.0063
Number of children: 12–17 years	–0.0154
Urban	0.0073
Distance to nearest district office ('100km)	0.0063
Main income: mining/quarrying	0.0004
Main income: processing/industry	0.0007
Main income: large trading/retail	–0.0011
Main income: services other than trade	–0.0023
Unemployment[#]	–0.0014

Notes. [#] Unemployment rate by region.
Source. Authors' calculations using SUSENAS and PODES

In order to apply the estimated life cycle effects (coefficients on age dummies) we also project the distribution of women across age groups.[10] We assume that the proportion of people living in each province remains constant.

We present two projections. The most optimistic projection assumes that trends in underlying variables observed between 1996 and 2013 will continue. The second, more pessimistic projection, reflects the fact the growth in FLFP flattens off after 2007 (see Figure 10.7), and so uses only data from 2007 to 2013 to project into the future.

---

10   We compared our projected figures for the percentage of population by age group against UN forecasts. They are broadly similar, particularly for women aged over 40 years, who constitute the majority of working women.

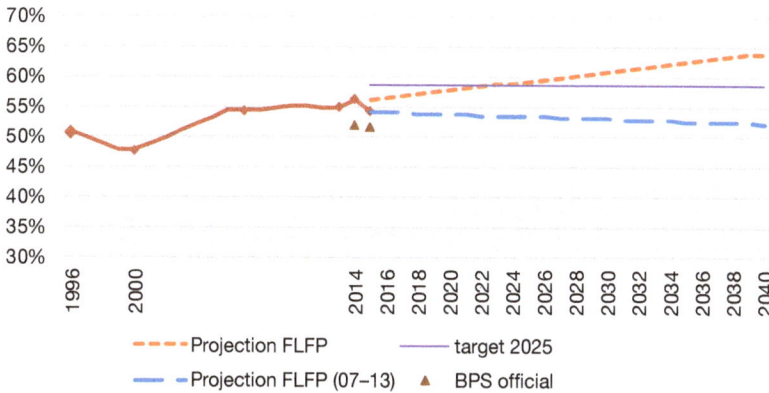

Figure 10.8. Projection of FLFP in Indonesia
Source. Authors' calculations using SUSENAS and BPS website

Figure 10.8 presents the results of both scenarios. The red line between 1996 and 2015 shows the observed levels. The brown triangles show the official Central Bureau of Statistics (BPS) estimated figures. The orange dotted line represents our estimated optimistic scenario and the blue dashed line represents the more pessimistic scenario. Under the optimistic scenario, FLFP just reaches the 58.5 per cent target by 2025. It is forecast that FLFP will reach 59 per cent by 2025. Under the less optimistic scenario, the FLFP will remain almost constant through to 2025 with FLFP *decreasing* slightly by 2025.[11]

Summary and policy implications

Female labour force participation in Indonesia has remained relatively constant from 1996 to 2013, even in the face of dramatic economic change. The analysis in this chapter, however, suggests that once individual, household and village characteristics are controlled for, there are signs that the underlying propensity for women to participate in the labour force has increased, particularly in urban areas. This is an interesting result and is consistent with societal attitudes changing to be more accepting of women participating in the labour market. Offsetting this secular increase in women's labour force participation are decreases in participation because

---

11   Note that both the predictions indicate an increase over the official BPS FLFP estimate for 2015. The BPS uses SAKERNAS information to calculate FLFP.

of the lesser importance of agriculture. If the underlying propensity for women to participate continues to increase then, as the older cohorts exit the labour market, we expect FLFP to eventually increase.

We nevertheless find that the G20 target of 58.5 per cent FLFP by 2025 is unlikely to be reached. Our projections show that the target will only just be reached under our most optimistic scenario. The less optimistic (and arguably more realistic) scenario suggests that the FLFP may even decrease if the most recent trends continue.

The main drivers of FLFP (cohort and age effects aside) were found to be marital status, the number of children between 0 and 2 years of age in the household, educational attainment (particularly tertiary education) and the village industrial structure (with agriculture and manufacturing being female-oriented industries).

Our results have several policy implications. That marital status and the presence of young children has such a large negative impact on FLFP suggests that policies that support women to return to work after childbirth are likely to increase FLFP. These policies include the provision of some form of child-care for women with young children and policies and laws that encourage employers to make part-time and family-friendly work available. Increasing the educational attainment of women, particularly in rural areas where educational attainment remains low, is also likely to assist.

The cohort analysis finding that the underlying propensity for women to participate in the labour market is increasing is promising. The ongoing movement of the Indonesian economy away from the agricultural sector, however, given the importance of the agricultural sector to female employment, will continue to offset this effect. Thus, policies designed to provide women with access to employment in non-traditional industrial sectors, for example, through the provision of subsidised vocational education and/or campaigns that provide and promote opportunities for women in these sectors, are also worthy of attention.

References

Afridi, F, Dinkelman, T & Mahajan, K (2016). *Why are fewer married women joining the work force in India? A decomposition analysis over two decades*, IZA Discussion Papers, 9722.

Alisjahbana, AS & Manning, C (2006). 'Labour market dimensions of poverty in Indonesia', *Bulletin of Indonesian Economic Studies*, 42(2), 235–61. doi.org/10.1080/00074910600873674.

Andres, L, Dasgupta, B, Joseph, G, Abraham, V & Correia, M (2017). *Precarious drop: Reassessing patterns of female labor force participation in India*, Policy Research Working Papers, World Bank Group, 8024.

Asian Development Bank (ADB) (2013). *Gender equality in the labor market in the Philippines*. Mandaluyong City, Philippines: Asian Development Bank.

——— (2015). Indonesia factsheet, 24 April. Mandaluyong City, Philippines: Asian Development Bank. www.adb.org/publications/indonesia-fact-sheet.

Asian Development Bank (ADB), International Labour Organization (ILO) & Islamic Development Bank (IDB) (2010). *Indonesia: Critical development constraints*. Mandaluyong City, Philippines: Asian Development Bank.

Cepeda, L (2013). 'Gender wage inequality in Indonesia', 1 August, Poverty and Social Protection Cluster, World Bank Study.

Comola, M & de Mello, L (2009). *The determinants of employment and earnings in Indonesia: A multinomial selection approach*, Economics Department Working Paper – OECD, No. 690.

Elias, S & Noone, C (2011). 'The growth and development of the Indonesian economy', December, *The Reserve Bank of Australia Bulletin*.

Euwals R, Knoef, M & van Vuuren D (2007). *The trend in female labour force participation: What can be expected for the future?*, IZA Discussion Paper Series, No. 3225.

Feridhanusetyawan, T & Aswicahyono, H (2001). 'Gender assessment of the Indonesian labour market', *East Asian Development Network*, No. 9.

Gaddis, I & Klasen, S (2014). 'Economic development, structural change, and women's labor force participation', *Journal of Population Economics*, 27(3), 639–81.

Gasparini, L, Marchionni, M, Badaracco, N & Serrano, J (2015). *Female labor force participation in Latin America: Evidence of deceleration*. Documentos de Trabajo del CEDLAS.

Islam, I & Chowdhury, A (2009). *Growth, employment and poverty reduction in Indonesia*. Geneva: International Labour Office (ILO).

Jayachandran, S (2015). 'The roots of gender inequality in developing countries', *The Annual Review of Economics*, 7, 63–88.

Klasen, S & Pieters, J (2015). 'What explains the stagnation of female labor force participation in urban India?', *The World Bank Economic Review*, 29(3), 449–78.

Manning, C (2000). 'Labour market adjustment to Indonesia's economic crisis: Context, trends and implications', *Bulletin of Indonesian Economic Studies*, 36(1), 105–36.

Schaner, S & Das, S (2016). *Female labor force participation in Asia: Indonesia country study*, Asian Development Bank Economics Working Paper Series, No. 474. www.adb.org/sites/default/files/publication/180251/ewp-474.pdf.

Van Klaveren, M, Tijdens, K, Hughie-Williams, M & Ramos Martin, N (2010). *An overview of women's work and employment in Indonesia*, AIAS Working Paper, Amsterdam.

Appendix

Table 10.A.1. Marginal effects by Java–Bali and the outer islands regions

Variables	Java–Bali region		Outer islands region	
	Female	Male	Female	Male
Household head	0.1181***	0.0370***	0.2093***	0.0485***
	(0.0040)	(0.0019)	(0.0032)	(0.0014)
Marital status: single (omitted)				
Marital status: married	−0.2316***	0.1153***	−0.1476***	0.0983***
	(0.0029)	(0.0023)	(0.0024)	(0.0017)
Marital status: divorced	−0.0467***	0.0134***	0.0126**	0.0139***
	(0.0059)	(0.0029)	(0.0050)	(0.0021)
Marital status: widowed	−0.2025***	0.0286***	−0.1586***	0.0238***
	(0.0051)	(0.0024)	(0.0042)	(0.0015)
Education: no schooling (omitted)				
Education: primary	−0.0363***	0.0156***	−0.0437***	−0.0015*
	(0.0022)	(0.0013)	(0.0018)	(0.0009)
Education: lower secondary	−0.1409***	−0.0404***	−0.1018***	−0.0548***
	(0.0026)	(0.0015)	(0.0018)	(0.0010)
Education: upper secondary	−0.0734***	0.0133***	0.0521***	−0.0215***
	(0.0027)	(0.0016)	(0.0030)	(0.0016)
Education: tertiary	0.1811***	0.0090***	0.2893***	−0.0122***
	(0.0037)	(0.0019)	(0.0025)	(0.0018)

Variables	Java–Bali region		Outer islands region	
	Female	Male	Female	Male
Household size	−0.0007	−0.0036***	−0.0076***	−0.0052***
	(0.0008)	(0.0003)	(0.0006)	(0.0002)
Number of women aged 45–65 years	0.0162***	−0.0009	0.0150***	0.0030***
	(0.0023)	(0.0009)	(0.0019)	(0.0006)
Number of elderly females	0.0177***	−0.0006	0.0228***	0.0022**
	(0.0028)	(0.0013)	(0.0026)	(0.0010)
Number of elderly males	0.0227***	0.0073***	0.0207***	0.0096***
	(0.0029)	(0.0015)	(0.0025)	(0.0011)
Number of children: 0–2 years	−0.1121***	0.0134***	−0.0676***	0.0130***
	(0.0021)	(0.0012)	(0.0015)	(0.0007)
Number of children: 3–6 years	−0.0304***	0.0132***	0.0000	0.0102***
	(0.0018)	(0.0010)	(0.0013)	(0.0006)
Number of children: 7–11 years	−0.0028*	0.0111***	0.0171***	0.0108***
	(0.0015)	(0.0008)	(0.0011)	(0.0005)
Number of children: 12–17 years	0.0035**	0.0088***	0.0159***	0.0083***
	(0.0014)	(0.0007)	(0.0010)	(0.0004)
Distance to office ('100km)	0.0454***	0.0192***	0.0071***	0.0023***
	(0.0052)	(0.0027)	(0.0008)	(0.0003)
Main income: agriculture (omitted)				
Main income: mining/quarrying	−0.0985***	−0.0303***	−0.1459***	−0.0188***
	(0.0181)	(0.0118)	(0.0063)	(0.0035)
Main income: processing/industry	−0.0264***	−0.0170***	−0.0727***	−0.0192***
	(0.0030)	(0.0017)	(0.0056)	(0.0031)
Main income: large trading/retail	−0.0615***	−0.0349***	−0.1163***	−0.0478***
	(0.0027)	(0.0016)	(0.0023)	(0.0014)
Main income: services other than trade	−0.0776***	−0.0454***	−0.1446***	−0.0587***
	(0.0025)	(0.0016)	(0.0018)	(0.0011)
Unemployment#	−0.0212***	−0.0026***	−0.0102***	0.0028***
	(0.0008)	(0.0004)	(0.0006)	(0.0002)
Observations	466,071	452,007	706,960	698,577

Notes. Standard errors in parentheses, *** p<0.01, ** p<0.05, * p<0.1. Estimations include province, age and date of birth fixed effects. # Unemployment rate by region.

Source. Authors' calculations using SUSENAS and PODES

Table 10.A.2. Marginal effects by year

Variables	1996		2000		2007		2011		2013	
	Female	Male	Female	Male	Female	Male	Female	Male	Female	Male
Household head	0.1621***	0.0315***	0.1769***	0.0439***	0.1786***	0.0485***	0.1659***	0.0463***	0.1447***	0.0469***
	(0.0063)	(0.0025)	(0.0069)	(0.0032)	(0.0045)	(0.0021)	(0.0043)	(0.0021)	(0.0092)	(0.0044)
Marital status: single (omitted)										
Marital status: married	-0.2299***	0.0915***	-0.1792***	0.1235***	-0.1663***	0.0987***	-0.1390***	0.1117***	-0.1444***	0.1279***
	(0.0039)	(0.0029)	(0.0045)	(0.0037)	(0.0034)	(0.0025)	(0.0035)	(0.0026)	(0.0073)	(0.0056)
Marital status: divorced	0.0093	0.0050	0.0048	0.0172***	-0.0213***	0.0113***	-0.0111	0.0142***	-0.0096	0.0247***
	(0.0086)	(0.0052)	(0.0093)	(0.0058)	(0.0071)	(0.0031)	(0.0070)	(0.0028)	(0.0141)	(0.0047)
Marital status: widowed	-0.1285***	0.0044	-0.1352***	0.0286***	-0.1886***	0.0237***	-0.1632***	0.0299***	-0.1554***	0.0374***
	(0.0081)	(0.0056)	(0.0083)	(0.0052)	(0.0060)	(0.0022)	(0.0060)	(0.0019)	(0.0124)	(0.0033)
Education: no schooling (omitted)										
Education: primary	-0.0474***	-0.0019	-0.0366***	0.0003	-0.0435***	0.0073***	-0.0556***	0.0019	-0.0619***	0.0067**
	(0.0028)	(0.0016)	(0.0033)	(0.0022)	(0.0027)	(0.0013)	(0.0026)	(0.0013)	(0.0053)	(0.0028)
Education: lower secondary	-0.1604***	-0.0781***	-0.1616***	-0.0790***	-0.1259***	-0.0436***	-0.1221***	-0.0455***	-0.1265***	-0.0493***
	(0.0036)	(0.0027)	(0.0039)	(0.0033)	(0.0031)	(0.0019)	(0.0030)	(0.0018)	(0.0061)	(0.0039)
Education: upper secondary	0.0270***	-0.0311***	-0.0350***	-0.0530***	-0.0807***	-0.0383***	-0.0746***	-0.0382***	-0.0840***	-0.0364***
	(0.0039)	(0.0023)	(0.0041)	(0.0030)	(0.0032)	(0.0018)	(0.0030)	(0.0017)	(0.0060)	(0.0035)

Variables	1996		2000		2007		2011		2013	
	Female	Male	Female	Male	Female	Male	Female	Male	Female	Male
Education: tertiary	0.2965***	0.0131***	0.2105***	-0.0037	0.2012***	-0.0097***	0.2467***	-0.0054**	0.2350***	-0.0148***
	(0.0059)	(0.0030)	(0.0078)	(0.0046)	(0.0040)	(0.0024)	(0.0034)	(0.0023)	(0.0069)	(0.0049)
Household size	-0.0062***	-0.0054***	-0.0113***	-0.0056***	-0.0052***	-0.0038***	-0.0061***	-0.0040***	-0.0102***	-0.0060***
	(0.0010)	(0.0004)	(0.0011)	(0.0005)	(0.0008)	(0.0003)	(0.0009)	(0.0004)	(0.0018)	(0.0008)
Number of women aged 45–65 years	0.0306***	0.0063***	0.0330***	0.0028*	0.0171***	-0.0006	0.0017	-0.0008	0.0201***	0.0007
	(0.0032)	(0.0011)	(0.0036)	(0.0015)	(0.0028)	(0.0009)	(0.0028)	(0.0009)	(0.0057)	(0.0020)
Number of elderly females	0.0215***	0.0001	0.0245***	0.0006	0.0240***	0.0016	0.0233***	-0.0015	0.0283***	0.0014
	(0.0041)	(0.0017)	(0.0044)	(0.0022)	(0.0035)	(0.0014)	(0.0036)	(0.0015)	(0.0072)	(0.0030)
Number of elderly males	0.0172***	0.0086***	0.0209***	0.0069***	0.0269***	0.0086***	0.0193***	0.0070***	0.0078	0.0146***
	(0.0043)	(0.0018)	(0.0047)	(0.0024)	(0.0035)	(0.0016)	(0.0035)	(0.0017)	(0.0070)	(0.0036)
Number of children: 0–2 years	-0.0835***	0.0158***	-0.0735***	0.0136***	-0.0706***	0.0130***	-0.0873***	0.0098***	-0.0783***	0.0108***
	(0.0027)	(0.0014)	(0.0032)	(0.0020)	(0.0023)	(0.0011)	(0.0023)	(0.0012)	(0.0049)	(0.0026)
Number of children: 3–6 years	-0.0033	0.0126***	-0.0065**	0.0134***	-0.0067***	0.0098***	-0.0048**	0.0095***	-0.0079*	0.0072***
	(0.0022)	(0.0011)	(0.0026)	(0.0016)	(0.0019)	(0.0009)	(0.0019)	(0.0010)	(0.0041)	(0.0021)
Number of children: 7–11 years	0.0149***	0.0129***	0.0161***	0.0151***	0.0096***	0.0080***	0.0125***	0.0094***	0.0169***	0.0117***
	(0.0019)	(0.0009)	(0.0022)	(0.0012)	(0.0017)	(0.0008)	(0.0017)	(0.0008)	(0.0035)	(0.0017)
Number of children: 12–17 years	0.0059***	0.0078***	0.0162***	0.0100***	0.0117***	0.0084***	0.0175***	0.0077***	0.0238***	0.0104***
	(0.0017)	(0.0007)	(0.0020)	(0.0010)	(0.0015)	(0.0006)	(0.0016)	(0.0007)	(0.0033)	(0.0015)

Variables	1996		2000		2007		2011		2013	
	Female	Male	Female	Male	Female	Male	Female	Male	Female	Male
Distance to office ('100km)	0.0091***	0.0022***	-0.0136***	0.0085***	-0.0084***	0.0052***	0.0076***	0.0028***	0.0079***	0.0029***
	(0.0012)	(0.0006)	(0.0022)	(0.0012)	(0.0014)	(0.0006)	(0.0010)	(0.0005)	(0.0021)	(0.0010)
Main income: mining/quarrying	-0.2362***	-0.0267**	-0.1681***	-0.0284**	-0.1894***	-0.0011	-0.1482***	-0.0118***	-0.1898***	0.0149
	(0.0172)	(0.0123)	(0.0168)	(0.0122)	(0.0103)	(0.0048)	(0.0083)	(0.0044)	(0.0450)	(0.0179)
Main income: processing/industry	-0.0415***	-0.0246***	-0.0280***	-0.0248***	-0.0277***	-0.0241***	-0.0195***	-0.0111***	-0.0096	-0.0065
	(0.0065)	(0.0038)	(0.0064)	(0.0041)	(0.0046)	(0.0025)	(0.0042)	(0.0021)	(0.0123)	(0.0061)
Main income: large trading/retail	-0.0988***	-0.0589***	-0.0984***	-0.0565***	-0.0946***	-0.0383***	-0.0588***	-0.0326***	-0.0213**	-0.0178***
	(0.0037)	(0.0025)	(0.0039)	(0.0028)	(0.0030)	(0.0017)	(0.0032)	(0.0018)	(0.0101)	(0.0053)
Main income: services other than trade	-0.1353***	-0.0698***	-0.1149***	-0.0674***	-0.1261***	-0.0525***	-0.0973***	-0.0445***	-0.0759***	-0.0329***
	(0.0031)	(0.0020)	(0.0035)	(0.0026)	(0.0027)	(0.0017)	(0.0027)	(0.0016)	(0.0061)	(0.0035)
Unemployment#	-0.0407***	-0.0021***	-0.0227***	-0.0011***	-0.0315***	-0.0029***	-0.0359***	-0.0034***	-0.0442***	-0.0035***
	(0.0006)	(0.0002)	(0.0007)	(0.0004)	(0.0007)	(0.0003)	(0.0008)	(0.0004)	(0.0016)	(0.0008)
Observations	230,355	219,045	179,665	174,903	328,629	325,065	347,342	345,598	87,040	85,973

Notes. Standard errors in parentheses, *** p<0.01, ** p<0.05, * p<0.1. Estimations include province fixed effects. # Unemployment rate by region.

Source. Authors' calculations using SUSENAS and PODES

Table 10.A.3. Probit estimation of FLFP for use in the projections

	All years (1996–2013)	Since 2007 (2007, 2011, 2013)
Household head	0.4517***	0.4703***
	(0.0070)	(0.0117)
Marital status: single (omitted)		
Marital status: married	−0.4557***	−0.4388***
	(0.0049)	(0.0083)
Marital status: divorced	−0.0079	−0.0404**
	(0.0095)	(0.0161)
Marital status: widowed	−0.4245***	−0.4762***
	(0.0087)	(0.0143)
Education: no schooling (omitted)		
Education: primary	−0.1069***	−0.1049***
	(0.0034)	(0.0061)
Education: lower secondary	−0.3067***	−0.2832***
	(0.0042)	(0.0071)
Education: upper secondary	−0.0868***	−0.1478***
	(0.0043)	(0.0073)
Education: tertiary	0.7147***	0.6466***
	(0.0068)	(0.0107)
Household size	−0.0122***	−0.0071***
	(0.0011)	(0.0019)
Number of women aged 45–65 years	0.0513***	0.0456***
	(0.0048)	(0.0081)
Number of elderly females	0.0522***	0.0491***
	(0.0048)	(0.0080)
Number of elderly males	0.0373***	0.0210***
	(0.0037)	(0.0063)
Number of children: 0–2 years	−0.2065***	−0.1992***
	(0.0031)	(0.0053)
Number of children: 3–6 years	−0.0221***	−0.0319***
	(0.0026)	(0.0045)
Number of children: 7–11 years	0.0283***	0.0163***
	(0.0022)	(0.0039)

	All years (1996–2013)	Since 2007 (2007, 2011, 2013)
Number of children: 12–17 years	0.0316***	0.0297***
	(0.0021)	(0.0036)
Urban	−0.2403***	−0.2589***
	(0.0036)	(0.0060)
Distance to office ('100 km)	0.0152***	0.0129***
	(0.0020)	(0.0036)
Main income: agriculture (omitted)		
Main income: mining/quarrying	−0.2425***	−0.2722***
	(0.0157)	(0.0288)
Main income: processing/industry	0.0160**	0.0237**
	(0.0068)	(0.0116)
Main income: large trading/retail	−0.0819***	−0.0815***
	(0.0050)	(0.0084)
Main income: services other than trade	−0.1491***	−0.1447***
	(0.0045)	(0.0076)
Unemployment#	−0.0141***	−0.0146**
	(0.0017)	(0.0070)
Constant	−0.4532***	−0.4119***
	(0.0249)	(0.0413)
Observations	1,173,031	415,669

Notes. Standard errors in parentheses, *** p<0.01, ** p<0.05, * p<0.1. Estimations include province, age and date of birth fixed effects. # Unemployment rate by region.

Source. Authors' calculations using SUSENAS and PODES

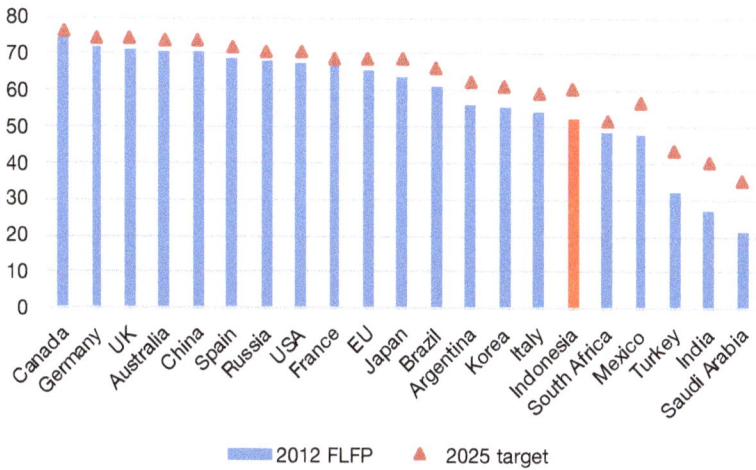

Figure 10.A.1. G20 FLFP targets

Source. ILO (2014) *Achieving stronger growth by promoting a more gender-balanced economy*. Report prepared for G20 Labour and Employment Ministerial Meeting, 10–11 September 2014. www.oecd.org/g20/topics/employment-and-social-policy/ILO-IMF-OECD-WBG-Achieving-stronger-growth-by-promoting-a-more-gender-balanced-economy-G20.pdf

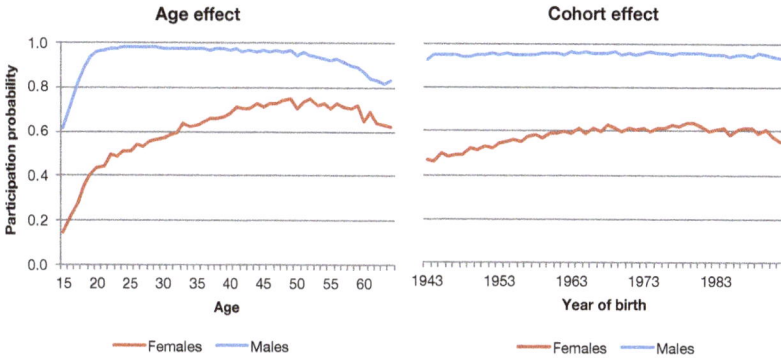

Figure 10.A.2. Age and cohort effects for rural Java–Bali region

Source. Authors' calculations using SUSENAS and PODES

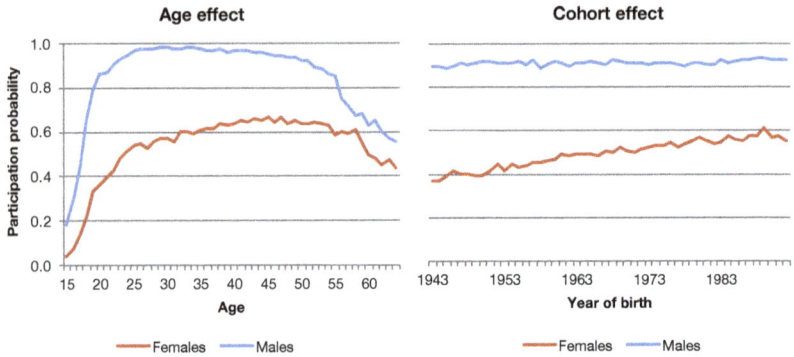

Figure 10.A.3. Age and cohort effects for urban Java–Bali region

Source. Author's calculations using SUSENAS and PODES

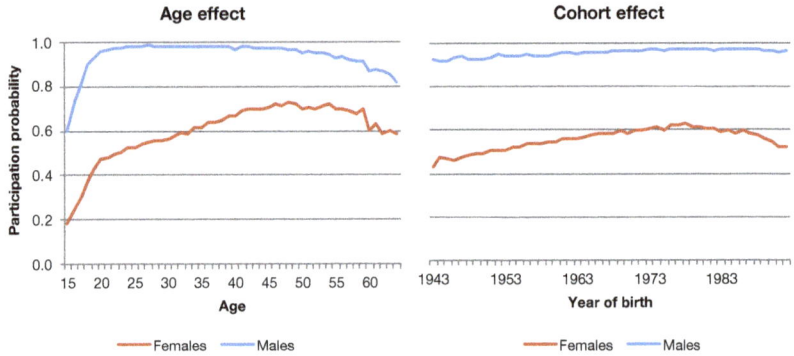

Figure 10.A.4. Age and cohort effects for rural outer islands region

Source. Authors' calculations using SUSENAS and PODES

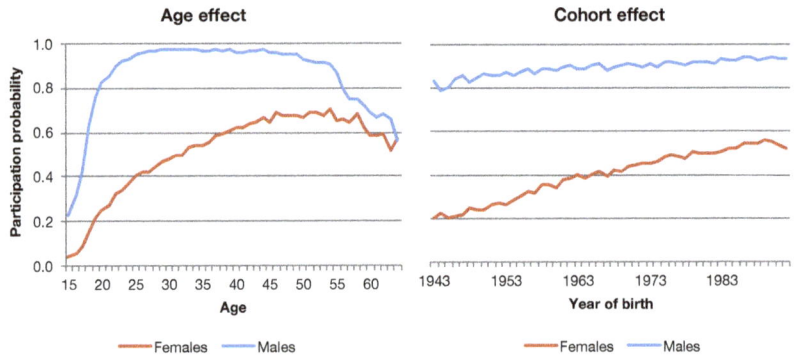

Figure 10.A.5. Age and cohort effects for urban outer islands region

Source. Authors' calculations using SUSENAS and PODES

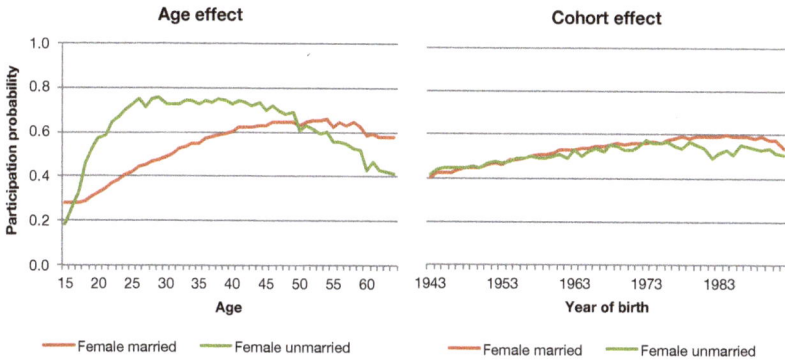

Figure 10.A.6. Age and cohort effects by marital status

Note. Unmarried includes single, divorced and widowed.

Source. Authors' calculations using SUSENAS and PODES

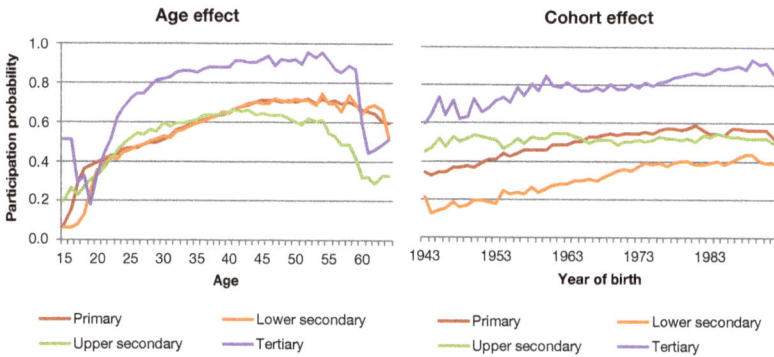

Figure 10.A.7. Age and cohort effects for females by educational attainment

Source. Authors' calculations using SUSENAS and PODES

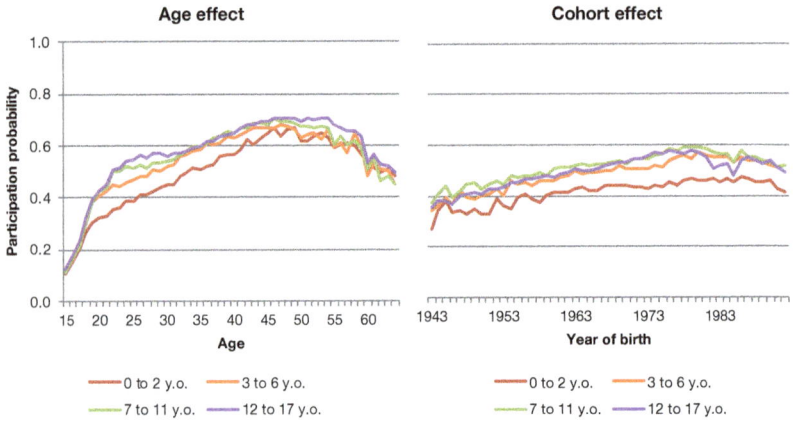

Figure 10.A.8. Age and cohort effects for females by number of children

Source. Authors' calculations using SUSENAS and PODES

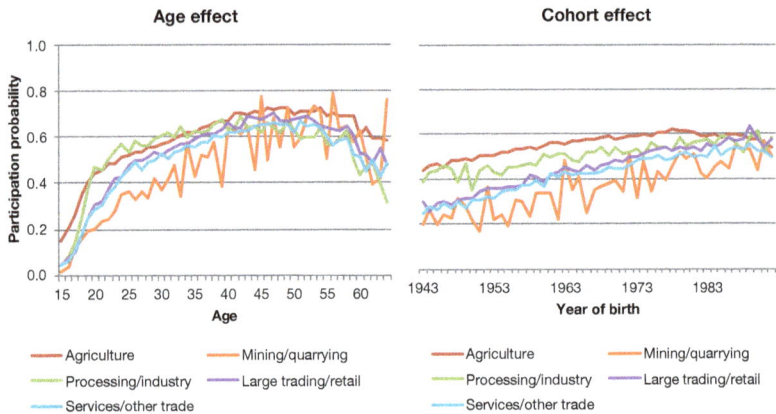

Figure 10.A.9. Age and cohort effects for females by village main income type

Source. Authors' calculations using SUSENAS and PODES

11

CONCLUSION

Adam Triggs and Shujiro Urata

Achieving inclusive growth is a major challenge for Asia–Pacific countries. Inclusive growth enables citizens to improve their standards of living, which in turn benefits us all. The realisation of inclusive growth supports social and political stability, which in turn promotes a virtuous cycle of economic growth. The realisation of a virtuous cycle of inclusive growth and social and political stability was the critical factor contributing to the 'East Asian miracle' of selected East Asian economies in the 1960s to 1980s. Conversely, it is the lack of recent inclusive growth in many of the advanced economies that has seen a sharp backlash against globalisation, openness, trade and foreign investment. Donald Trump, Brexit and the rise of the far right in Europe are the result.

Inclusive growth, which East Asian economies achieved previously, has been the focus of attention recently because many economies have experienced increasing inequality across income, wealth, gender, age and location. A variety of reasons, such as globalisation and technological progress, are proposed as having contributed to increasing inequality. The chapters of this book examine these issues.

A rigorous definition of inclusive growth is important so as to add precision to discussions of the concept and make academic and policy discussions more meaningful. What does 'inclusive growth' mean? What does it mean to reduce inequality and promote equality?

The push for equality is a challenging political topic in many Asian countries. Much of this debate hinges on defining equality and the policy solutions that flow from it. One 'definition' of equality that tends to be more agreeable across the political spectrum is the notion of equality of opportunity.

Theorists and philosophers continue to debate the definition of equality of opportunity, relying as it does on an inherent value judgement to distinguish between 'circumstance' and 'effort'. The notion of equality of opportunity, however, rings true at some basic level for many citizens, regardless of their origins and political persuasion. For this reason, Miles Corak argues, practitioners should firmly grasp theories that offer practical indicators of problems and policy solutions.

One commonly used indicator of equality of opportunity is intergenerational earnings elasticity. A high elasticity implies a significant fraction of income inequality will be passed on across generations. Corak presents the estimated results of intergenerational earnings elasticity in Asia. This provides a useful starting point for thinking about where inequality is particularly problematic and what can be done to address it.

Corak's analysis shows that, in the Asia–Pacific, India is at the upper end of this ranking with an intergenerational elasticity of 0.596. The elasticity in China is 0.399, which is somewhat lower than India and the United States, but is nonetheless a relatively high elasticity. Corak explores the reliability and usefulness of this and other measures of equality of opportunity and argues that properly measuring equality of opportunity is critical for achieving inclusive growth.

Intergenerational equity is an important issue because it not only locks in existing inequality but also worsens it. Under such situations, social and economic dynamism fall, and economic growth cannot be realised. Inter-generational equity is an important issue in many Asia–Pacific economies that have experienced a decline in fertility, resulting in ageing populations. In such societies, the voices of aged people get louder and stronger, putting fiscal and other burdens on younger generations.

When it comes to inequality, what we choose to measure can be just as important as how we choose to measure it. What we choose to measure will often direct policy. If we take a narrow measure of inequality, we will deliver narrow policy responses. But if we measure inequality incorrectly or too broadly, or use measurements that are open to criticism, then we may do more harm than good.

'Inclusive wealth', outlined by Kevin Mumford, provides a holistic measure of inclusive growth. Mumford presents inclusive wealth measures, which he argues is appropriate for the measurement of intergenerational well being for several Asia–Pacific countries for the 1990–2010 period. The computed results make it clear that GDP growth does not necessarily indicate growth in inclusive wealth. Indonesia and Malaysia, for example, have both had periods of high gross domestic product (GDP) growth. Yet, this growth has occurred simultaneously with decreases in inclusive wealth. GDP growth rates tend to be larger than inclusive wealth growth for most countries, with the exception of Japan.

Governments should prepare annual wealth accounts, just as firms create annual balance sheets. Such an initiative could play a critical role in helping governments to track and measure whether their growth is inclusive or whether it is failing to deliver benefits throughout the community.

But identifying and measuring, whether growth is inclusive or not, is only half the story. The critical question explored in this book is what factors make growth more inclusive and what this means for policymakers. The impact on inclusive growth by multiple dimensions is considered, including trade, financial liberalisation, technological advances, automation, education, caste, religion, geography, ageing, intergenerational equity, gender and participation.

According to Juzhong Zhuang, inequality of opportunity is a crucial factor in widening income inequality. Zhuang argues that the three driving forces of economic growth – technological change, globalisation, and market-oriented deregulation – should not be obstructed, even if they result in rising inequality. Anything that generates wealth is a good thing. The key focus of policy should be to ensure that this wealth is distributed fairly. Zhuang recommends a series of policies to achieve this goal, including creating more high-quality jobs for the broader population, interventions that narrow spatial disparity, fiscal policies that reduce inequality in human capital and policy reforms that make the tax system more effective and fairer. Reforms that strengthen governance and institutions are critical. Levelling the playing field, strengthening the social safety net and eliminating social exclusion will help ensure that the wealth generated by technological change, globalisation, and market-oriented deregulation is shared broadly throughout the community.

A critical question that has persisted for many years regards the influence of trade and financial openness on inequality. Do they promote inclusive growth or hinder it?

Aekapol Chongvilaivan examines the redistribution effects of trade and financial openness in the context of South-East Asian economies. His empirical analysis, like much before it, suggests that trade has a statistically insignificant relationship with inequality. In aggregate, it neither improves nor worsens it. When breaking down trade into its export and import components, however, an interesting result appears. Chongvilaivan argues that exports and imports have opposing effects on inequality in the context of South-East Asian economies. While export openness mitigates inequality, more exposure to imports results in higher inequality.

Additionally, Chongvilaivan finds that financial liberalisation, measured by the ratio of foreign assets to GDP, helps reduce inequality. Opening South-East Asian economies to global financial markets has assisted those countries to promote more inclusive growth. Reducing the cost of capital and opening lower-cost international financial markets to households and firms, it seems, plays a critical role in helping these economies get a foothold on the development ladder.

These empirical results draw two policy implications. First, export promotion policy could be the effective impetus for South-East Asian governments to address the challenge of rising inequality and promoting inclusive growth. Second, freer flows of cross-border capital may provide the poor with greater access to financial resources and economic opportunities.

These results are consistent with the broader literature. Research shows that, when it comes to manufacturing-job losses in the advanced economies, trade is often unfairly blamed. A study found that technological change – largely automation – rather than trade caused 85 per cent of US manufacturing-job losses between 2000 and 2010. While this result might ease concerns with regard to trade, what does it mean for technological innovation in Asia?

Yixiao Zhou examines the impact of recent technological developments on employment and income distribution and identifies important trends for the future of inequality in the Asia–Pacific region. Zhou observes that, despite sluggishness in the growth of total factor productivity in major economies since the global financial crisis, a new round of technological revolution – characterised by automation, robotics, artificial intelligence, big data analytics and Industry 4.0 – is approaching at a rapid rate. The full impact of these new technologies, he argues, is yet to be realised. Zhou argues that, although technological progress positively impacts a firm's competitiveness and economic growth, it may lead to negative impacts on income inequality. Zhou concludes that staying open and connected, investing in human capital, improving the business environment and stimulating entrepreneurship are strategies that will help firms in the Asia–Pacific region to prosper in the new wave of technological progress.

Yang Yao and Zhi-An Hu highlight the critical role that education plays in reducing inequality and promoting inclusive growth. They analyse intergenerational mobility in education in China by using the results of a broad survey conducted in 2010, which covered 62,219 people born between 1930 and 1985.

They find that the education level has largely improved since the establishment of new China in 1949, except for a temporary setback around the ending of the Cultural Revolution. Intergenerational mobility in terms of education accelerated for people born before the mid-1950s. But the situation reversed after the 1950s and mobility remained stagnant for birth cohorts between 1955 and 1980.

This U–shape educational transmission reflects rapid economic growth based on efficiencies pursued by the Chinese Government since the late 1970s. They argue that a crucial reason for the decline in intergenerational mobility is the disadvantageous educational environment that prevails in rural compared to urban areas and they call for improvement in rural education. Above all, Yao and Hu stress the need for the government to reintroduce social progress into its programs. Their results highlight the importance of education in reducing inequality and represent a case study for the region.

Himanshu analyses inequality in India from various aspects, including caste, religion, geography and gender. Himanshu shows that, in the long run, inequality is not just a matter of moral and philosophical concern.

It is also instrumental in sustaining the growth of the economy through allowing a larger majority of disadvantaged individuals to participate in and benefit from the growth process.

Himanshu finds that inequality is much higher in India compared to other countries with similar level of economic development. This has now been confirmed especially in the economic dimensions, such as in income, consumption and assets, but also in areas of human development, such as education, health and nutrition. For Himanshu, more worrying are the trends over time, which suggest a secular rise in inequality in almost all dimensions with some moderation in the most recent period.

Himanshu finds that inequality in India has largely been driven by changes in the labour market. The rise in profit share of national income has accompanied the decline in wage share. Inequality in access to public services, such as health and education, has also risen in recent years. Whether the process of growth will be sustained or not depends on policies related to the economy, human development and inclusion. Evidence of intergenerational mobility is mixed, with an overall increase in access to non-farm jobs by the poor and the disadvantaged. It also shows the persistence of caste-based rigidities.

A critical area of inequality is that which persists between generations. The challenge of ageing populations throughout Asia will continue to strain this important dimension. Sumio Saruyama, Saeko Maeda, Ryo Hasumi and Kazuki Kuroiwa conduct a simulation analysis of different scenarios involving timing of retirement and collecting pensions to examine intergenerational equity in Japan, where life expectancy is increasing. Their main interests are the impacts on consumption, generational accounting, government finance and GDP. With extended working years and delays in when people move onto the pension, they find that increased longevity results in increased consumption and improvements in the government's fiscal position. Importantly, it also reduces the burden on the young and on future generations. They propose that Japan needs to build a system enabling people to work at least an additional 10 years. They also point out that extending people's healthy lifespan is critical to enjoying a longer life.

Lisa Cameron, Diana Contreras Suarez, and William Rowell use the interesting case of Indonesia to examine the issue of gender inequality. Despite the dramatic economic advances that have occurred since the late 1990s, female labour force participation in Indonesia has barely increased. They analyse the drivers of female labour force participation and disentangle the factors that have contributed to female participation remaining largely unchanged for two decades, at around 51 per cent. By applying a cohort analysis to separate life-cycle effects from changes over time in women's labour market participation, over the period 1996 to 2013, they find that the raw labour market participation figures, which show little change over time, mask changes that offset one another in the current population.

There is evidence of social norms changing to support women's participation, but this is offset by the effect of the changing industrial structure. Projections show that with the current policy settings, Indonesia is unlikely to reach the G20 target of decreasing the gender gap in participation by 25 per cent between 2014 and 2025. According to the authors, policies that support women to return to work after child birth are likely to have the most dramatic effects in increasing female labour force participation. These policies include the provision of some form of child care for women with young children and policies and laws that encourage employers to make part-time and family-friendly work available. Increasing the educational attainment of women, particularly in rural areas, is also likely to assist. Moreover, policies designed to provide women with access to employment in non-traditional industrial sectors, for example, through the provision of subsidised vocational education or campaigns that provide and promote opportunities for women in these sectors, are worthy of special attention.

This book began with the story of the advanced economies. The backlash against globalisation has spread quickly from one country to the next. It has most profoundly affected the United States, the United Kingdom and countries throughout Europe. The common denominator, more often than not, is inequality and the belief that globalisation and openness has made it worse.

Asia's recent experience of rapid growth has come at the cost of higher inequality. Asia has a small window of opportunity to learn from the experiences of the advanced economies and put in place the policies that are necessary to reduce inequality and promote more inclusive growth. This will be the key determinant in deciding whether Asia, too, will see a backlash against globalisation and an attack on the very things that have given Asia its prosperity: trade, investment, immigration, technology and international collaboration.

This book has clear messages on how this can be done. Inequality is an increasingly politically sensitive topic in Asia. But focusing on equality of opportunity frames the debate in a way that is palatable to different political persuasions. Equality can be considered in terms of outcome and opportunity. Although achieving reasonable equality in outcome may be important to maintain social and political stability, attempting to achieve complete equality in outcome could deter economic growth. It may result in the loss of economic dynamism by reducing an incentive for achieving success in business. While equality of opportunity is difficult to define, it nevertheless provides a starting place to begin a conversation on how we think society should look and how we think its resources should be shared.

On the other hand, achieving equality in opportunity, which is closely related to intergenerational equality, is important to generate dynamism in an economy and society. Inequality in opportunity makes it difficult for people to realise their potential in business, academia and elsewhere, leading to a lack of economic growth. Inequality in opportunity tends to result in intergenerational inequality, reducing social and economic mobility.

The chapters in this book provide several policy suggestions to remove barriers for achieving equality of opportunity. The provision of soft infrastructure, such as education in rural areas, is important to overcome the disadvantage faced by rural populations compared to their urban counterparts. Access to financial and human resources and information, such as market information by small and medium enterprises (SMEs), needs to be improved if they are to be able to compete against large firms on a level playing-field. In this regard, enforcement of competition policy is necessary for providing equal business opportunities to SMEs compared to large firms. Female workers need to be given the same opportunities as their male workers by eliminating discrimination, improving workplace flexibility and improving access to affordable child care.

The authors agree on the importance of promoting openness in trade and finance; on the importance of technological progress in order to achieve and maintain economic growth, by maintaining open trade and investment systems and competitive economies; and they agree that globalisation and technological progress continue to advance in the future. Each of these processes will be important sources of wealth. But, without carefully calibrated policies, that wealth may not be shared equally. The focus of governments should not be to undermine these sources of growth, but to ensure that their fruits are distributed broadly throughout the community, reinforcing social and economic stability and cohesion. Two-time Pulitzer Prize winner Nicholas Kristof once remarked that 'Inequality causes problems by creating fissures in societies, leaving those at the bottom feeling marginalized and disenfranchised'. The challenge for Asian governments over the next decade is to close those fissures before it is too late.

www.ingramcontent.com/pod-product-compliance
Lightning Source LLC
Chambersburg PA
CBHW051442270326
41932CB00032B/3401